CHRISTIANITY FOR MODERN PAGANS

PETER KREEFT

CHRISTIANITY
for
MODERN PAGANS

Pascal's *Pensées*
Edited, Outlined and Explained

IGNATIUS PRESS   SAN FRANCISCO

Selections from Pascal's *Pensées*
translated by A. J. Krailsheimer
© 1966 by A. J. Krailsheimer
London: Penguin Classics, 1966
Used with permission

Cover design by Riz Boncan Marsella

© 1993 Ignatius Press
ISBN 0-89870-452-9
Library of Congress catalogue number 93-78533
Printed in the United States of America

CONTENTS

OUTLINE

(For an explanation of the boldface type, see p. 21 below.)

PREFACE

I have snored my way through far too many student papers beginning "Pascal was born . . ." to even think of beginning this book with the usual biographical trivia. I hope you are reading it (or considering reading it) *not* to hear some gossip about the life of another person who happened to be Pascal but to taste and maybe swallow some of his wisdom about *your* life.

The only biographical details that seem to me important for appreciating his thoughts are these:

1. He was a seventeenth-century contemporary of Descartes, "the father of modern philosophy", and the *only* philosopher until the nineteenth century who did *not* climb onto Descartes' new methodological bandwagon, which the eighteenth century misnamed "the Enlightenment"—namely, trying to do philosophy and even life by the scientific method.

2. He was himself a great scientist. He did major work in physics and mathematics, especially probability theory, and invented the world's first working computer, vacuum cleaner and public transportation system. He knew the power of science but also its impotence to make us wise or happy or good.

3. He was a child prodigy, well educated by a wise and loving father.

4. One of his sisters became a nun and a Jansenist. His best friends were Jansenists, but he was *not* a Jansenist. More of this later (p. 14).

5. He died in his thirties, after a long and painful illness.

6. He had always been a nominal and worldly Catholic but had a "second conversion" (recorded in *pensée* no. 913, pp. 325–26), which gave direction and vocation to his life. The *Pensées* could never have been written without it.

Enough about Pascal. The point of this book is his *book*. Or, rather, his nonbook. For in 1662 God in his infinite mercy struck Pascal dead at the tender age of thirty-nine, before he could complete the greatest book of Christian apologetics ever written.

We stand stupefied most of the time at the way God runs the world; but occasionally we get a hint, a little lifting of the curtain and a glimpse backstage. I think we have such a glimpse here. Why didn't God let Pascal finish the book for which the *pensées* are only the scattered notes, like a scholar's storm-struck study? Everyone who reads the *pensées* can sense the reason: they are too lively, too *alive*, to be contained in a book. They are like St. Francis of Assisi rather than like St. Thomas Aquinas.

Chesterton describes the difference:

> If we actually saw the two human figures in outline, coming over the hill in their friar's gowns, we should find that contrast even comic. It would be like seeing, even afar off, the sil-houettes of Don Quixote and Sancho Panza, or of Falstaff and Master Slender. St. Francis was a lean and lively little man; thin as a thread and vibrant as a bowstring; and in his motions like an arrow from the bow. All his life was a series of plunges and scampers: darting after the beggar, dashing naked into the woods, tossing himself into the strange ship, hurling himself into the Sultan's tent and offering to hurl himself into the fire. In appearance he must have been like a thin brown skeleton autumn leaf dancing eternally before the wind; but in truth it was he that was the wind.
>
> St. Thomas was a huge heavy bull of a man, fat and slow and quiet; very mild and magnanimous but not very sociable; shy, even apart from the humility of holiness; and abstracted, even apart from his occasional and carefully concealed experiences of trance or ecstasy. St. Francis was so fiery and even fidgety that the ecclesiastics before whom he appeared quite suddenly thought he was a madman. St. Thomas was so stolid that the scholars in the schools which he attended regularly thought he was a dunce (*St. Thomas Aquinas*, chap. 1).

To ask such a man to write an ordinary book is like asking lightning to sit for its portrait.

Yet we have a sort of semibook from St. Francis: the *Fioretti*, or "Little Flowers", the "sayings" of St. Francis, as the Gospels contain the "sayings" of Jesus. The *pensées*, though written by Pascal, are more like "sayings" than a book.

No one of the three greatest teachers and most influential men in history—Jesus, Socrates or Buddha—ever wrote a word, except in sand (Jn 8:6). I think the reason why is the same reason God didn't let Pascal live long enough to tame the tiger, to string the raw pearls that are the *pensées* into a necklace: their very artlessness is the highest art.

There is a higher and a lower mode of teaching. Books are the lower; living is the higher. "Sayings" are halfway between. They reflect and approximate the higher, the mode of Christ and Socrates and Buddha. That's why Socrates is the greatest philosopher, according to St. Thomas (*S.T.* III, 42, 4): because he taught like Christ, in the higher mode. That's why he wrote no books.

Pascal's "thoughts" are living. They dart like sparks among reeds, or like bolts of lightning. Each bolt is short. The sustained continuity needed for a long book requires a mind more like a mapmaker's mind, like St. Thomas': angelic, transcendent, detached, infinitely patient. Pascal has the passionate impatience of a lover. He writes lyrics, not maps—like St. Francis.

I can think of only two philosophers as lively as Pascal who ever ordered their passion into great books: Augustine, in the *Confessions*, and Nietzsche, in *Thus Spake Zarathustra*—ironically, the most passionate Christian and the most passionate anti-Christian. (The only *novelist* whose words seem to leap off the page with as much life as Pascal's words is Dostoyevsky, especially in *The Brothers Karamazov*.)

How to describe Pascal's style? I began by listing twenty or thirty adjectives, then tried to outline them and found that they fit naturally into three categories corresponding to the three great ideals of style and of life itself: the true, the good and the beautiful. Take the beautiful first. Pascal is eloquent, lyrical, delicate yet potent, witty, gemlike, incisive, stunning, biting, provocative, arresting, sharp, haunting, even terrifying. He is also precise, rigorous, accurate, objective, concrete, empirical, enlightening, scientific, brilliant, wise, intelligent— that is, true. Yet he is also warm, personal, passionate, loving, tender, heartening, curative, disarming, intimate, earnest, loving—that is, good. His prose is like the prose of Jesus, his master. I think the burning bush must have sounded like that.

There are two ways to describe a book or an author. The usual one is to describe what is said or how it is said. Sometimes this is memorable. But the most memorable thing about a really great author is how he makes *you* feel when you read him. What does it feel like to read Pascal? What *happens* when you read Pascal? Let me tell you.

It is like a roller coaster or like an Irish country road or like an underwater cave: you don't know what to expect. Something new and striking lurks around every corner.

Suddenly, without warning, an arrow pierces your heart. You instantly become very, very quiet. You stop breathing. Time stands still. You listen, really listen. To your heart. Pascal no longer speaks from the page of a book, or from history, from the past. It is exactly as if you are haunted, possessed by his ghost.

And you know, you just absolutely know, you have touched Truth.

Pascal for Today

Pascal is the first postmedieval apologist. He is "for today" because he speaks to modern pagans, not to medieval Christians. Most Christian apologetics today is still written from a medieval mind-set in one sense: as if we still lived in a Christian culture, a Christian civilization, a society that reinforced the Gospel. No. The honeymoon is over. The Middle Ages are over. The news has not yet sunk in fully in many quarters.

It has sunk in to Pascal. He is three centuries ahead of his time. He addresses his apologetic to modern pagans, sophisticated skeptics, comfortable members of the new secular intelligentsia. He is the first to realize the new dechristianized, desacramentalized world and to address it. He belongs to us. This book is an attempt to reclaim him.

I thought of titling this book "A Saint for All Skeptics"—but Pascal was no saint, and he wrote for nonskeptics as well as for skeptics. But I know no pre-twentieth-century book except the Bible that shoots Christian arrows farther into modern pagan hearts than the *Pensées*. I have taught "Great Books" classes for twenty years, and every year my students sit silent, even awed, at Pascal more than at any other of the forty great thinkers we cover throughout the history of Western philosophy and theology.

Why then is he not better known? Why was I taught every major philosopher *except* Pascal in studying the history of philosophy in four colleges and universities? "Late have I loved thee", Pascal; why did I have to discover you so late, as a maverick?

Because that's what Pascal is: a maverick philosopher in today's Establishment; a sage rather than a scholar; a human being rather than a "thinker"; not just *smart* but *wise*. That's what philosophy is supposed to be—"the love of *wisdom*"—but we've come a long way since Socrates, alas.

There are also religious reasons for ignoring Pascal. For one thing, he's too Protestant for Catholics and too Catholic for Protestants. Yet he's not somewhere in the muddled middle.

Protestants who read the whole of the *Pensées* cannot help noticing that Pascal was totally, uncompromisingly, unapologetically and enthusiastically Catholic. On everything that separates Protestants from Catholics (Church, saints, sacraments, Pope, and so forth) he took the Catholic side in unquestioning assent and obedience to the Church, even to the extent of submitting to the Church when, with doubtful fairness, she condemned his Jansenist friends' writings.

Catholics see that code word, "Jansenism", and see red. Isn't Jansenism a heresy, and wasn't Pascal a Jansenist? Yes, Jansenism is a heresy, but Pascal was not a Jansenist.

Those who dismiss Pascal with the label of "Jansenist" are like those who call all orthodox Christians "fundamentalists": the label reveals more about the labeler than about the labeled. (It usually reveals these three things: that he does not seek truth, facts or accuracy; that he rejects orthodox, supernaturalistic Christianity; and that he thinks of himself as a "progressive", which today means a decadent.)*

What are the facts? What was Jansenism, and what was Pascal?

Jansenism, as defined and condemned by the Church, was not simply the emphasis, in Bishop Jansenius' *Augustinus*, on otherworldliness or detachment. That's simply Christianity, if Christianity is defined as what Christ actually taught.

Nor was Jansenism simply the fanatical, wholehearted love of God and sanctity. That's what Moses taught (Dt 6:5) and Jesus reaffirmed as "the whole law and the prophets" (Mt 22:37).

Nor was Jansenism simply the emphasis on the seriousness of sin and divine judgment; that, too, is simply Christ's emphasis.

Yet these are things nearly everyone means when dismissing "Jansenism", rather than the highly technical theological errors about moral maximalism and theological Calvinism that the Church condemned as heretical. "Jansenism" in the popular sense (otherworldliness, "fanaticism", and divine "judgmentalism") is the single most hated teaching in the Western world

---

* *Note on "sexist" language:* Those who insist on changing the centuries-old convention by which "he" is shorthand for "he or she" are invited to pay their dues to the newly neutered grammar god and add a "she" to each "he" in the following sentence, then read it aloud. If he (or she) does not have a tin ear for language, he (or she) will change his (or her) mind about his (or her) linguistic "improvement", I (or we) think.

today. The world will do anything to get rid of the consciousness of sin, for the smell of its sins stinks to high Heaven and
makes Sodom and Gomorrah look like a church service.

There is enormous social and psychological pressure, inside
the Church as well as outside her, to ignore, deny or minimize
sin, as Molina and the Jesuits did in Pascal's day. (You can read
Pascal's brilliant satire on them in his *Provincial Letters*. But
beware: though they are beautifully rhetorical, they are also
very technical.) It seems that the most important question in
the world, "What must I do to be saved?" (Acts 16:30), is
never asked; and if it is, the answer is *not* to be born again but
just born; not otherworldly but this-worldly; not repentant but
respectable; not self-denying but self-affirming (see Mt 16:24).
Yet even if every voice in the world should preach the gospel
of spiritual auto-eroticism, there are two voices that tell us we
are sinners in need of a Savior: the voice of conscience within
and the voice of God without: in Scripture, in all the prophets
and saints and above all in the teaching of Jesus and his living
Church. And these two voices, not society's, are the only two
we can never escape, in this world or the next. Better to make
peace with them even if it means war with the whole world,
rather than vice versa. That is not Jansenism, it is simply Christianity.

Catholics who read this may suspect that Pascal was really a
kind of Protestant evangelical spy. This is two-thirds true. He
was an "evangelical", like Jesus, and he was a spy, like Kierkegaard, whose mission was "to smuggle Christianity back into
Christendom". But he was not a Protestant.

His uncompromising Catholicism seems at first to burn
bridges rather than build them between Catholics and Protestants. But he does build bridges between some Catholics and
some Protestants and burn the bridges between another kind.
Both very liberal and very conservative Protestants are deeply
threatened by Catholicism. For the liberals, "the only good
Catholic is a bad Catholic", as Fr. Rutler gibes. And for many
fundamentalists, Catholics are pagans, not even Christians:

Church-worshipers, Pope-worshipers, Mary-worshipers, saint-worshipers, superstition-worshipers, sacrament-worshipers, idol-worshipers, and works-worshipers. But Pascal builds bridges to evangelical Protestants by showing them how evangelical a Catholic mind can be, and how deeply Christocentric. (See point 28.) What Pascal does in the *Pensées*, without consciously trying, is the same thing C. S. Lewis did in *Mere Christianity*: to show us the infinite importance of the common core beneath the denominational differences.

Honest reunion between Catholics and Protestants—which is clearly close to Christ's own heart: see John 17:21 and 1 Corinthians 1:10–13—can come about only in one way: without compromise; in strength, not in weakness. The fact that Pascal, like Augustine, seems both too Catholic and too Protestant points the way to this reunion. Its secret is simple: the Christian orchestra will play in harmony (not necessarily unison) if and only if all the instrumentalists have the "purity of heart" to "will one thing" (in Kierkegaard's perfect phrase), have one absolute will to follow the will of their common conductor, Christ. The absolute center of Catholicism is Christ. The absolute center of Protestantism is Christ. The Catholic and Protestant circles can join only from the center outward. The two wheels can be aligned only on a common hub.

And that common hub—Christ—is precisely the single point to which Pascal drives us through all his points in the *Pensées*. Every *pensée*, every word in every *pensée*, is a cobblestone in the road leading to the same Christ, a sign pointing to the same home. The whole structure of Pascal's argument is Christocentric. I shall now let the whole cat out of the bag and state Pascal's ultimate conclusion right here at the beginning:

> Not only do we only know God through Jesus Christ, but we only know ourselves through Jesus Christ; we only know life and death through Jesus Christ. Apart from Jesus Christ we cannot know the meaning of our life or our death, of God, or of ourselves. (no. 417)

The only other two Christian writers who may be more powerful ecumenical bridges than Pascal are Augustine and C. S. Lewis. And both of them shared the same simple secret of the centrality of Christ. Pascal always thought of himself as an Augustinian. When he became ill, he gave away all his books, a very large library for his day, and kept only two to be his sole nourishment until he died, two he could not part with: the Bible and the *Confessions*. "A wise choice", comments Muggeridge. A wise comment.

What and Why This Book Is

This is not just a book *about* Pascal or an editing *of* Pascal. It is an original work of apologetics addressed to our own time and using Pascal as cavalry is used in battle. Pascal is a very fast horse. (I have always thought the horse to be marvelously courteous to allow a man to ride him. I thank Pascal for letting a little boy ride a stallion.)

This book is not an "explanation" of Pascal. Pascal needs no explanations. Rather, it is a *festooning* of Pascal, like decorating a Christmas tree.

Oh, so this book is a book about another book. That sounds deadly dull and terribly scholarly. No. Why not? Let me try to explain. We can classify books about other books into seven categories. First, there are simply new *editions* of the old book. Second, the editor may add a new *outline*, as is often done in editions of books of the Bible. Third, there are *condensations*. Fourth, there are *rearrangings*, reorderings. This is rarely called for, unless the old book is something like what Pascal left us in the *Pensées*: a thousand scattered "thoughts" like the pieces of an unassembled crystal chandelier, a jigsaw puzzle of jewels. Fifth, there are *commentaries*, explanations and interpretations of what the author meant. The clearer the author is, the less this is necessary. It is nearly superfluous for Pascal. Seventh, there are *festoonings*: free-flowing extensions of his thought, *discipleship*.

This book is that: Pascalian discipleship. It is close to what the rabbinical tradition calls *midrash*. This is a literary form that is strangely absent from modern writing, probably because of our desperate cultivation of originality and scorn of tradition and the past.

The reader may wonder why I included only about half of the original pages of the *Pensées* and only 203 of the 993 original *pensées*. Why half-Pascal and half-Kreeft instead of all Pascal? Why buy and use this version rather than the original, unadorned, complete *Pensées*? Why not drink Pascal straight?

First, you *should* drink Pascal straight, and buy Krailsheimer's translation of the complete *Pensées* (Penguin). That's like going out and cutting down a great fir tree for Christmas. *This* is like cutting off its superfluous branches (there are many) and decorating it. The most beautiful thing about any Christmas tree, however well decorated, is always the tree itself. "Poems are made by fools like me,/ But only God can make a tree." That's why I have printed Pascal's words in boldface type. It is symbolic.

You should also take Pascal "straight" by reading just his words, *not* mine, either (a) before you read both together, (b) after you read both together or (c) instead of reading both together. The last thing I want to do in this book is to get in the way, like a fussy matchmaker. Pascal's words ring like a bell. I do not want to put my snow on the bell and muffle its clear sound. I only want to point to it, like a tour guide.

Second, half the *pensées* (the half I left out) are *not* great, not even very interesting, except to specialists. They are either technical, redundant, outdated or obscure—for example, the interminable details of his Old Testament exegesis. This is not a personal judgment call; nearly all readers agree about which *pensées* are great and interesting. They are all here.

Third, my "festoonings" of the essential *pensées* are my attempt to bring you into my college classroom. My students and I read, interpret and discuss "the beef" of a book. We have always found this method (*explication de texte*) to be by far the most successful and most interesting method of teaching. By reading this book you can take my course without traveling to Boston and paying tuition. I bring it to your house, put it into your hands.

My notes are the equivalent of my class lectures. They are usually short and subdivided into small, distinct parts, like the *Pensées* itself. This is like Mommy cutting up Baby's meat into small pieces for easier digestion. St. Thomas used the same method in the *Summa*. Pascal was a master of epigram and condensation. Much of the secret of his stylistic success is knowing what to leave out—as in Japanese flower arranging or Chinese landscape painting.

*

This book is addressed to two different audiences, just as the original *Pensées* was three centuries ago. It is first of all for skeptics, unbelievers, modern pagans. It is a program for a private "retreat for skeptics", an extended experiment for skeptics, even a prayer for skeptics. But it is also for Christians: both for apologetics and for self-examination.

Christian apologetics is weak today because it usually takes one of two incomplete forms. If it is orthodox in content, it is usually naively impersonal in form; while if it is psychologically deep, it is usually theologically shallow. Pascal, like Christ, has double depth, of both mind and heart. Christ was Pascal's immediate model in all things, even style. Compare their styles with each other and then with that of professional psychologists and philosophers or theologians, and you will see the kinship.

*

The overall outline, plot and strategy of the *Pensées* is clearly visible in my Outline. It moves from The Bad News to The Good News, from problem to solution, from diagnosis to cure:

I. PROBLEMS: wretchedness, vanity, injustice, irrationality, alienation, death, sin, selfishness

For Pascal, all the phenomena in our lives were pointing fingers converging on Christ. The *pensées* teach us the art of following the fingers. Pascal sees things as signs, not just as things. Cosmic sign-reading was an essential art that most ancients had and most moderns miss.

We desperately need these signs, for we find ourselves "lost in a haunted wood":

> Faces along the bar
> Cling to their average day;
> The lights must never go out,
> The music must always play;
> Lest we know where we are:
> Lost in a haunted wood—
> Children afraid of the dark
> Who have never been happy or good.
> (W. H. Auden, "September 1939")

The *Pensées* takes us through and out of the haunted wood; it takes us Home. The *pensées* are prophetic; they were written for our time more than for Pascal's. They become more up-to-date the more the date is "down" rather than up.

In this book I invite you to walk with Pascal on this journey, a journey that looks strangely like your life. Here is a road map—rather, something far better: an experienced and canny seventeenth-century trail guide, accompanied by his twentieth-century American apprentice.

The Structure of the *Pensées*

Only nine of the *pensées* stand out as finished essays or chapters. They are:

1. no. 149: Greatness and Wretchedness (pp. 65–69)
2. no. 131: Dogmatism and Skepticism (pp. 107–9)
3. no. 199: Disproportion of Man (pp. 120–26)
4. no. 978: Self-Love (pp. 149–51)
5. no. 136: Diversion (pp. 172–76)
6. no. 427: Indifference (pp. 189–96)
7. no. 418: The Wager (pp. 293–95)
8. no. 449: The Two Essential Truths (pp. 283–86)
9. no. 919: The Mystery of Jesus (pp. 327–30)

If the reader wants a "Cook's tour" of only the finished highlights of the *Pensées*, he could read just these nine essays. If he wants a little more—all the famous and powerful *pensées*—he can read just the fifty-one numbers printed in boldface in my Outline. That Outline, in turn, selects just 203 of the 993 original *pensées*.

When I reflect on my education in college and graduate school and ask myself what I have learned, what was lastingly worthwhile, what I still remember from thirty years ago, what I will remember as I lie dying, I always come up with just a few Big Ideas rather than a thousand little ones. That is why I have organized my whole Outline around the twenty-six Big Ideas in the *Pensées*. This reduction of 993 to twenty-six is really a plus, not a minus. It carries on Pascal's strategy. That strategy is to crowd us into a narrow way with only two exits (Up or Down) rather than putting us on a broader, freer way with many options. This strategy culminates in the "Wager". Like Christ, Pascal brings us to life's one absolute "either/or", to the place where the options are narrowed to two: to the crossroads; to the Cross.

I

INTRODUCTION

1. Order

Pascal made quite clear in his notes that his book was to begin, not with my first points, Order and Method, but with a much more interesting "grabber", death. The *pensées* he classified under the title "Beginning" (nos. 150–166) are all about death. If the reader wants to be "grabbed", and/or to be faithful to Pascal's original intention, he should turn to those *pensées* (my point 11) first.

In my Outline, the dullest points come first. We begin slowly. The airplane has a long, slow taxi before it gets off the ground. This is obviously not good psychological technique (no "grabber"), but it is logically clearer and "upfront" about what Pascal means to do and where he means to go.

6*
First part: Wretchedness of man without God.
Second part: Happiness of man with God.
   otherwise
First part: Nature is corrupt, proved by nature itself.
Second part: There is a Redeemer, proved by Scripture.

(60)

[6]
The *structure* of the *Pensées* follows from its *strategy*.

The strategy is to bring us to this absolute either/or: happiness or misery, God or no-God. It is the same absolute that life itself brings us to.

Therefore the structure/outline mirrors these two points.

These two great primal truths—that man is happy with God and wretched without God—is an unfolding into two truths of the single great Augustinian truism that "Thou hast made us

---

* The first number of each *pensée* is that of the Penguin/Krailsheimer translation; the last number, in parentheses, is that of the Brunschvicg French edition.

for Thyself, and our hearts are restless until they rest in Thee"
(*Confessions* I, 1, 2).

The two truths are simply the two most important things
we can possibly know. They define the two alternatives that
constitute Augustine's two "cities", the "City of God" and the
"City of the World". These are invisible but real spiritual com-
munities, and everyone who has ever lived is a member of one
or the other of them. This choice is our "fundamental option"
(Rahner). Ultimately it is the choice between salvation and
damnation, Heaven or Hell, for the "happiness with God" and
the "wretchedness without God" refer to lives that begin in
this world indeed but continue into eternity.

C. S. Lewis puts this fundamental teaching (of Jesus, Augustine, Pascal and every orthodox Christian thinker) this way in
The Great Divorce: "There are only two kinds of people in the
end: those who say to God, 'Thy will be done', and those to
whom God says, in the end, '*Thy* will be done.' "

Every orthodox Christian apologetic, from Paul (Letter to
the Romans) to Augustine (*Confessions*, *City of God*) to Aquinas
(both *Summas*) to Pascal (*Pensées*) to Kierkegaard to Chesterton
to C. S. Lewis, has always circled around these two foci,
rotated around these two poles: sin and salvation.

All the different forms of Modernist, revisionist Christianity
have in common the rejection of the first of these two points,
sin. Instances include radical feminism, pop psychology mask-
ing as religion, "creation spirituality", wicca, the New Age
Movement and classical theological "demythologizing".

In the past, the difficulty in accepting Christianity was its
second point, salvation. Everyone in premodern societies
knew sin was real, but many doubted salvation. Today it is the
exact opposite: everybody is saved, but there is no sin to be
saved from. Thus what originally came into the world as "*good
news*" strikes the modern mind as *bad* news, as guilt-ridden,
moralistic and "judgmental". For the modern mind is no
longer "convinced of sin, of righteousness and of judgment"
(Jn 16:8).

Yet the "bad news" is the only part of Christianity that is empirically verifiable, just by reading the newspapers. As Pascal puts it, the first of his two truths can be "proved by nature itself". The first half of the *Pensées* is like Ecclesiastes, who used no faith, only experience, to discover that life without faith "under the sun" was "vanity of vanities". You don't need faith to see the consequences of faithlessness.

*

Pascal uses "wretchedness" (unhappiness) and "happiness" here in their deep, ancient meanings rather than in their shallow, modern meanings. There are three important differences:

1. To us moderns, "happiness" connotes a subjective feeling, not an objective state, like health. To the ancients, happiness was to the soul what health was to the body. The test case is *suffering*: if happiness is objective, it can include suffering, as in Job and Greek tragedy; if it is merely subjective, then by definition it cannot.

2. Our word "happiness" comes from the Old English "hap" (chance, luck, fortune: it "happens"). It comes from without and from the material world rather than from within our own souls. It comes from what used to be called "the gifts of Fortune", who was traditionally pictured as a whore and a cheat (see, for example, Boethius' *The Consolation of Philosophy*). Thus happiness is not under our own control—a terrifying and pessimistic conclusion indeed, as it is in Freud.

3. To us, happiness is present and transitory rather than permanent: a momentary "high" rather than the quality of a whole life, as Aristotle defines it.

Like the ancients, Pascal means by "happiness" (1) a state of real perfection (2) of soul (3) in a complete life, including eternity. Aristotle's word for this was *eudaimonia*: the lasting state (*-ia*) of true goodness (*eu-*) of soul (*daimon*). That is why Pascal offers religion instead of psychology as the way to happiness; for psychology can make us *feel* good, but religion can make us *be* good.

Like St. Paul in Romans 1, and like Aquinas in the *Summa*, Pascal here distinguishes between that part of the Christian claim that *can* be proved by natural reason alone without faith in divine revelation (the first of his two points) from that part which can't (the second). Pascal seems to draw this line at a different place than Aquinas does, for he doubts whether unaided reason can prove the existence of God with any certainty (see no. 429). But the *Pensées* includes much "natural theology", or "rational theology", on the near side of the line. It does not presuppose faith; it is addressed to unbelievers, to bring them to faith through reason (though this "reason" is not so much abstract syllogistic *reasoning* as *sanity*; not *calculation* but *vision*—the ancient, broad meaning of the word).

Pascal's first point, the consciousness of sin, is the absolutely necessary "narrow gate" to his second point, salvation. For "those who [think they] are well have no need of a physician, but those who are sick. I came not to call the righteous, but sinners" (Mk 2:17–18). Free heart surgery is good news to one who knows he has a fatal heart disease but not to one who denies it (Ps 51:10).

12

Order. **Men despise religion. They hate it and are afraid it may be true. The cure for this is first [1] to show that religion is not contrary to reason, but worthy of reverence and respect.**

Next [2] make it attractive, make good men wish it were true, and then [3] show that it is.

Worthy of reverence because it really understands human nature.

Attractive because it promises true good.   (187)

[12]

The root of most atheism is not argument but attitude, not intellection but feeling, not the love of truth but the fear of truth.

Any evangelistic or apologetic effort that ignores this psychological fact is naive and doomed to ineffectiveness, except with the small minority who are utterly honest and objective. (They are a small minority among believers too.) Pascal, like Augustine, was too good a psychologist to make that mistake.

The point—that atheism's origin is not intellectual but volitional and moral—follows from Christ's promise that all who seek (God) will find (him). For unless this promise is a lie, and Christ a liar, there can be only two causes for not having found God, that is, for unbelief: (1) not seeking him, or (2) time. For eventually, however long the delay, all seekers find. (See no. 160, p. 211.) And seeking is an act of will, that is, a moral choice. Computers do not seek, they only obey their programming. For they have no will. (See no. 741, p. 225.)

One of the things that delay our finding God is ignorance. That can indeed be addressed by purely rational apologetics. But the primary obstacle is an attitude of the will, and this must be addressed by a different kind of apologetics: Pascal's kind.

Purely rational apologists like Aquinas are often far greater masters than Pascal was in dealing with the factor of ignorance or misunderstanding of the truth, assuming the love of truth. But Pascal is much more effective in dealing with the prior factor, the fear of truth. Perhaps Aquinas was just too saintly to experience the depths of human self-deception, too merely honest. Augustine also was passionately honest, but he also knew from his own experience, and told us in utter honesty, about his own dishonesty in all its devious deceptions and twisting tentacles. He too was a great saint, but unlike Aquinas he had also been a great sinner. This made him vividly aware of the point Pascal makes in this *pensée*: see, for example, *Confessions* X, 23, 2.

Pascal's honesty reminds me more of Wittgenstein than of any other twentieth-century philosopher. This is surprising only if you know Wittgenstein from his "disciples" in linguistic analysis and not from his own private writings. His diaries are full of confessions like this:

> The edifice of your pride has to be dismantled. And that is terribly hard work. . . . Lying to oneself about oneself, deceiving yourself about the pretense in your own state of will, must have a harmful influence on [your] style; for the result will be that you cannot tell what is genuine in the style and what is false.

You can always tell with Pascal. The transparency and directness of the style reflect that of the author. Style is like body language. Often, you can fool adults, who listen to your mind and your words, but not children, who listen to your body and your tone of voice.

If Pascal is so utterly honest, why does he appeal to our desire for happiness (point 2) and not just our desire for truth (point 3)?

It is dishonest to ignore truth for the sake of happiness, but it is not dishonest to seek happiness. It is dishonest to believe anything for any other reason than that it is true, but it is not dishonest to consider other "selling points" (happiness, goodness) when wondering whether it is worth your while to inquire. A complete apologetic does not ignore happiness (point 2) any more than it ignores truth (points 1 and 2).

The three points in this *pensée* are not the *outline* of the *Pensées* but its *strategy*. There is, however, a rough correspondence between the strategy (the three points of no. 12) and the outline (the two points of no. 6):

1. That Christianity is "worthy of respect" on a human level because it understands the problem, human unhappiness, the human heart—this corresponds to the first of the two points of the Outline, man's "wretchedness without God".

2. That Christianity "promises true good"—this is the point of the "Wager", which is the transition or turning point from the problem to the solution.

3. That the Christian solution, though learned by faith, is also reasonable; that the "happiness of man with God" is true and credible—this is the second of the two points of the outline.

Thus Pascal shows that Christianity is

1. psychologically respectable, because it understands the truth about man;

2. psychologically attractive, because it promises true happiness, the good for man; and

3. objectively true, tells the truth about God (the point of traditional apologetics).

Thus the *Pensées* is not an *alternative* to or a *subtraction* from traditional apologetics but an addition to it.

The order of the three points is of more than scholarly importance. It helps account for why the *Pensées* "works". Pascal first (1) shows that Christianity is a viable candidate. Then (2) he shows that it is an *attractive* candidate. Perhaps it is "too good to be true"—we have not proved its truth yet—but at least it is good, and good for us. The crucial strategic point is that once you get past point (2), the only obstacles remaining are intellectual: ignorance, misunderstanding and myopia. The inclusion of points (1) and (2) is crucial, for before Pascal convinced you of them, you *wanted* Christianity to be false, because you hated and feared it. After (1) and (2), if they work, you love it and want it to be true.

Of course this alone is not enough. Wanting something to be true does not make it true, and believing anything just because you like it is simple dishonesty. Step (3) is essential. But (1) and (2) enable us to be open to (3) instead of closed to it. Pascal first opens your mind, then feeds it. Most apologetics tries to feed spinach to a reluctant baby who stubbornly closes his mouth. (Ever try it? Watch sometime.) What you have to do is make the baby *hungry*.

Someone may object that it is just as dishonest to make us want Christianity to be true as it is to make us want it to be false. Why not cultivate neutrality instead?

Because neutrality is impossible once you are addressed with a claim as total, as intimate, as life-changing and as sin-threatening as Christianity. Christianity is not a *hypothesis*, it is a proposal of marriage.

Our intellect lives off our will and emotions as a plant lives off the earth. Reason is not a balloon floating loose in the air of truth; it is the leaves of a tree that lives from its trunk (the heart) and its roots in the earth (its feelings). If psychology has learned anything since Plato, it has learned that. And so has Pascal, long before Freud.

If (a) Christianity is true, and if (b) there are *two* obstacles to believing it, namely, the irrational obstacle (hate and fear) and the rational obstacle (ignorance and misunderstanding), and if (c) neutrality is impossible, then it follows that replacing this hate with love and this fear with fascination (which is Pascal's step 2) is honest and serves the truth just as much as rational arguments do (Pascal's step 3). If a man is dying of both cancer and pneumonia, the cure of either disease is just as much in the service of his life and health as the cure of the other.

298

Order. Against the objection that there is no order in Scripture.

The heart has its order, the mind has its own, which uses principles and demonstrations. The heart has a different one.[A] We do not prove that we ought to be loved by setting out in order the causes of love; that would be absurd.[B]

Jesus Christ and St Paul possess the order of charity, not of the mind, for they wished to humble, not to teach.[C]

The same with St Augustine. This order consists mainly in digressions upon each point which relates to the end, so that this shall be kept always in sight.   (283)

[298]

A

It is a prejudice of rationalism (not of reason) that rational order is the only kind of order. In fact, the heart's order is just as much *order*, but a different kind.

The head seeks truth, the heart seeks goodness. This is why reason's order is that of a map or outline of truth, while the heart's order is that of a journey to its goal, its heart's desire. Reason's order is static, the heart's is dynamic. Reason's order is spatial, the heart's is temporal. Reason's order naturally takes the shape of a grid, a square shape; the heart's order naturally takes the shape of a spiral, a round shape. The hunter spirals in on his quarry, his beloved, from every angle; thus, the form of his journey is "digressions upon each point which relates to the end" like the wheel's spokes leading to the hub.

The order of theoretical thinkers is from premise to conclusion; the order of practical thinkers is from problem to solution, from unhappiness to happiness, from diagnosis to prognosis, from disease to cure.

B

Lovers have never yet been heard to propose in syllogisms.

C

Perhaps this is why Socrates taught so few doctrines; he, too, wanted to humble more than to teach. The most important thing he taught was humility (*Apology* 21–23b).

By "teaching" here Pascal means filling the mind with new ideas, and by "humbling" he means emptying it of old ones. Scripture, Socrates, Pascal and the mystics are all first of all "humblers", and only after that are they "teachers".

How can "humbling" be better than "teaching"? This makes no sense with regard to things below us (nature), only with regard to things above us (God) or things beside us (other people, God's images). In regard to nature, the highest stage of knowledge is knowledge. But in regard to God and his images, the highest stage of knowledge is love. We know God and man only by loving them.

St. Thomas says that it is better to know a stone than to love a stone but better to love God than to know God, because love conforms the lover to the beloved, while knowledge conforms the known object to the way-of-knowing of the knower (*S.T.* I, 82, 3). When we love a dog, we become more doggy, but when we know a dog, we raise it up to our own level: thought. When we know God, we drag him down to our anthropomorphic level, we make God more humanoid than he really is; but when we love God, we are raised up more closely to his level, we become more God-like than we were (for "God *is* love").

Humility ("humbling") goes with love. Therefore, although knowledge ("teaching") is the best relation to nature, love and humility ("humbling") are the best relation to God.

And man. Who knows you best: the intellectual who does not love you or your dear friend who is not too bright but loves you deeply? No contest.

2. Method

Much ink has been spilled lately on questions of theoretical methodology. Pascal confines himself to practical points.

55

Inconstancy. **We think playing upon man is like playing upon an ordinary organ. It is indeed an organ, but strange, shifting and changeable. Those who only know how to play an ordinary organ would never be in tune on this one. You have to know where the keys are.** (111)

[55]

There is a double meaning here to "playing": (1) playing a game and (2) playing an instrument.

1. Games can be serious (war) as well as nonserious (charades). Apologetics is a serious game, part of spiritual warfare to win (save) human souls.

2. Apologetics is also playing an instrument: the soul organ. There is a double meaning here to "organ": (a) a musical instrument and (b) a part of a living organism: here, the heart. This *pensée* describes how to play the organ of the human heart.

Playing on the heart differs from playing on a pipe organ. It is like playing on a living organ, a squirming organ. To win, you must control its squirming. You must create silence.

Kierkegaard said that if he were a doctor and were allowed to prescribe just one remedy for all the ills of the modern world, he would prescribe silence. For even if the Word of God were proclaimed, it would not be heard or heeded, for there is too much noise and busyness in our world. "Therefore, create silence."

Pascal planned to begin his book by talking about death because death creates silence—not just when it happens but also before that, when we contemplate it.

Unless the apologist creates internal silence in his reader, unless he produces somehow that precious moment of sudden, standstill shock, his apologetics is only chatter or scholarship, not power. "The kingdom of God is not in words but in power" (1 Cor 4:20). And the purpose of apologetics is to help establish *that* Kingdom in the human heart (though it does this *through* words).

Knowing how to create this silence through words is like knowing how to touch a wild animal to quiet it, knowing where the sensitive bodily organ is. It is also like knowing how to play a pipe organ: knowing where the right keys are. That is the secret of Pascal's power: he knows where our keys are. He "pushes our buttons".

He also knows the music. The music is Christianity. You need to know and love both the student and the subject, both psychology and theology. Few know both as Pascal does. These two things are like flint and steel: touch them together and they spark. They are like man and woman: made for each other.

91

One must have deeper motives and judge everything accordingly, but go on talking like an ordinary person.

(336)

[91]

Every spy needs a cover.

The "deeper motives" are the Christian spy's real mission: to win souls. The "talking like an ordinary person" is the spy's cover: witty writing on human affairs. This is precisely what St. Paul advised: "Let your speech always be gracious, seasoned with salt, so that you may know how you ought to answer every one" (Col 4:6). Pascal is a "salty dog" like Paul, like Jesus.

Especially today the Christian apologist needs to be a spy and work in the catacombs. It was not so in the Christian world of the Middle Ages. But our world has returned to paganism—or rather, to something much worse, for a divorcée is not a virgin. We need to return to the catacombs and undermine the modern world from within. We must do the same spy work in the world as the world is now doing in the Church: planting secret agents inside. Kierkegaard defined his spy mission this way: to smuggle Christianity back into Christendom (that is, our nominally Christian but really post-Christian society).

Kierkegaard seems to have learned his method, which he calls "indirect communication", from Pascal. Pascal uses the equivalent of Kierkegaard's pseudonyms for the same end, namely, to speak from within the opposite point of view, that of alienated, skeptical modern man, rather than speaking only from the passionate, committed point of view of the Christian believer. This is his "cover".

Walker Percy and Flannery O'Connor are two twentieth-century American writers who use this same method. Lovers of Pascal will also likely love especially Percy's *Lost in the Cosmos*, a wonderfully wise and funny book that Pascal might have written if he had lived three centuries later, read pop psychology and watched Woody Allen movies and TV soaps.

130

If he exalts himself, I humble him.
If he humbles himself, I exalt him.
And I go on contradicting him
Until he understands
That he is a monster that passes all understanding.   (420)

[130]

This is exactly what Jesus did. When his disciples were "down" or fearful, he lifted up their spirits with a "fear not". When they were "up" and thought they were ready for instant sanctity, he dashed cold water on them. The Gospels are crammed full of examples of both.

Why did he do this? For Truth. To teach them who they

really were: neither angels nor beasts, neither Heavenly nor Hellish, neither sages nor fools, but both. To keep them from the Devil's twin pits of pride and despair, and also his most popular pit, contented mediocrity in the muddled middle.

Pascal has learned his strategy from his Master. Therefore, he, too, constantly contradicts our natural tendency to rest in either mere self-exaltation ("the greatness of man") or mere self-humbling ("the wretchedness of man"). He goes on contradicting us, bothering us, bugging us, until we understand the truth about ourselves. And the truth about ourselves is that we are a mystery, not a problem; a monster, not a puzzle; a living self-contradiction who *needs* to be contradicted if he is to understand himself.

Like Socrates and Jesus, Pascal does not leave us at rest, because he knows that the restless heart is the second best thing in life, for it is the road to the Best Thing.

696

Let no one say that I have said nothing new; the arrangement of the material is new. In playing tennis both players use the same ball, but one plays it better.   **(22)**

[696]

All honest Christian apologists must be "conservative" or traditional or unoriginal in this basic sense: we cannot make a new ball or a new game. God gave us the ball (the truth he revealed in Christ) and the game (the task to preach the "good news"). Those who are so "original" that they invent new games or new balls are by biblical standards "faithless" (Mt 17:17), unfaithful. They were entrusted to wrap and deliver God's gift; instead, they went out and exchanged it for another. They were told to deliver God's mail; instead, they edited it. Who do they think they are? Do they think they are greater than Christ? Christ never thought of being original! As he heard from his Father, so he spoke (Jn 8:28; 12:50; 14:10). He came not to do his own will but his Father's (Jn 4:34; 5:30; 6:38).

But the "arrangement" is new. The *strategy* of playing the old game can be new. In this way, Pascal is very original.

Originality and unoriginality are not mutually exclusive. They are not even opposed tendencies. Fidelity is precisely the secret of originality—in apologetics as in marriage. Kierkegaard saw that point clearly too—read his Judge William on marriage in *Either/Or*. C. S. Lewis says:

> No man who bothers about originality will ever be original; whereas if you simply try to tell the truth (without caring two-pence about how often it has been told before) you will, nine times out of ten, become original without ever having noticed it. The principle runs through all life from top to bottom. Give up yourself, and you will find your real self.
>
> (*Mere Christianity* IV, 11)

701

When we want to correct someone usefully and show him he is wrong, we must see from what point of view he is approaching the matter, for it is usually right from that point of view, and we must admit this, but show him the point of view from which it is wrong. This will please him, because he will see that he was not wrong but merely failed to see every aspect of the question. (9)

[701]

Compare what Pascal says here with what Kierkegaard says in *The Point of View*:

> An illusion can never be destroyed directly, and only by indirect means can it be radically removed. If it is an illusion that all are Christians, and if there is anything to be done about it, it must be done indirectly, not by one who vociferously proclaims himself an extraordinary Christian, but by one who, better instructed, is ready to declare that he is not a Christian at all. That is, one must approach from behind the person who is under an illusion. Instead of wishing to have the advantage of

being oneself that rare thing, a Christian, one must let the prospective captive enjoy the advantage of being the Christian, and
for one's own part have resignation enough to be the one who
is far behind him—otherwise one will certainly not get the man
out of his illusion, a thing which is difficult enough in any
case. . . .

A direct attack only strengthens a person in his illusion and,
at the same time, embitters him. There is nothing that requires
such gentle handling as an illusion, if one wishes to dispel it. If
anything prompts the prospective captive to set his will in
opposition, all is lost. And this is what a direct attack achieves,
and it implies moreover the presumption of requiring a man to
make to another person, or in his presence, an admission which
he can make most profitably to himself privately. This is what is
achieved by the indirect method which, loving and serving the
truth, arranges everything dialectically for the prospective captive, and then shyly withdraws (for love is always shy), so as not
to witness the admission which he makes to himself alone
before God—that he has lived hitherto in an illusion.

The religious writer must, therefore, first get in touch with
men. That is, he must begin with aesthetic achievement. . . .

If real success is to attend the effort to bring a man to a
definite position, one must first of all take pains to find him
where he is and begin there. This is the secret of the art of helping others. Anyone who has not mastered this is himself
deluded when he proposes to help others. In order to help
another effectively I must understand more than he—yet first of
all surely I must understand what he understands. If I do not
know that, my greater understanding will be of no help to him.
If, however, I am disposed to plume myself on my greater
understanding, it is because I am vain or proud, so that at bottom, instead of benefitting him, I want to be admired. But all
true effort to help begins with self-humiliation: the helper must
first humble himself under him he would help, and therewith
must understand that to help does not mean to be a sovereign
but to be a servant, that to help does not mean to be ambitious
but to be patient, that to help means to endure for the time

being the imputation that one is in the wrong and does not understand what the other understands.

Take the case of a man who is passionately angry, and let us assume that he is really in the wrong. Unless you can begin with him by making it seem as if it were he that had to instruct you, and unless you can do it in such a way that the angry man, who was too impatient to listen to a word of yours, is glad to discover in you a complaisant and attentive listener—if you cannot do that, you cannot help him at all. . . .

So it is with respect to what it means to become a Christian— assuming that the many who call themselves Christians are under an illusion . . . the religious writer, whose all-absorbing thought is how one is to become a Christian, starts off rightly in Christendom as an aesthetic writer.

For . . . one does not reflect oneself into being a Christian, but out of another thing in order to become a Christian; and this is more especially the case in Christendom, where one must reflect oneself out of the semblance of being a Christian.[1]

Your prospective captive's point of view, or world view, is of first importance because it is the hidden premise behind all his arguments.

It is of first importance not only logically but also psychologically, personally. It is more important to the person than what he explicitly says and argues about, because it is the conviction held so close to his heart that he feels he does not need to argue for it, only to assume it.

We find Jesus constantly responding to the other's point of view rather than to his words: for example, Matthew 19:3–9, 16–22; 21:23–27; 22:15–46; John 8:2–11.

What Kierkegaard describes above is also exactly Socrates' method. Kierkegaard and Pascal apply it to Christianity.

*

A happy corollary of the last part of this *pensée* is that *everyone* sees *some* truth. Therefore we can learn some truth from every

[1] Translated by Walter Lowrie, from *A Kierkegaard Anthology*, edited by Robert Bretall.

one and every philosophy, even those most disastrously in error. Error teaches truth, too, by contrast. See John Stuart Mill on this (*On Liberty*, chap. 2).

St. Thomas is constantly applying this principle in the *Summa*. Nearly every answer to every objection takes the form of distinguishing two points of view, or two meanings of a term, and admitting that the objection is right from one point of view (a less adequate one) but wrong from another.

For Aquinas, this consisted mainly in distinguishing two *meanings of a term*, two *logical* points of view or horizons of *meaning*—two different world views. For Pascal (and for Kierkegaard, who follows him here), it is broadened to include contrasting two different *life* views or horizons of values. (In Kierkegaard it is the three "stages" of "aesthetic, ethical and religious".)

The apologist must read between the lines and see his opponent's point of view, assumptions, horizons or world-and-life view, for the same reason a general must know the opposing army's base camp and supply lines. In both cases I want to know "where you're coming from". For philosophy, unlike science, does not go forward to discover new empirical truths, but backward to illuminate where arguments come from. Science builds skyscrapers, philosophy inspects foundations.

737
We are usually convinced more easily by reasons we have found ourselves than by those which have occurred to others. (10)

[737]
Therefore it is a more effective apologetic strategy to get your opponent to discover the truth for himself than for you to give it to him. (See the Kierkegaard quotation a few pages back.) How is this to be done? We have just seen Pascal's answer: indirect communication, spying, looking at things from your opponent's point of view and drawing out the consequences of his premises. In other words, the Socratic method.

842

Our religion is wise and foolish: wise, because it is the most learned and most strongly based on miracles, prophecies, etc., foolish, because it is not all this which makes people belong to it. . . . What makes them believe is the Cross. . . .

And so St. Paul, who came with wisdom and signs, said that he came with neither wisdom nor signs, for he came to convert, but those who come only to convince may say they come with wisdom and signs. (588)

[842]

Pascal's method spiritually speaking is that of St. Paul in 1 Corinthians 2. All we can do, really, is to be street-sweepers for grace. The street we sweep is Via Crucis, the Way of the Cross.

All we can be is John the Baptists, smoothing the Lord's way (Mk 1:1–4); Palm Sunday children strewing palm branches before him; or donkeys letting him ride us.

This is especially true in addressing skeptics and scholars— the toughest nuts to crack because of intellectual pride. (See no. 562, p. 158.) Pride can never defeat pride; only humility can defeat pride.

869

To make a man a saint, grace is certainly needed, and anyone who doubts this does not know what a saint, or a man, really is. (508)

[869]

The world thinks men are good and saints are better. Pascal knows men are sinners and saints are miracles.

II

THE PROBLEM:

THE HUMAN CONDITION

3. Wretchedness

Pascal begins his apologetic with, and rests its argument on, one simple and undeniable fact: that we are unhappy.

The point is obvious yet full of surprising consequences. Pascal is going to argue that man is like a very strangely shaped lock, with weird protuberances and indentations; and that Christianity is like a key—an equally strangely shaped key—that fits the lock; that Christianity alone explains both the protuberances and the indentations, man's greatness and his wretchedness; and that Christ alone can actually lead us from wretchedness to happiness. That is the "bottom line" or fundamental point of the whole argument of the *Pensées*.

Wretchedness, or unhappiness, is the opposite of blessedness, or happiness. (See page 27 for three important differences between what Pascal and the ancients in general meant by these terms and what moderns mean.) Unhappiness is perhaps the most obvious and pervasive feature of experience. It was for Buddha, another deep and canny scientist of the soul; his very "first noble truth" was that "to live is to suffer; life is suffering [*dukkha*, out-of-joint-ness]".

Though this is life's most obvious fact, it is also the fact that Americans and Englishmen cover up the most, as if it were a disgrace, like a running sore.

Paradoxically, this fact of unhappiness is both the strongest argument against belief in God (if there is an all-good, all-loving God, how could he let his children suffer so?) and also the starting point and premise for Pascal's argument *for* faith in God.

Pascal does not say our wretchedness is total or infinite or as bad as it can be or unrelieved by happiness; only that it is real and that it is ubiquitous. We can not call Pascal a pessimist, but we can call him a paradoxicalist. In his vision man is a living paradox, both very great and very wretched at once.

401

We desire truth and find in ourselves nothing but uncertainty.

We seek happiness and find only wretchedness and death.

We are incapable of not desiring truth and happiness and incapable of either certainty or happiness.   (437)

[401]

These are the four fundamental truths, the *data*, about the human condition always and everywhere. No philosophy that ignores them is worth a first glance; no philosophy that has no explanation for them is worth a second. Ultimately, no philosophy except Christianity is worth a third glance and our belief, because only Christianity has a satisfactory explanation for these four facts. This is another way of summarizing Pascal's fundamental overall argument in the *Pensées*.

Truth (our head's food) and happiness (our heart's food) are the two things everyone wants, and not in crumbs but in great loaves; not in raindrops but in waves. Yet these are the two things no one gets except in little crumbs and droplets. The human predicament is summarized nicely by two quotations from the songs of that quintessentially American philosopher Mick Jagger (actually, he's British): "You can't always get what you want", and "I can't get no satisfaction."

Since no one can change human nature, no one can make us stop desiring truth and happiness; and no mere human being can give us truth or happiness. We may mediate these two things, but we cannot create them; we are aqueducts, not fountains. (See C. S. Lewis, *The Great Divorce*, chapter 11, for evidence for the terrible, suppressed truth that "human beings can't make one another really happy for long".)

Tremendous disappointments in life have come from believing the opposite. Dictators or gurus, husbands or wives, friends or lovers, are treated like gods. To place divine expectations on human shoulders is an infallible recipe for ruin and bitter disappointment.

Science and technology shield modern man from a clear knowledge of these four fundamental truths of Pascal, for science (or rather scien*tism*) offers us the illusion that we now know the Truth when in fact we only know some truths, and technology has given us comforts but not contentment. We have confused these two things; that's why these two servants have turned into our masters, like Dr. Frankenstein's monster, more and more in the three centuries since Pascal's words were written.

403

Wretchedness. **Solomon and Job have known and spoken best about man's wretchedness, one the happiest, the other the unhappiest of men; one knowing by experience the vanity of pleasure, and the other the reality of afflictions.** **(174)**

[403]

The best background for the *Pensées* is Ecclesiastes.

It is instructive to compare Job and Ecclesiastes. For this is the comparison between ancient and modern man. Ecclesiastes, like modern man, has everything and yet has nothing because it is only "vanity". Job, like ancient man, has nothing but has everything because he has God.

75

Ecclesiastes shows that man without God is totally ignorant and inescapably unhappy. **(389)**

[75]

The major obstacle to faith for modern man is the secular utopian idea that he can find wisdom and happiness without God. Ecclesiastes demolishes this illusion. (See my *Three Philosophies of Life*, chap. 1.)

412
Men are so inevitably mad that not to be mad would be to give a mad twist to madness.   **(414)**

[412]
Therefore when we find a man who is *not* mad—Jesus, Socrates, Ghandi, the saints—we declare him so mad that he must be martyred.

53
Man is vile enough to bow down to beasts and even worship them.   **(429)**

[53]
What could be more mad, monstrous and miserable than God's image bowing down to snakes? It is the King's kid bowing to his pet reptile instead of to his Father.

Ancient idolatry seems to be getting a new life and a new form today in currently fashionable Earth-worship and environment-worship. "Wanted" whales have more "right" to life than "unwanted" babies. And Earth is called "Gaia"—a proper name, as if for a goddess.

The explanation is obvious: if you don't know the true God, you must sooner or later find some false god to worship. To be human is to worship.

The alternative to theism is not atheism but idolatry.

4. The Paradox of Greatness and Wretchedness

613

Greatness, wretchedness. The more enlightened we are the more greatness and vileness we discover in man. . . .

Philosophers: they surprise the ordinary run of men.
Christians: they surprise the philosophers.   (443)

[613]

Philosophers should not be divided into "optimists" and "pessimists", or into philosophers of human greatness and philosophers of human wretchedness, but into paradoxicalists and nonparadoxicalists. Paradoxicalists are philosophers like Pascal, whose vision is wide-angled enough to see deeply in both directions at once. They are like giants with arms outstretched farther than smaller thinkers *both* right and left, both up and down, into both the Heaven and the Hell in the human heart.

The spiritual family of Paul, Augustine, Pascal, Kierkegaard and Dostoyevsky are prominent paradoxicalists.

To look at man with both eyes open is terrifying and wonderful, like a roller-coaster ride. It yields a great sense of depth, a third dimension, just as two physical eyes do. Most philosophers by comparison are flat and one-dimensional because they cover one eye. They are optimists or pessimists, rationalists or empiricists, spiritualists or materialists.

629

Man's dualism is so obvious that some people have thought we had two souls:

Because a simple being seemed to them incapable of such great and sudden variations, from boundless presumption to appalling dejection.   (417)

[629]

Even the deadly sins of pride and despair, or "boundless presumption" and "appalling dejection", perceive a deep though

51

one-sided truth about ourselves—a truth most of us dare not
face because either one of these two truths without the other is
dangerous and destructive.

Thus we can learn from and include even great one-sided
optimists like Rousseau and Walt Whitman and great one-
sided pessimists like Hobbes and Camus.

678
**Man is neither angel nor beast, and it is unfortunately the
case that anyone trying to act the angel acts the beast.**

(358)

121
**It is dangerous to explain too clearly to man how like he is
to the animals without pointing out his greatness. It is also
dangerous to make too much of his greatness without his
vileness. It is still more dangerous to leave him in ignorance
of both, but it is most valuable to represent both to him.**

**Man must not be allowed to believe that he is equal
either to animals or to angels, nor to be unaware of either,
but he must know both.** (418)

[678, 121]
The two fundamental human heresies, the two banes of modern philosophy, are animalism and angelism. Man has lost his
place in the cosmos, the place *between* angel and beast.

Chesterton says, describing St. Thomas' philosophy of man,
that "man is not like a balloon, floating free in the sky, nor like
a mole, burrowing in the earth, but like a tree, with its roots
firmly planted in the earth and its branches reaching up into
the heavens."

Some examples of "angelism", which ignore the concrete,
earthy, embodied nature of man, are Platonism, Gnosticism,
Pantheism and New Age humanism. Some examples of "animalism", which ignore the spiritual nature of man, are Marx-
ism, Behaviorism, Freudianism, Darwinism, and Deweyan
Pragmatism.

The two most life-changing revolutions in modern times were the scientific-industrial revolution, which taught man to live and think abstractly, like an angel; and the sexual revolution, which taught man to live and think like an animal. The first knows only the head, the second knows only the hormones. Neither knows the heart.

The angelist reduces the world to a projection of the self; the animalist reduces the self to a species in the animal world. Thus angelists find Pascal's Christian man too animalistic, too earthly, too wretched; and animalists find him too unearthly, too idealistic, too hopeful.

Chesterton says:

> Suppose we heard an unknown man spoken of by many men. Suppose we were puzzled to hear that some men said he was too tall and some too short; some objected to his fatness, some lamented his leanness. . . . One explanation . . . would be that he might be an off shape.
>
> But there is another explanation. He might be the right shape. Outrageously tall men might feel him to be short. Very short men might feel him to be tall.   (*Orthodoxy*)

Modern philosophy has lost its sane anthropology because it has lost its cosmology. Man does not know himself because he does not know his place in the cosmos; he confuses himself with angel or with animal. He is alienated, "lost in the cosmos". (See point 10 in my Outline. All twenty-six of Pascal's main points have multifarious subterranean connections with each other.)

54

Nothing presented to the soul is simple, and the soul never applies itself simply to any subject. That is why the same thing makes us laugh and cry.   (112)

[54]

This is why life is neither a tragedy nor a comedy but a tragicomedy.

If we do not both laugh and cry at life, we do not understand it. For example, Samuel Beckett's *Waiting for Godot* and Dylan Thomas' *Under Milk Wood* both show that even an honest nihilist-atheist-existentialist and an honest pagan can see this tragicomic vision and move us to both tears and laughter.

People are never simple. They are good-and-evil, happy-and-wretched. We are also flesh-and-spirit.

God is not simple either. He is one-and-three, person-and-nature, just-and-merciful, eternal-and-dynamic, transcendent-and-immanent.

Only abstractions are simple. The only language with no ambiguity, no analogy and no poetry is mathematics. That's why it's the only language computers can "understand": it doesn't require *understanding* at all.

131

There are in faith two equally constant truths. One is that man in the state of his creation, or in the state of grace, is exalted above the whole of nature, made like unto God and sharing in his divinity. The other is that in the state of corruption and sin he has fallen from that first state and has become like the beasts. . . .

Whence it is clearly evident that man through grace is made like unto God and shares his divinity, and without grace he is treated like the beasts of the field. **(434)**

[131]

Everything else in all reality is secure in its essence: God, angels, animals, plants, minerals, concepts—everything except man. Man is either divinized or brutalized; he is either raised to share in divinity (2 Pet 1:4) or lowers himself to animality (2 Pet 2:12). He is either pre-Heavenly or pre-Hellish; "all that seems earth is Hell or Heaven" (C. S. Lewis).

For man is not just nature but freedom. It is his essence to choose his essence. And there are only these two possibilities.

200

Man is only a reed, the weakest in nature, but he is a thinking reed.^A There is no need for the whole universe to take up arms to crush him: a vapour, a drop of water is enough to kill him. But even if the universe were to crush him, man would still be nobler than his slayer, because he knows that he is dying and the advantage the universe has over him. The universe knows none of this.^B

Thus all our dignity consists in thought. It is on thought that we must depend for our recovery, not on space and time, which we could never fill. Let us then strive to think well; that is the basic principle of morality.^C   (347)

[200]
A

Man is a living oxymoron: wretched greatness, great wretchedness, rational animal, mortal spirit, thinking reed.

There are three oxymorons here, which should be distinguished:

1. Metaphysically, man is both an object and a subject. He is one of many objects in nature: a *thing*, like a reed—in fact, a very small and weak thing, like a reed. Yet he is also subject: mind, spirit, ego, thought, consciousness. Think of it: a blade of grass that philosophizes!

2. Psychologically, man is both great and wretched, exalted and miserable.

3. Morally, man is both very evil and very good, capable of Hell or Heaven, spiritually dead without grace yet destined to be married to God forever in infinite and eternal glory.

In all three ways man is *unstable*. His nature is double (body and spirit), his consciousness is double (exalted and wretched), and his potentiality is double (Heaven or Hell). In all three ways he us unlike all the things in nature, which rest stably within their nature. Roses can no more be unrosy than triangles can be nontriangular; but humans can be inhuman. As the existentialists put it, man's essence does not determine his exis-

tence, but his existence determines his essence. We determine
our nature, our character, our personality, by the free choices
in our existence, our life, our career in time, our history.
Everything in nature has its life and history determined by its
timeless pattern, plan or essence; with us it is the reverse. This
formula—existence determines essence—is Sartre's, and the
Christian will not buy into everything Sartre means by it—for
instance, that we have no essence at all because there is no God
to design it—but in itself it is true and profound.

True, we have a natural essence, we belong to a species, and
we cannot change that. We cannot become angels or animals.
But we can change our character. We must be men, but we
can be two different kinds of men. To be a man instead of an
angel or a beast is to be able to choose to be an angelic man or
a beastly man. Man can choose to be beastly; beasts cannot
choose to be human. A cat cannot be a man, but a man can be
catty. ("Man" here includes "woman", of course.)

B

C. S. Lewis was asked by a media interviewer during World
War II what he would think if the Germans got the atom
bomb, dropped one on England, and he saw it falling right on
top of him. "If you only had time for one last thought, what
would it be?" Lewis replied that he would look up at the
bomb, stick out his tongue at it, and say, "Pooh! You're only a
bomb. I'm an immortal soul."

C

The crucial importance of *thought* for morality was well known
to the ancients. They enumerated "intellectual virtues" as well
as "moral virtues" and tied the two very closely together. We
moderns have scorned or forgotten this tie because we tend to
be nominalists, reducing thought to the calculation of particu-
lars, not the understanding of universals. Morality needs universals, therefore it needs thought, understanding, wisdom,
seeing.

One obvious example of how thought is a key to morality is Pascal's thought about *thought* versus *things*: we can never fill space by accumulating things, or time by accumulating money to control the future, but we can control our present thoughts and choices.

Morality is first the regulation of our inner world and only secondarily the regulation of our outer world. All outer wars are outworkings of inner wars. All outer works are outworkings of inner works, both good and evil. Modern materialism reduces morality to rules for regulating our outer world, visible society, because this outer world is the only one it believes in or cares about. This is like propping up a corpse, pushing it in the right direction and wondering why it doesn't work. It has no soul.

113

Thinking reed. **It is not in space that I must seek my human dignity, but in the ordering of my thought. It will do me no good to own land. Through space the universe grasps me and swallows me up like a speck; through thought I grasp it.** (348)

[113]

Therefore Socrates, whose body was ugly but whose soul was beautiful with wisdom, has more beauty than Alcibiades, the handsome decadent. And Mother Teresa is far more beautiful with all her wrinkles than Madonna with all her blasphemies.

How remarkable that the same being (man) who is physically grasped and swallowed up by a universe vastly superior spatially can at the same time spiritually grasp and swallow that same universe, simply by thought. We can swallow our swallower.

We can perform this paradox because the universe is even more vastly inferior to man spiritually than man is inferior to it physically. Which is greater, which is it better to be: one tiny man about to die but *knowing* this fact and many others; or the blind, dumb eighteen-billion-light-year-long universe about to kill that man but *not* knowing this fact or any others?

114

Man's greatness comes from knowing he is wretched: a tree does not know it is wretched.

Thus it is wretched to know that one is wretched, but there is greatness in knowing one is wretched.   (397)

[114]

Thus the greatness and high dignity of Greek drama. It is not only that the wise sufferer is rewarded in the end, like Oedipus (and Job), but that even *in* the act of suffering well there is dignity, because the suffering is not just a negative event in the physical world but also a positive event in the spiritual world. By the sufferer's understanding and will, his suffering is granted entrance into this second world. It becomes not merely an event in space but an event in consciousness. It is taken up to Heaven: the Heaven of thought, even if not the Heaven of bliss.

How utterly low and brutish is the level to which a human mind has to sink before it can look at an old lady in a nursing home bed suffering some incurable disease and call this life and this suffering "meaningless", lacking in "quality of life". To call this the "quality of life *ethic*" is like calling a cannibal a chef.

If this sneeringly snobbish judgment is true of the old lady, it is true a fortiori of Christ. If her cross of suffering, her death-bed, lacks "quality", then his Cross and death-tree also lack "quality".

"Quality" is thus used as a professional euphemism for sex and money. We find this brutish mentality only in the "upper" classes, the professional and "educated" people, especially journalists and professors, not among the poor, not among real people. Such "intellectuals" are as intelligent as radical "feminists" are feminine.

115

Immateriality of the soul. When philosophers have subdued their passions, what material substance has managed to achieve this?   (349)

[115]

I fast, therefore I am.

Here is empirical proof of our doubleness, proof of an immaterial and thus immortal soul, and refutation of materialism. It is a fact that wise men are not driven by their animal passions as a car is driven by a driver; but they control them. *They* are the drivers. The materialist wants us to believe that the body is a car that drives itself, or that the driver is just another one of the parts of the engine; that the *mind* is merely the *brain*. How absurd! How could a mere machine negate its own drives and overcome its passions? Only a double being can oppose itself—something like a "thinking reed". *A* cannot oppose *A*. Only *A* in *AB* can oppose *B* in *AB*.

116

All these examples of wretchedness prove his greatness. It is the wretchedness of a great lord, the wretchedness of a dispossessed king.   **(398)**

[116]

Only the very great can be very wretched.
Man can suffer more than any animal.
Christ can suffer more than any man.

117

Man's greatness is so obvious that it can even be deduced from his wretchedness, for what is nature in animals we call wretchedness in man,[A] thus recognizing that, if his nature is today like that of the animals, he must have fallen from some better state which was once his own.[B]

Who indeed would think himself unhappy not to be king except one who had been dispossessed? . . . Who would think himself unhappy if he had only one mouth and who would not if he had only one eye? It has probably never occurred to anyone to be distressed at not having three eyes, but those who have none are inconsolable.   (409)

[117]

Our doubleness is itself double. First, we are both mind and body. (This is proved in no. 115.) Second, we are both great and wretched. (This is explored in no. 117.)

St. Paul makes this same distinction. The distinction between *mind* (*nous* or *psyche*) and *body* (*soma*) is not the same as the distinction between *spirit* (*pneuma*) and *flesh* (*sarx, sakra*). "Flesh" does not mean "body" but fallenness, soul as well as body. "The works of the flesh" (Gal 5:19–21) include spiritual sins, as the works of the Spirit include corporal works of mercy.

Pascal's distinction between greatness and wretchedness is part of Paul's distinction between spirit and flesh. Wretchedness is of the flesh; but it is more a matter of the soul and consciousness and feeling than a matter of body and molecules.

Pascal proceeds to *interpret* the data of doubleness; to read it, like a riddle. It is a sign; what does it signify?

It certainly seems to signify the Fall. It is a spiritual fossil, a clue to the past height from which we have fallen.

One who had never been a prince would not be unhappy to be a peasant. But a dispossessed prince would never be happy as a peasant. We are not happy as we are—that is, as fools, wretches and sinners. Therefore we must have some dim collective memory of a time when we were wise, happy and innocent. Otherwise, if we were in no contact with such a higher state, we "just wouldn't know any better". To judge A is to compare A with standard B, and this is to know B. Thus to judge Earth as inadequately Edenic is to know Eden.

A

For instance, animals "accept" death as natural, like good Stoics or pop psychologists, while man does not. Animals struggle against death, of course, but they are not scandalized or outraged by it. But man is—if he still has a heart that pumps blood rather than psychobabble, and if he listens to this inner prophet rather than to his outer prophets, social propaganda from secularist ideologies. His outer prophets tell him to "make friends with the necessity of dying" (Freud); but his inner prophet tells him: "Do not go gentle into that good-night./ Rage, rage against the dying of the light" (Dylan Thomas). The same applies to sin and suffering as to death.

B

Here is our "disinherited prince" principle again, as in no. 116. The conclusion may seem to be a non sequitur, to go beyond the evidence in the premise. Can you really prove a past Paradise from our present unhappiness? But the conclusion logically follows from the premise if we only add one other premise, as our missing link. The complete syllogism would then look like this:

A. No one would be unhappy not to be king (king of life—perfectly happy) unless he had once been king and been dethroned.

B. But man is unhappy not to be king. "All men complain" (no. 148, par. 3).

C. Therefore man must have once been this king of happiness and fallen from this state, that is, been dethroned.

If we never had X, we would not miss X. If we miss X, we once had X. Thus we are unhappy to have one eye instead of two, but not two instead of three.

119

Let man now judge his own worth, let him love himself, for there is within him a nature capable of good; but that is no reason for him to love the vileness within himself. Let him despise himself because this capacity remains unfilled; but that is no reason for him to despise this natural capacity. Let him both hate and love himself;[A] he has within him the capacity for knowing truth and being happy, but he possesses no truth which is either abiding or satisfactory.[B]

I should therefore like to arouse in man the desire to find truth, to be ready, free from passion, to follow it wherever he may find it, realizing how far his knowledge is clouded by passions. I should like him to hate his concupiscence which automatically makes his decisions for him, so that it should not blind him when he makes his choice, nor hinder him once he has chosen.^C   (423)

[119]

A

G. K. Chesterton says that no one can love his own soul too much or hate his own self too much. Pascal makes the same distinction, for he is taught by the same Master. We are to despise our selves, because we have chosen not to fulfill our capacity for good; but we are not to despise our souls, which have that capacity.

In other words, we are metaphysically very good and morally very bad. Modern paganism says exactly the opposite: it tells us to despise our souls but love our selves, our "rights" and demands and desires and passions. Its euphemism for passion is "freedom". That is, it identifies freedom with what is really enslavement. It would be horribly offended by C. S. Lewis' statement: "I was not born to be free. I was born to adore and to obey." How scandalously Christlike! And how liberating!

We are metaphysically very good because we are created in the image of the absolutely good God. But we are morally very bad because we have despised our Creator. Modern paganism says we are *not* metaphysically very good at all, because we are merely trousered apes; and not morally very bad at all because there is no divine law to judge us as very bad. There is only man-made societal law, that is, our own pagan society's expectations, and these are quite low, negotiable and revisable. "Here, kid. Take a condom. We know you're incapable of free choice and self-control. We expect you to play Russian roulette with AIDS, so we're giving you a gun with twelve chambers instead of six."

There are only four possibilities:

1. Optimistic humanism: love both your self and your soul.
2. Pessimistic misanthropy: hate both your self and your soul.
3. Christianity: love your soul, hate your self.
4. Modern paganism: love your self, hate your soul.

Only (3) is wholly true; (1) and (2) are half true; (4) is wholly false.

Pascal's dissatisfaction with our achievements and satisfaction with our nature rather than vice versa is far more relevant to our age of psychopaganism (position 4) than it ever was to his age of optimistic humanism and pessimistic misanthropy (positions 1 and 2). For we have combined the errors his age separated. We have misplaced both our satisfactions and our dissatisfactions.

If there is any one message all our psychopagan prophets insist on, it is that we must love our selves. But if there is any one message that Jesus and all his saints insist on, it is that we must deny our selves. In Christ's psychology, the absolute oxymoron is "St. Self".

B

See the four fundamental truths, no. 401 (pp. 48–49).

C

If we seek the truth without realizing how far we are from it, we will be dogmatists. If we realize how far we are from it but do not seek it, we will be skeptics. If we both seek the truth and realize how far we are from it, we will be wise.

What most powerfully hinders our knowledge of the truth? Pascal's answer is utterly realistic and practical, unlike the answers of the philosophers. The answer is not ignorance or finitude or social conditioning or the mysteriousness of truth or the weakness of reason or even of *our* reason. It is our passions. An addict cannot see truly and clearly and realistically; his mind is blinded by his passions. His brains are scrambled and skewered—not by his drug but by his addiction to his drug.

We are all addicts to something. "A man is a slave to whatever he cannot part with that is less than himself" (George Macdonald).

122

Since wretchedness and greatness can be concluded each from the other, some people have been more inclined to conclude that man is wretched for having used his greatness to prove it, while others have all the more cogently concluded he is great by basing their proof on wretchedness. Everything that could be said by one side as proof of greatness has only served as an argument for the others to conclude he is wretched, since the further one falls the more wretched one is, and vice versa.[A] One has followed the other in an endless circle, for it is certain that as man's insight increases so he finds both wretchedness and greatness within himself.[B] In a word man knows he is wretched. Thus he is wretched because he is so, but he is truly great because he knows it.   (416)

[122]

A

The two truths of man's greatness and wretchedness are not only true together simultaneously, but each includes the other. Each can be "concluded" from the other—not by *deduction* but by *seeing*, by insight. The height of the mountain and the depth of the valley measure each other.

B

Corollary: the *least* wise and insightful philosophy of man must be one that finds man *neither* great *nor* wretched but bland and comfortable, "acceptable".

Psychopaganism is infinitely inferior to existentialist nihilism because it does not even rise to the dignity of despair. It cannot be great, because it does not know it is wretched. It cannot be saved, because it denies sin.

127

Man's nature may be considered in two ways; either according to his end,[A] and then he is great beyond compare, or according to the masses, as the nature of horses and dogs is judged by the masses from seeing how they run or ward off strangers,[B] and then man is abject and vile. These are the two approaches which provoke such divergent views and such argument among philosophers, because each denies the other's hypothesis.

One[C] says: 'Man was not born for this end, because everything he does belies it.' The other[D] says: 'He is falling far short of his end when he acts so basely.'   (415)

[127]

A

Union with God. This is his potentiality for eternity.

B

Behavior. This is his actuality in time.

C

The materialist-"realist"-naturalist—the modern pagan.

D

The spiritualist-"idealist"-supernaturalist—the classical pagan and the Christian.

149

Man's greatness and wretchedness are so evident that the true religion must necessarily teach us that there is in man some great principle of greatness and some great principle of wretchedness.

It must also account for such amazing contradictions.[A]

To make man happy it must show him [1] that a God exists whom we are bound to love; that our true bliss is to be in him, and our sole ill is to be cut off from him. It

must acknowledge [2] that we are full of darkness which
prevents us from knowing and loving him, and so, with
our duty obliging us to love God and our concupiscence
leading us astray, we are full of unrighteousness. It must
account to us for the way in which we thus go against
God and our own good. It must teach us [3] the cure for
our helplessness and the means of obtaining this cure. Let
us examine all the religions of the world on that point
and let us see whether any but the Christian religion
meets it.[B]

Do the philosophers, who offer us nothing else for our
good but the good that is within us? Have they found the
cure for our ills? Is it curing man's presumption to set him
up as God's equal? . . .

What religion . . . will teach us our true good, our
duties, the weaknesses which lead us astray, the cause of
these weaknesses, the treatment that can cure them, and
the means of obtaining such treatment?[C] All the other
religions have failed to do so. Let us see what the wisdom
of God will do.

'Men', says his wisdom, 'do not expect either truth or
consolation from men. It is I who have made you and I
alone can teach you what you are.[D]

'But you are no longer in the state in which I made you.
I created man holy, innocent, perfect, I filled him with
light and understanding, I showed him my glory and my
wondrous works. Man's eye then beheld the majesty of
God. He was not then in the darkness that now blinds his
sight, nor subject to death and the miseries that afflict him.

'But he could not bear such great glory without falling
into presumption. He wanted to make himself his own
centre and do without my help. He withdrew from my
rule, setting himself up as my equal in his desire to find
happiness in himself,[E] and I abandoned him to himself.
The creatures who were subject to him I incited to revolt
and made his enemies,[F] so that today man has become like

the beasts, and is so far apart from me that a barely glimmering idea of his author alone remains of all his dead or flickering knowledge.[G] The senses, independent of reason and often its masters, have carried him off in pursuit of pleasure. All creatures either distress or tempt him, and dominate him either by forcibly subduing him or charming him with sweetness, which is a far more terrible and harmful yoke.

'That is the state in which men are today. They retain some feeble instinct from the happiness of their first nature,[H] and are plunged into the wretchedness of their blindness and concupiscence, which has become their second nature.

'From this principle which I am disclosing to you, you can recognize the reason for the many contradictions which have amazed all mankind, and split them into such different schools of thought.[I] Now observe all the impulses of greatness and of glory which the experience of so many miseries cannot stifle, and see whether they are not necessarily caused by another nature.

'Men, it is in vain that you seek within yourselves the cure for your miseries. All your intelligence can only bring you to realize that it is not within yourselves that you will find either truth or good.

'The philosophers made such promises and they have failed to keep them.

'They do not know what your true good is, nor what your true state is.

'How could they provide cures for ills which they did not even know?[J] Your chief maladies are the pride that withdraws you from God, and the concupiscence that binds you to the earth; all they have done is to keep at least one of these maladies going. If they gave you God for object it was only to exercise your pride; they made you think that you were like him and of a similar nature.[K] And those who saw the vanity of such a pretention cast you into the other abyss, by giving you to understand that your nature was like that of the beasts, and they induced you to seek your good in concupiscence, which is the lot of the animals. . . .' ᴸ

If you are united to God, it is by grace, and not by nature.ᴹ

If you are humbled, it is by penitence, not by nature. . . .ᴺ

Incredible that God should unite himself to us.ᴼ

This consideration derives solely from realizing our own vileness, but, if you sincerely believe it, follow it out as far as I do and recognize that we are in fact so vile that, left to ourselves, we are incapable of knowing whether his mercy may not make us capable of reaching him. For I should like to know by what right this animal, which recognizes his own weakness, measures God's mercy and keeps it within limits suggested by his own fancies. . . . There is thus undoubtedly an intolerable presumption in such arguments, although they seem to be based on patent humility,ᴾ which is neither sincere nor reasonable unless it makes us admit that, since we do not know of ourselves what we are, we can learn it only from God. . . .Q

'If he had wished to overcome the obstinacy of the most hardened, he could have done so by revealing himself to them so plainly that they could not doubt the truth of his essence, as he will appear on the last day with such thunder and lightning and such convulsions of nature that the dead will rise up and the blindest will see him. This is not the way he wished to appear when he came in mildness, because so many men had shown themselves unworthy of his clemency, that he wished to deprive them of the good they did not desire. It was therefore not right that he should appear in a manner manifestly divine and absolutely capable of convincing all men, but neither was it right that his coming should be so hidden that he could not be recognized by those who sincerely sought him.

He wished to make himself perfectly recognizable to them. Thus wishing to appear openly to those who seek him with all their heart and hidden from those who shun him with all their heart, he has qualified our knowledge of him by giving signs which can be seen by those who seek him and not by those who do not.

'There is enough light for those who desire only to see, and enough darkness for those of a contrary disposition.'[R]

(430)

[149]

A

An acceptable religion, like an acceptable scientific theory, must account for all the data. Pascal's argument here is that only Christianity, with its doctrine of the Fall, accounts for all three pieces of essential data that permeate the whole human condition, namely, greatness, wretchedness and the "amazing (but real) contradictions" between these two.

B

Here are the three essential truths that we must admit as our data and explain in our religion:

First, the eternal truth about God: that he is our *summum bonum*, our end.

Second, the bad news about us: that we are fallen away from God.

Third, the good news about us: how we can be saved.

We find the same essential strategy and structure in all orthodox Christian apologetics, from Sts. Peter and Paul in their sermons in Acts to C. S. Lewis in *Mere Christianity*.

C

These three points are now expanded into six:

1. our true end: God
2. true morality, our duty: to love God
3. our situation: sin, alienation from God

4. the causes of sin: pride and concupiscence
5. how to cure sin: Christ
6. how to get the cure: faith

D

The golden key that alone unlocks the closed door of the riddle of the paradoxical greatness and wretchedness of man—the key the world will not accept—is right here: that God alone can tell us what we are. To understand and repair any machine, you must read the repair manual written by the inventor.

The world judges what is natural and normal to man empirically, from observing his present state. This is the world's base line. Christianity begins with a completely different base line and therefore judges everything differently. Its assumption is that what we see is not normal but abnormal; not natural but unnatural, inhuman, fallen.

The reason it judges so differently is that it judges human experience by divine revelation, while the world judges divine revelation by human experience. Christianity sees the present experience of human behavior as abnormal, while the world judges this religion as abnormal. Each implicates the other's standard.

The key to all anthropology, for Christianity, is the sentence: "You are no longer in the state in which I made you."

E

The primal, original sin was (and is) pride, that is, playing God, willing ourselves as our own ends, trying to find our happiness and fulfillment in ourselves—in other words, being good little yuppie disciples of pop psychology, being our own best friends.

F

Once the Duke rebels against the authority of the Emperor, the Duke's vassals, no longer held by the Imperial chain of authority, rebel against the Duke.

G

What we take as our normal situation—"a barely glimmering idea of his Author"—is as far from the beatific vision that Adam had, the vision that the greatest mystics fitfully recapture and the vision that we are destined to live in Heaven, as a kazoo is from a symphony orchestra.

H

Thus both their greatness (for they remember Paradise) and their wretchedness (for they no longer experience it). And thus their dissatisfaction with their present experience. It is the "disinherited prince" principle: see pages 59–60.

I

Some (the idealists) look only at the greatness, others (the cynics) look only at the wretchedness. Today's idealists are New Age pantheists, and today's cynics are scientific materialists.

J

No philosophy can save us because no philosophy can understand us. When even the diagnosis is wrong, how can the prescription be right?

K

Various idealisms, pantheisms, Eastern mysticisms and Gnosticisms. Even Platonism holds that the soul is inherently divine.

L

Various materialisms: biologism, pragmatism, hedonism, "the playboy philosophy", and so forth.

M

Here is the deep truth and the deep error in half the world's religions, those of the Orient. They know that "you are united to God" but not that this union is "by grace, and not by nature".

N

Here is the deep truth and the deep error in modern Western scientism. It knows that "you are humbled" but not that it is "by penitence, not by nature". We should not be humbled by our nature, our essence; for that is made in the image of God, not the image of apes. But we should be humbled by penitence, by repentance; for we have sinned against our all-good Father. We are metaphysically better and morally worse than we dream.

O

This is the objection of the skeptic. The reply follows.

P

Notice the paradox: the apparently humblest, most animalistic and materialistic philosophies are really not humble at all, but proud.

Q

Pascal assumes the skepticism of Christianity's critics and deduces from it the reasonable conclusion that our ignorance is then all the more reason to listen to God instead of to our own unreliable knowledge.

R

See point 19 in our Outline.

5. Vanity

By "vanity" Pascal means something between mere self-regard or self-flattery (as in a "vanity mirror") and the total meaninglessness and purposelessness of life that Ecclesiastes means by "vanity of vanities, all is vanity". He means pettiness, thinness, shallowness, hollowness, insubstantiality. This is the condition of man without God, that is, of the modern pagan.

Gabriel Marcel has said that the most important distinction is not "the one and the many" or good vs. evil or even life vs. death, but "the full vs. the empty", that is, the real vs. the unreal. If God's essence is existence, being, reality, then the absence of God will be reflected in all forms of unreality. One gets the impression that beneath the pagan playboy's sophisticated and cultivated façade, there's just nobody home, nobody there.

We are all infected with this disease, more or less. For instance, *pensée* no. 40 shows our tendency to prefer the unreal, or the less real, to the real: painted imitations (today, photographs or TV reports) to the real. And *pensée* no. 47 shows our preference for the two unreal moments of time to the one real one; the dead past or the unborn future to the living present.

40
How vain painting is, exciting admiration by its resemblance to things of which we do not admire the originals!
(134)

[40]
Pascal, like Plato and many of the ancients, has a rather primitive and naive philosophy of art because he reduces it to imitation of nature. But this does not invalidate his point that here is an example of vanity; for most people are artistically unsophisticated and do value art chiefly for its natural realism (thus the paintings of Norman Rockwell and Andrew Wyeth are

73

immensely popular), and Pascal's analysis applies well to this art.

I think, by the way, that there is a naive realist in all of us. We spontaneously admire a good seascape, for example: "It doesn't look like oil, it looks like water."

Pascal does not want us to admire art less but nature more.

47

We never keep to the present. We recall the past; we anticipate the future as if we found it too slow in coming and were trying to hurry it up, or we recall the past as if to stay its too rapid flight. We are so unwise that we wander about in times that do not belong to us, and do not think of the only one that does; so vain that we dream of times that are not and blindly flee the only one that is. The fact is that the present usually hurts. We thrust it out of sight because it distresses us, and if we find it enjoyable, we are sorry to see it slip away. We try to give it the support of the future, and think how we are going to arrange things over which we have no control for a time we can never be sure of reaching.

Let each of us examine his thoughts; he will find them wholly concerned with the past or the future. We almost never think of the present, and if we do think of it, it is only to see what light it throws on our plans for the future. The present is never our end. The past and the present are our means, the future alone our end. Thus we never actually live, but hope to live, and since we are always planning how to be happy, it is inevitable that we should never be so.   (172)

[47]

Pascal does not mean that we should live *for* the present but that we should live *in* the present; not irresponsibility and whim-gratification, but the wise counsels of the Sermon on the Mount: "Do not be anxious about tomorrow, for tomorrow will be anxious for itself. Let the day's own trouble be sufficient for the day" (Mt 6:34).

Jesus practiced what he preached about living in the present when he forgave the thief on the cross. The bystanders who heard this probably complained about Jesus ignoring all the thief's past crimes, for they were still living in the past. But Jesus, living in the present, saw only the present paradise of repentance in the thief's heart; and when he said to him, "Truly I say to you: Today you are to be with me in Paradise", he was seeing and saying only the real present, with its seed of the immediate future, not the dead past. This "today" did not even mention the duration of the thief's Purgatory or how long he would have to wait until the general resurrection at the end of the world; such chronological considerations became irrelevant when the two of them stood face to face, blood to blood, in the living and dying present.

The thought-experiment Pascal suggests in paragraph 2 of this *pensée* can be tremendously enlightening and (after the first shock) healing to us if only we actually do it instead of just thinking about doing it.

18
An inch or two of cowl can put 25,000 monks up in arms.
(955)

[18]
Most wars—between nations, spouses or even factions in monastic orders—are over little things. This, too, is vanity.

43
A trifle consoles us because a trifle upsets us. (136)

[43]
Therefore take no comfort in the consolation of a trifle. If shooting 90 on the golf course consoles you, shooting 100 will upset you. Why sell your happiness hostage to fortune?

The alternative? The beginning of the Heidelberg Catechism: " 'What is your only comfort in life and in death?' 'That I, both in life and in death, belong unto my faithful Savior Jesus Christ.' "

522

How is it that this man so distressed at the death of his wife and his only son, deeply worried by some great feud, is not gloomy at the moment and is seen to be so free from all these painful and disturbing thoughts? There is no cause for surprise: he has just had a ball served to him and he must return it to his opponent. He is intent on catching it as it falls from the roof so that he may win a point. How could you expect him to think of his personal affairs when he has this other business in hand? Here is a concern worthy of occupying this great soul and driving every other thought out of his mind![A] Here is this man, born to know the universe, to judge everything, to rule a whole state, wholly concerned with catching a hare.[B] And if he will not stoop to that and wants always to be keyed up, the more fool he, because he will be trying to rise above man's estate and he is only a man when all is said, that is to say capable of little and of much, of all and nothing. He is neither angel nor beast, but man.[C]   (140)

[522]

A

How much of our busyness and our business has this—diversion—as its deepest psychological root? (See point 13.) It is not only when something terrible happens, like a death, that we seek diversion, but always. This indicates that there is a pervasive presence of death and despair in our lives that we are always seeking diversion from.

B

Notice the comic and tragic contrast between our nature and

our lives, between what we are born to do ("born to know the universe, to judge everything") and what we do ("wholly concerned with catching a hare"), between our greatness and pettiness. (See no. 127.)

C

Pascal does not counsel us to abandon diversions, because he knows this is impossible. He is not some unrealistically serious prig, but a realistic observer. We cannot "rise above man's estate" any more than water can rise above its source. It is our very nature to be more than a beast regarding our end, our destiny, and less than an angel regarding our lives. We are philosophers contemplating hangnails.

16

Vanity. **That something so obvious as the vanity of the world should be so little recognized that people find it odd and surprising to be told that it is foolish to seek [worldly] greatness; that is most remarkable.** (161)

[16]

Simple escape from vanity is impossible to human nature. Pascal "sticks it to us" by his dilemma. The denial of vanity can come only from a very, very vain man. It takes greatness to recognize pettiness.

"Are you vain?" "Yes." "Q.E.D. You are vain."

"Are you vain?" "No." "Then you are all the more vain for being unable to recognize it."

The funniest and vainest thing about us in our vanity is that "we behave seriously!" (no. 33). Only a snob is funny tripping on a banana peel, not a humble saint.

661

The mind naturally believes and the will naturally loves, so that when there are no true objects for them they necessarily become attached to false ones. (81)

[661]

Here is the deep *root*, in our nature, of our vanity. Pascal's favorite philosopher, St. Augustine, put it this way in the most famous Christian line outside Scripture: "Thou hast made us for Thyself, and (therefore) our hearts are restless until they rest in Thee" (*Confessions* I, 1, 2).

A shark cannot stop swimming and hunting and eating. It is a perpetual-motion machine. If its proper food is not available, it will eat *anything*, even empty metal containers.

St. Thomas says: "Man cannot live without joy. That is why it is necessary that a man deprived of spiritual joys goes over into carnal pleasures."

95

It is not mere vanity to be elegant, because it shows that a lot of people are working for you. Your hair shows that you have a valet, a perfumer, etc. . . . It means more than superficial show or mere accoutrement to have many hands in one's service.

The more hands one employs the more powerful one is. Elegance is a means of showing one's power.   (316)

[95]

We seek power more than beauty, elegance, honor, fame or pleasure. Kierkegaard made the same point when he wrote: "If I had a servant whom I asked for a glass of water, and he brought me instead the world's costliest wines blended in a chalice, I would fire him, to teach him that true pleasure consists in getting my own way."

The point is crucial for our era and our civilization, which begins with Bacon's redefinition of the end of all knowledge ("knowledge for power") and of life itself ("man's conquest of nature"). In petty princedoms, power is over *others*. In a giant industrial democracy, it is power over *nature* (hence the demand for technology), over fate and the future (hence the demand for wealth), and over guilt (hence the new morality and psychobabble), and even over divine revelation (hence theological "dissent").

It is no longer fashionable to be honest enough to call the thing we lust after "power". So we substitute a more exalted and idealistic-sounding word: "freedom". But what do we mean by "freedom" but power, control over our own lives? Surely we do not mean what Scripture means, freedom from *sin* by faith and obedience!

806

We are not satisfied with the life we have in ourselves and our own being. We want to lead an imaginary life in the eyes of others, and so we try to make an impression.[A] We strive constantly to embellish and preserve our imaginary being, and neglect the real one.[B] And if we are calm, or generous, or loyal, we are anxious to have it known so that we can attach these virtues to our other existence; we prefer to detach them from our real self so as to unite them with the other. We would cheerfully be cowards if that would acquire us a reputation for bravery.[C] How clear a sign of the nullity of our own being! (147)

[806]

A

Why? Most of all, deep down, we fear damnation. Damnation is the loss of your soul, true self, image of God, real "I". In this life, perhaps the closest we come to that is emptiness, hollowness, "nobody there", "nobody home". We fear we are really insubstantial ghosts, deep down.

To prove we are real, we make splashes in others' pools. Especially by the two things no ghost can do: sex and violence. This is the deep, unconscious source of our obsession with sex and violence: a secular society has no other way of overcoming the fear of damnation. (Except for diversion and indifference, the two other modern pseudo-solutions. See points 13 and 14.)

B

This is the deepest meaning behind Socrates' opposition to the
Sophists' preference for *seeming* over *being*. We are in the same
spiritual battle today with those modern Sophists and nihilists,
the "deconstructionists". The source of this most worthless of
all philosophies is the same as the source of more outrageous
but spectacularly evil ones such as neo-Nazism: "the nullity of
our own being".

C

Test yourself. Use Plato's thought-experiment at the beginning
of book 2 of the *Republic*. Ask yourself which you would
rather be: a good soul whom everyone thought evil, hated,
misunderstood, persecuted and victimized? Or an evil soul
whom everyone thought good, loved and rewarded? Would
you rather be really good but apparently evil, like Socrates; or
really evil but apparently good, like the perfectly successful
tyrant? Would you rather be brave and thought to be a coward, or cowardly but thought to be brave?

Would you rather be a Catholic or a Kennedy?

77

**Curiosity is only vanity. We usually only want to know
something so that we can talk about it; in other words, we
would never travel by sea if it meant never talking about
it, and for the sheer pleasure of seeing things we could
never hope to describe to others.**   **(152)**

[77]

Thus we take vacations only to take pictures. We use reality as
a means to the end of producing appearances of it.

627

**Vanity is so firmly anchored in man's heart that a soldier,
a rough, a cook or a porter will boast and expect admir-
ers, and even philosophers want them; those who write**

against them want to enjoy the prestige of having written well, those who read them want the prestige of having read them, and perhaps I who write this want the same thing, perhaps my readers. . . .   (150)

[627]

No escape! No exceptions.

Pascal, too, is sucked into the same syndrome he observes, by observing it only in order to *be* observed, read and praised.

So am I, who observe and read and write about him.

So are you, who read us.

688

What is the self?

A man goes to the window to see the people passing by; if I pass by, can I say he went there to see me? No, for he is not thinking of me in particular. But what about a person who loves someone for the sake of her beauty; does he love *her*? No, for smallpox, which will destroy beauty without destroying the person, will put an end to his love for her.

And if someone loves me for my judgement or my memory, do they love me? *me*, myself? No, for I could lose these qualities without losing myself. Where then is this self, if it is neither in the body nor the soul? And how can one love the body or the soul except for the sake of such qualities, which are not what makes up the self, since they are perishable? Would we love the substance of a person's soul, in the abstract, whatever qualities might be in it? That is not possible, and it would be wrong. Therefore we never love anyone, but only qualities.   (323)

[688]

This is an extremely disturbing thought: that perhaps, as Hume and Buddha say, beneath the attributes of the self, there is no substance; that beneath our many masks there is no face but only an emptiness that we constantly construct covers for.

Even if this is *not* true, in the end, no one can identify or define the true self. "Know thyself" is an unsolvable puzzle, our universal *koan*. For how could the true self, the subject, the "I", ever be an object, a "that"? And if it cannot be an object, it cannot be an object of thought or grasped.

I do not know whether or not it was Pascal's settled judgment that we never touch the real self, even in love; or whether he is only throwing out a challenge here, a question without an answer. (Romans 7:14–25 is similarly ambivalent.) I think it is only a challenge, to which true charity is his answer; otherwise his praise of charity (see point 16) would be pointless and invalidated by this abyss remaining under it. So would his category of the "heart" (point 17).

Eros may be only the love of a quality or of an act or of a relationship. When you become ugly or abusive or unfaithful, I naturally cease to have *eros* (desire) toward you. But *agapē* "never fails" (1 Cor 13:8). Only *agapē* is the love of the other *self*; the natural loves are loves of its qualities.

413

Anyone who wants to know the full extent of man's vanity has only to consider the causes and effects of love. The cause is a *je ne sais quoi*.[1] And its effects are terrifying. This indefinable something, so trifling that we cannot recognize it, upsets the whole earth, princes, armies, the entire world.[A]

Cleopatra's nose: if it had been shorter the whole face of the earth would have been different.[B]   (162)

[413]
A

Nothing in the world has such tiny and invisible causes, and such great and visible effects, as human love.

---

[1] "I know not what."

No psychologist, to this day, has ever explained why Romeo falls in love *with Juliet*. Yet this is literally a matter of life or death. Let us pray that no one ever *will* explain it.

B

—because Mark Antony would then not have fallen in love with her, fought a war for her, upset the Empire and changed all subsequent history, including ours today.

Every one of us is an illustration of the Cleopatra's Nose Principle. If one of a million sperm cells had not successfully hailed the taxi of your mother's ovum but another had gotten in instead, you would be a totally different person. If your grandfather hadn't gotten a crick in his neck and turned his head the wrong way one day and noticed your grandmother walking down the street with a pleasing girlish gait, he would never have met her and married her, and you would never have been born.

No other philosopher has ever so pointedly *noticed* this common truth: that enormous things constantly depend on tiny things. Perhaps this is because most philosophers seldom get their heads out of the comfortable clouds of thought and ideology and look at life as it really is. Cleopatra's nose, Cromwell's kidney stone, flies, the heel of a shoe—what philosopher takes these as his data?

Pascal's mind, like his nose, was pointed: cunning, like Machiavelli's. Pascal is Machiavelli converted.

750

Cromwell was about to ravage the whole of Christendom; the royal family was lost and his own set for ever in power, but for a little grain of sand getting into his bladder. Even Rome was about to tremble beneath him. But, with this bit of gravel once there, he died, his family fell into disgrace, peace reigned and the king was restored.

(176)

[750]

War, like baseball, is "a game of inches". If Lee had only occupied Little Round Top, he would have won at Gettysburg,
would probably have won the war, and we might be two
nations today. "For want of a nail, a shoe was lost; for want of
a shoe, a horse was lost; for want of a horse, a battle was lost;
for want of a battle, a war was lost; for want of a war, a kingdom was lost."

This is *data*. This is the nature of the world. There are only
two possible explanations for the data. As Thornton Wilder
says, in *The Bridge of San Luis Rey*, "Some say that to the gods
we are like flies idly swatted by boys on a summer day. Others
say that not a hair falls from our head without the will of the
Heavenly Father."

22

**Flies are so mighty that they win battles, paralyse our
minds, eat up our bodies.   (367)**

[22]

The species that will survive a nuclear holocaust the longest
will be the cockroaches.

What other philosopher in all of history has seen the profound and comic absurdity of *flies*? They are all too caught up
in their abstractions.

35

Heel of a shoe. 'How well-made that is! What a skilful
workman! What a brave soldier!' That is where our inclinations come from, and our choice of careers. . . .   (117)

[35]

To understand this *pensée*, imagine a small child at a parade
being deeply impressed by the heels of the boots of the march-
ing soldiers (just at his height). This child will become a shoe-
maker.

The three most important choices we make in life are: (1) the choice of a God to worship, if any; (2) the choice of a mate to marry, if any; and (3) the choice of a career to pursue, if any. The last two usually depend on unpredictable and uncontrollable trivia like Cleopatra's nose and the heel of a shoe. Only the first is truly free. If there is no God, we easily become determinists.

48

The mind of this supreme judge of the world is not so independent as to be impervious to whatever din may be going on near by. It does not take a cannon's roar to arrest his thoughts; the noise of a weathercock or a pulley will do. Do not be surprised if his reasoning is not too sound at the moment, there is a fly buzzing round his ears; that is enough to render him incapable of giving good advice. If you want him to be able to find the truth, drive away the creature that is paralysing his reason and disturbing the mighty intelligence that rules over cities and kingdoms.

What an absurd god he is! Most ridiculous hero! (366)

[48]

Socrates, Plato and Aristotle all say that philosophy begins with wonder. A philosopher is someone who wonders at things everyone else takes for granted, someone who is astonished at what we all see but fail to notice, someone who makes us astonished, too. Pascal is a true philosopher. What else could be more astonishing than ourselves, the "absurd gods"?

The nihilist-pessimist-existentialist sees man as an absurd nongod. The rationalist-optimist-spiritualist sees man as a non-absurd god. The philosopher with the nonblunted nose smells out man as an absurd god.

6. Vanity of Human Justice

We usually take for granted our relics, the remnants of the Christian heritage that still exist in our post-Christian society. One of these is our notions of justice: a justice that is not mere power or convention but is objectively and universally right, a "natural law". As religion declines, so does belief in this real justice or natural law. It is now the greatest *fear* in the minds of many of our Senators that a prospective Supreme Court judge might actually believe in a real and not merely conventional justice! This is exactly like a seminary voting against an applicant for a teaching job because he might believe in a real God. (That happens, too!)

Pascal's strategy here is to expose the horror of man without God, just as Ecclesiastes did. Without God, man is not even man but a beast. Pascal does not, however, teach the "Divine Command Theory" of justice, which is that there is no universal objective "natural law" but only God's revealed will as the source of true justice. That is the position of Euthyphro in Plato's dialogue by that name, and easily refuted by Socrates. Most Calvinists and many Fundamentalists also believe this. But Pascal explicitly says that there *is* a natural law (middle of no. 60, p. 89); but our *knowledge* of it and our *use* of it are so fallen and wretched that *empirical* justice is power dressed in propaganda. De facto justice is not de jure justice. Thus, man without God is wretched and hopeless, de facto. Without Daddy's help, Johnny can't read or get his simple arithmetic homework right.

659
Must one kill to destroy evildoers?

That is making two evildoers in place of one. *Overcome evil with good* (St. Augustine). (911)

[659]

There may be a just *warring*—a defending of the innocent against the bully—but how can there be a just *war*? War is an attempt to solve some people's problems by killing other people. It is the attempt to destroy evil by doing evil. Thus all wars are lost. War is the attempt to make one evil into zero evils, but it makes one evil into two evils.

Scripture is not clear about the *social* and *political* solution to war; but Scripture is very clear about the spiritual solution. The solution is "spiritual warfare", a war against war and all other evils. "Overcome evil with good" (Rom 12:21). If we see that incarnated evil (bullies) has no power over us, we will not fear, and we will not fight fire with fire, evil with evil, but will fight evil with good, aware of the true identity of our enemies: *not* flesh and blood but "principalities and powers" (Eph 6:12).

Pacifism is apparently not usually practical for societies—Ghandi would not have been successful in Hitler's Germany. But it is very practical for individuals.

51
'Why are you killing me for your own benefit? I am unarmed.' 'Why, do you not live on the other side of the water? My friend, if you lived on this side, I should be a murderer, but since you live on the other side, I am a brave man and it is right.'   (293)

[51]

(Dialogue between two soldiers.)

What makes the difference between what society calls justice and what it calls injustice? Simply, where a river runs, which side of the river you were born on. It would be murder for a German to kill a German, but it would be heroism for a German to kill a Frenchman in a war. Substitute "Arab" and "Jew" or anyone else.

9

On injustice:

The absurdity of the eldest son having everything. 'My friend, you were born on this side of the mountain, so it is right that your elder brother should have everything.'

(291)

[9]

This particular injustice—primogeniture—has been abolished in our society, but injustice has not. Is it any less unjust for the child born to rich parents to inherit a vastly different life than one born to poor parents? Yet all ways of abolishing this injustice seem to be only substituting a new injustice for an old one. Ambrose Bierce says, "A conservative is one enamored of existing evils; a liberal wants to replace them with new ones."

Pascal is not a social revolutionary. He does not suggest a new and better social order, in which the State compensates for such private economic injustices. For that would be only a new and greater injustice to families. Like Augustine, Pascal is a realist. He knows that injustice is inevitable in a fallen world, and he believes the sober teaching of his primary Teacher, that "the poor you will have always with you" (Mt 26:11). Against utopian reformers, Pascal is verified by history.

We don't *want* to believe that the evils of our age are only another version of perennial injustice. We want to believe either that they are far worse than those of the past or far lighter. If we believe they are worse, the past becomes our Utopia; if they are lighter, the future does.

60

What basis will he take for the economy of the world he wants to rule? Will it be the whim of each individual? What confusion! Will it be justice? He does not know what it is. If he did know he would certainly never have laid down this most commonly received of all human maxims: that each man should follow the customs of his own country. True equity would have enthralled all the peoples of the world with its splendour, and lawgivers would not have taken as their model the whims and fancies of Persians and Germans in place of this consistent justice. We should see it planted in every country of the world, in every age, whereas what we do see is that there is nothing just or unjust but changes colour as it changes climate. Three degrees of latitude upset the whole of jurisprudence and one meridian determines what is true. . . .[A] It is a funny sort of justice whose limits are marked by a river; true on this side of the Pyrenees, false on the other.

They confess that justice does not lie in these customs, but resides in natural laws common to every country. They would certainly maintain this obstinately if the reckless chance which distributed human laws had struck on just one which was universal, but the joke is that man's whims have shown such great variety that there is not one.[B]

Larceny, incest, infanticide, parricide, everything has at some time been accounted a virtuous action. Could there be anything more absurd than that a man has the right to kill me because he lives on the other side of the water, and his prince has picked a quarrel with mine, though I have none with him?

There no doubt exist natural laws,[C] but once this fine reason of ours was corrupted, it corrupted everything. . . .

Custom is the whole of equity for the sole reason that it is accepted. That is the mystic basis of its authority. Anyone who tries to bring it back to its first principle destroys it. . . . The art of subversion, of revolution, is to dislodge established customs by probing down to their origins in order to show how they lack authority and justice. There must, they say, be a return to the basic and primitive laws of the state which unjust custom has abolished. There is no surer way to lose everything; nothing will be just if weighed in these scales. Yet the people readily listen to

such arguments, they throw off the yoke as soon as they
recognize it, and the great take the opportunity of ruining
them and those whose curiosity makes them examine
received customs.[D] That is why the wisest of legislators
used to say that men must often be deceived for their own
good. . . . The truth about the usurpation must not be
made apparent; it came about originally without reason
and has become reasonable. We must see that it is
regarded as authentic and eternal, and its origins must be
hidden if we do not want it soon to end.   (294)

[60]

A

Geography determines opinions about what is just and true.
Pascal is not a moral relativist; he does not reduce objective
truths to subjective opinions. But he is not a naive idealist
either; he clearly sees the relativity of moral opinions to social
conditioning. He is demeaning not justice itself but human justice, "a funny sort of justice where limits are marked by a
river".

B

Natural law is not to be found in nations. True justice, or natural law, is not a lowest common denominator observable in
all societies.

C

Proof that Pascal is not a relativist, subjectivist, skeptic or
cynic. Human nature tolerates, but then rejects, injustice as the
human body tolerates, but then rejects, diseases.

D

Revolutionaries can always show the defects in de facto justice
or established custom or mores. That is their moral appeal.
This, by the way, presupposes and proves the existence in us of
a natural law or de jure justice or true morality, known at least

unconsciously; for that is the operative standard by which all revolutionaries judge existing conditions defective. If we did not innately know an ideal "better", we would not be able to judge existing conditions as "worse".

But Pascal says our grasp of this ideal is so tenuous that we cannot run states by it. Custom is a surer and more concrete basis for social order. Pascal is a social conservative for the intensely practical reason that revolutions almost always have done more harm than good, brought more suffering than happiness.

What follows (the need for deception) is shocking but seems to follow from the preceding points and from historical example. Do we really think we who believe newspapers and TV are less deceived than our ancestors, who believed Popes and kings?

81

The only universal rules are the law of the land in everyday matters and the will of the majority in others. How is that? Because of the power implied. . . .^A

As men could not make might obey right, they have made right obey might. As they could not fortify justice they have justified force.^B (299)

[81]

A

The de facto universal is not justice but power, whether located in the will of one or in the will of many. A democracy can be just as totalitarian as a monarchy; Rousseau's "general will" can be (and has been) far more powerful and repressive than any dictator in history.

B

The central political point of the most famous political book ever written, Plato's *Republic*, is that wisdom and power must join, therefore philosophers must rule. Plato could not make might obey right, even when he tried it, in Syracuse. Nor can anyone else. Why? *Pensée* no. 103 tells us why (next).

The ancient Sophists like Thrasymachos, the Renaissance Sophist Machiavelli and the modern Sophists, like most sociologists, have a point: all societies do in fact enact justice by power. Mao Tse-Tung put it with elegant bluntness: "Justice comes out of the barrel of a gun." Peace is created by war, justice by injustice, as Machiavelli argues in *The Prince*. The foundation of all states, which make the laws, is force. Rome was founded on Romulus' murder of his brother, Remus, just as all of our history began with Cain's murder of his brother Abel. Pascal is as brutally realistic as the Bible.

103
Right without might is helpless, might without right is tyrannical.

Right without might is challenged, because there are always evil men about. Might without right is denounced. We must therefore combine right and might, and to that end make right into might or might into right.

Right is open to dispute, might is easily recognized and beyond dispute. Therefore right could not be made mighty because might challenged right, calling it unjust and itself claiming to be just.

Being thus unable to make right into might, we have made might into right.   (298)

[103]
It is easier to pin a new label ("right") on an old powerful thing (might) than to persuade the powerful thing to obey true labels. It is easier to pin a slogan on a cannon than to make a cannon obey a slogan. Easier for the navigator to chart a new course in accordance with how the battleship is actually moving than for the whole ship to change its course in accordance with the old charts.

520

I spent much of my life believing that there was such a thing as justice,[A] and in this I was not mistaken, for in so far as God has chosen to reveal it to us[B] there is such a thing. But I did not take it in this way, and that is where I was wrong, for I thought that our justice was essentially just,[C] and that I had the means to understand and judge it,[D] but I found myself so often making unsound judgements that I began to distrust myself and then others. I saw that all countries and all men change. Thus, after many changes of mind concerning true justice I realized that our nature is nothing but continual change and I have never changed since. And if I were to change I should be confirming my opinion.[E]   (375)

[520]

A

That is, natural law.

B

By conscience and reason as well as by miraculous intervention in history via Moses and the Ten Commandments.

C

The first mistake of the idealist: confusing "our" justice with justice, positive law with natural law.

D

Mistake number 2: forgetting the noetic consequences of sin. Not only is our *practice* of justice fallen, not only are our law and customs fallen, but our *knowledge* of true justice is also fallen and fallible. Otherwise why would there be moral arguments and moral uncertainties?

E

As Heraclitus saw, the only unchanging law (*logos*) is the law that "all things change" (*panta rhei*). True justice does not change, but that is not a *thing*. Our minds are spiritual things and change. Minds are not in space, but they are in time. We change our minds more often than we change our clothes (unless we are either professional models or very dull).

697

Those who lead disorderly lives tell those who are normal that it is they who deviate from nature, and think they are following nature themselves; just as those who are on board ship think that the people on shore are moving away. Language is the same everywhere; we need a fixed point to judge it. The harbour is the judge of those aboard ship, but where are we going to find a harbour in morals?

(383)

[697]

How often have we not heard modern pagans prefer a "life-style" supposedly more "natural" and "normal" than the heroically supernatural one Christ commands—above all in the modern pagan's one nonnegotiable absolute, sexual "freedom". But "natural" and "normal" are relative terms. The whole question is: What is the true standard of naturalness and normalcy in morality? What is the absolute to which everything is relative? Where but in God can we ever find this "harbour in morals"?

Thus we return again to Dostoyevsky's terrifying little truism: "If there is no God, everything is permissible."

The very things that lead many *away* from God—the problems of evil, injustice, ignorance and relativity—are what Pascal uses to drive us in desperation to his arms. The atheist argues: "If there were a God, how could there be injustice?" To which Pascal replies: "If there is injustice, there must be true justice for it to be relative to and a defect of; and this true justice is not found on Earth or in man, therefore it must exist in Heaven and God." Either there or nowhere; and if nowhere, then "everything is permissible". But not everything is permissible. Therefore there must be a God.

Pascal does not use this "moral argument" as an *argument* but as a *prod*.

699

When everything is moving at once, nothing appears to be moving, as on board ship. When everyone is moving towards depravity, no one seems to be moving, but if someone stops he shows up the others who are rushing on, by acting as a fixed point.   (382)

[699]

Since "everything flows", everything is relative. This is Einsteinianly true of all physical things. Relative to the sun, the earth moves, but relative to the earth, the sun rises and sets. This is not a problem but a principle in physics; but it is a problem in ethics. Clearly Pascal's description of the whole ship sailing down into depravity describes our society; but it also describes human history as a whole. Only a fixed point above the flow of time and history can judge the flow. Concretely, these fixed points are the saints, who navigate not by the waves of history and the winds of fortune but by the fixed stars of Heaven. Therefore we windswept, sinking relativists call them "religious fanatics", all because of the principle of relativity Pascal describes here: to a cold-blooded reptile, 98.6 degrees is a high fever.

7. Vanity of Human Reason

Pascal deflates human reason *not* to establish skepticism (see point 8, especially no. 131, pp. 108–9), and not to demean the mind God made in us as part of his own image, but for the same reason he deflated human justice.

De jure, justice is great; de facto, it is weak. Natural law is great, human law is weak. Similarly, reason de jure, reason essential, reason in its nature, is great; but reason de facto, reason existential, reason in its exercise, is weak and pushed around by passion, imagination, habit, diversion and random chance.

There have always been two emphases in Christian philosophy: the Augustinian emphasis on the existential inadequacy and wretchedness of natural things like human reason, justice and philosophy; and the Thomistic emphasis on the essential adequacy and greatness of these things. The two emphases are opposites but complementary; they do not contradict but complete each other. By temperament and emphasis Pascal is "Augustinian". So were Paul, Luther, Dostoyevsky, Kierkegaard and many of the saints.

Pascal's strategy in deflating reason (rather, I should say, deflating reason's pretensions) can best be stated by quoting these lines by W. B. Yeats: "Now that my ladder's gone,/ I must lie down where all ladders start:/ In the foul rag-and-bone shop of the heart." His strategy is not architectural but spelunking; he does not build a tower but digs a cave, explores the heart and the heart's road to God (Ps 84:5).

This is the necessary strategy today, because reason's ladder to God is gone for most people. Remember, apologetics is not just science, not just statements of objective truth. It is seduction; it is matchmaking; it is spying.

Reason's ladder is far thinner today because of what happened in Pascal's day: under Bacon, Descartes and the Great Darkness (universally misnamed the "Enlightenment"), reason narrowed from "wisdom" to "science", from "understanding" to "calculation", from exploring mysteries to solving problems. Descartes implicitly redefines reason in the very first sentence of his enormously influential *Discourse on Method* by declaring it equal in all men—something obviously untrue of wisdom and obviously true of the laws of logic. This newly narrowed, sharpened, laser-like, this-worldly reason is a poor power for climbing Jacob's ladder to Heaven—that is, for Pascal's purpose in the *Pensées*. (Jacob's ladder is explained in John 1:51.)

In fact, even the older, broader, deeper, fuller "reason" is not sufficient for that, as freely admitted by the most rational of all Christian theologians, St. Thomas (see *S.T.* I, 1, 1).

410

This internal war of reason against the passions has made those who wanted peace split into two sects. Some wanted to renounce passions and become gods, others wanted to renounce reason and become brute beasts. But neither side has succeeded, and reason always remains to denounce the baseness and injustice of the passions and to disturb the peace of those who surrender to them. And the passions are always alive in those who want to renounce them. **(413)**

[410]

Freud was far from being the first to discover the weakness of reason and the power of passion. He saw the impossibility of living the Platonic and Stoic philosophy, which says the war can be won by reason. What Freud failed to see was the impossibility of living his own animalistic philosophy, which says that the war can be won by passion and that we can overcome the guilt that arises from the reason. Pascal pulls no punches in labeling all such philosophies (like those of Hobbes, Marx, Darwin and Skinner) ones that "wanted [us] to renounce reason and become brute beasts".

Like the war between Might and Right, the war between Reason and Passion can never end this side of Heaven. The materialists and the spiritualists, the animalists and the angelists, are all dreamers. Pascal is the realist.

The fact that we cannot *renounce* passions does not mean, however, that we cannot control, direct or ride them, like wild horses or Bonzai Pipeline waves. We cannot dry up the waves, nor can we build on them, but we can learn to surf on them. We cannot renounce our passions, nor can we live on the basis of passion, but we can ride them.

But no surfer can avoid all wipe-outs.

21

If we are too young our judgement is impaired, just as it is if we are too old.

Thinking too little about things or thinking too much both make us obstinate and fanatical.

If we look at our work immediately after completing it, we are still too involved; if too long afterwards, we cannot pick up the thread again.

It is like looking at pictures which are too near or too far away. There is just one indivisible point which is the right place.

Others are too near, too far, too high, or too low. In painting the rules of perspective decide it, but how will it be decided when it comes to truth and morality?   (381)

[21]

Human reason is not invalid but weak.

Ideal reason, purely objective reason, divine reason, reason essential, is not so weak that it can know truth only through a tiny, narrow window. But human reason is like human eyesight: only a narrow range of color is visible to it. All extremes are invisible to the eye and incomprehensible to the mind. (See also no. 199, p. 120.)

As the last line shows, this situation is not critical in sensory or aesthetic realms, but in morality it is crucial, and tragic, especially in our age of moral relativism.

542

Thoughts come at random, and go at random. No device for holding on to them or for having them.

A thought has escaped: I was trying to write it down: instead I write that it has escaped me. (370)

[542]

Plato (in the *Theaetetus*) compared the mind to an aviary and thoughts to birds. We have only a little control over them. Reach for one, and you may scare it away and get another. The highest and most God-like thing in us—that which understands eternal Truth—is subjected to the lowest thing in us, random chance, which neither understands nor is understood.

This is more evidence for the Fall, another example of our looking suspiciously like disinherited princes (see pp. 59ff.). The fact that we are *used* to the fact that blind molecules bumping into each other condition our thoughts to be or not to be, to be thoughts of this or thoughts of that, makes our condition more, not less, wretched. The fact that we do not see our weakness is our deepest weakness. (See no. 16, p. 77.)

821

For we must make no mistake about ourselves: we are as much automaton as mind. As a result, demonstration is not the only instrument for convincing us. How few things can be demonstrated! Proofs only convince the mind; habit provides the strongest proofs and those that are most believed. It inclines the automaton, which leads the mind unconsciously along with it.[A] Who ever proved that it will dawn tomorrow, and that we shall die? And what is more widely believed?[B] It is, then, habit that convinces us. . . . We must resort to habit once the mind has

seen where the truth lies, in order to steep and stain ourselves in that belief . . . , for it is too much trouble to
have the proofs always present before us. . . .[C] When we
believe only by the strength of our conviction and the
automaton is inclined to believe the opposite, that is not
enough. We must therefore make both parts of us believe:
the mind by reasons, which need to be seen only once in
a lifetime, and the automaton by habit. . . .[D]

  Reason works slowly. . . . Feeling does not work like
that, but works instantly, and is always ready.   (252)

[821]

A

Pascal is not a determinist, behaviorist, mechanist or materialist. We are not *only* automaton, or *essentially* automaton. But
our reason is so weak that it needs help from habit. Habit
moves us much more effectively than reason. There is almost
nothing people cannot be habituated, almost hypnotized, into
accepting: genocide, slavery, infanticide, abortion, sodomy,
suicide.

B

Here Pascal anticipates Hume's critique of causality—
completely valid on the sensory level. The past tells us only the
probable, not the certain future; we risk the remote possibility
of miracles.

C

See C. S. Lewis' essay "On Obstinacy in Belief" and also the
last page of *Miracles*.

D

See the conclusion of the "Wager" (p. 295): once reason has
convinced us to believe, we require the aid of good habits to
overcome bad habitual tendencies in the opposite direction.
Therefore we must *act as if* we believed, go to church and so

forth, thus habituating the automaton to obey what reason has discovered to be true. Habit is not an honest *substitute* for reason, but it is an honest and needed *servant* to reason. If we try to fight against irrationality with reason alone, we will lose. We need cruder weapons too.

44

Imagination.[A] It is the dominant faculty in man, master of error and falsehood, all the more deceptive for not being invariably so; for it would be an infallible criterion of truth if it were infallibly that of lies. Since, however, it is usually false, it gives no indication of its quality, setting the same mark on true and false alike. . . .

This arrogant force, which checks and dominates its enemy, reason, for the pleasure of showing off the power it has in every sphere, has established a second nature in man. . . . Nothing annoys us more than to see it satisfy its guests more fully and completely than reason ever could. Those who are clever in imagination are far more pleased with themselves than prudent men could reasonably be. They look down on people with a lofty air; they are bold and confident in argument, where others are timid and unsure, and their cheerful demeanour often wins the verdict of their listeners, for those whose wisdom is imaginary enjoy the favour of judges similarly qualified. Imagination cannot make fools wise, but it makes them happy. . . .

Who dispenses reputation? Who makes us respect and revere persons, works, laws, the great? Who but this faculty of imagination? . . . Would you not say that this magistrate, whose venerable age commands universal respect, is ruled by pure, sublime reason, and judges things as they really are, without paying heed to the trivial circumstances which offend only the imagination of weaker men? See him go to hear a sermon in a spirit of pious zeal, the soundness of his judgement strengthened by the ardour of his charity, ready to listen with exemplary respect. If, when the preacher appears, it turns out that nature has given him a hoarse voice and an odd sort of face, that his barber has shaved him badly and he happens not to be too clean either, then, whatever great truths he may announce, I wager that our senator will not be able to keep a straight face.[B]

Put the world's greatest philosopher on a plank that is wider than need be: if there is a precipice below, although his reason may convince him that he is safe, his imagination will prevail. Many could not even stand the thought of it without going pale and breaking into sweat.

I do not intend to list all the effects of imagination. Everyone knows that the sight of cats, or rats, the crunching of a coal, etc., is enough to unhinge reason. The tone of voice influences the wisest of us and alters the force of a speech or a poem. . . .

How absurd is reason, the sport of every wind![C] . . . Men . . . hardly stir except when jolted by imagination. . . .

Reason never wholly overcomes imagination, while the contrary is quite common.[D]

Our magistrates have shown themselves well aware of this mystery. Their red robes, the ermine in which they swaddle themselves like furry cats, the law-courts where they sit in judgement, the fleurs de lys, all this august panoply was very necessary. If physicians did not have long gowns and mules, if learned doctors did not wear square caps and robes four times too large, they would never have deceived the world, which finds such an authentic display irresistible.[E] If they possessed true justice, and if physicians possessed the true art of healing, they would not need square caps; the majesty of such sciences would command respect in itself. But, as they only possess imaginary science, they have to resort to these vain devices in order to strike the imagination, which is their real concern, and this, in fact, is how they win respect. . . . (82)

[44]

A

Imagination depends on images. Images come from sense experience. Thus we find ourselves upside down: the highest thing in us—reason, the prophet of truth—is at the mercy of sensory imagination. This enslavement of the soul to the body provides more evidence for the "disinherited prince" principle. (See pp. 59ff.)

B

Israel loved and wanted Saul as king because he was tall and handsome. America chooses its President by the "image" he projects. Few Greeks listened to Socrates because he was short, fat, bald, bulbous-nosed and frog-eyed. Christ himself "had no form or comeliness that we should look at him, and no beauty that we should desire him" (Is 53:2).

C

This was Freud's most traditional yet most radical and disturbing discovery.

D

The rider, when triumphant, only tames the wild horse; the horse, when triumphant, throws off the rider.

E

Who would fear and obey policemen without uniforms?

551

Imagination magnifies small objects with fantastic exaggeration until they fill our soul, and with bold insolence cuts down great things to its own size, as when speaking of God.   (84)

[551]

When one is traveling on a train, the nearest telephone pole always looms the largest. We are constantly deluded by this illusion of perspective—in space, in time (present dangers and opportunities are like those telephone poles) and in importance. Imagination makes little things (like a cross word or a kiss) big, and big things (like Heaven and Hell) small.

Why? Because we are upside down, abnormal, fallen, disinherited princes.

8. Vanity of Dogmatism

Dogmatism and skepticism both make the same mistake: confusing reason essential (or reason de jure) with reason existential (or reason de facto). Dogmatism ascribes the same trustworthiness and power to reason de facto as to reason de jure, and skepticism ascribes the same untrustworthiness and impotence to reason de jure as to reason de facto. It is a case in point of the paradox of greatness and wretchedness; neither side sees the whole picture. Pascal does.

The case for Christianity is often built upon the foundation of the power of reason to establish truth with certainty in traditional Catholic apologetics. Protestant (especially Reformed) apologetics, on the other hand, is often fideistic. Luther called reason "the devil's whore". Calvin thought it shared in the Fall into "total depravity". Kierkegaard exalted the transcendence of religion over reason and rational ethics, especially in *Fear and Trembling*. Karl Barth called natural theology, especially the doctrine of analogy (by which our reason can understand at least some meaningful truths about God by metaphor, analogy or proportion), "theology's original sin". Pascal follows neither the traditional medieval Scholastic Catholic approach nor the Protestant one, but the Augustinian tradition, which is the common root of both. He strongly emphasizes reason's fallenness de facto, but not de jure, and even carefully balances the claims of faith and reason de facto in nos. 170, 173 and 174 (pp. 236–37; 238).

Pensées about the vanity of human reason (point 7) are part of the "bad news" of our wretchedness and are evidence of our fallenness and need of salvation. But an even stronger indication than reason's weakness (point 7) is our tendency to ignore this truth. As Pascal says in no. 33 (p. 106), the strongest argument for skepticism is the existence of dogmatists.

(We mean by "dogmatism" here not firm belief in revealed dogma [that is simply orthodox Christianity] but naive or arrogant confidence in human reason's power and trustworthiness de facto.)

709

We know so little about ourselves that many people think they are going to die when they are quite well, and many think they are quite well when they are on the point of death, not sensing the approach of fever or the abscess ready to form.   (175)

[709]

Two reasons for skepticism:

(1) If we are not even certain whether we are about to die or live, how can we claim to know ourselves?

(2) And if we do not even know ourselves, how can we claim to know what is infinitely farther above us?

33

What amazes me most is to see that everyone is not amazed at his own weakness. We behave seriously. . . .^A It is a good thing for the reputation of scepticism that there are so many people about who are not sceptics, to show that man is quite capable of the most extravagant opinions, since he is capable of believing that he is not naturally and inevitably weak, but is, on the contrary, naturally wise.

Nothing strengthens the case for scepticism more than the fact that there are people who are not sceptics. If they all were, they would be wrong.^B   (374)

[33]
A

The snob who slips on a banana peel would not be funny if he were not a snob. The funniest thing in the world is how seriously we silly bugs take ourselves. Sin, death, vanity, ignorance—these are our banana peels. And we take our fall as *normal*; we are not amazed at our weakness. This is the most amazing thing of all and our greatest weakness, just as impenitence and insensitivity to sin is the greatest sin.

B

If there were no dogmatists, skepticism would have no balloons to stick its pins into and would win no arguments. Only the folly of dogmatism makes for the truth in skepticism.

Skepticism of reason de jure is self-contradictory and absurd, for it is a piece of the very thing it destroys: reasoning. But skepticism of reason de facto, that is, skepticism of dogmatic confidence in our reason, is true and right and necessary.

131

The strongest of the sceptics' arguments, to say nothing of minor points, is that we cannot be sure that these principles[A] are true (faith and revelation apart) except through some natural intuition.[B] Now this natural intuition affords no convincing proof that they are true. There is no certainty, apart from faith, as to whether man was created by a good God, an evil demon, or just by chance, and so it is a matter of doubt, depending on our origin, whether these innate principles are true, false or uncertain.

Moreover, no one can be sure, apart from faith, whether he is sleeping or waking, because when we are asleep we are just as firmly convinced that we are awake as we are now. As we often dream we are dreaming, piling up one dream on another, is it not possible that this half of our life is itself just a dream, on to which the others are grafted, and from which we shall awake when we die? That while it lasts we are as little in possession of the principles of truth and goodness as during normal sleep? . . . And who can doubt that, if we dreamed in the company of others and our dreams happened to agree, which is common enough, and if we were alone when awake, we should think things had been turned upside-down? . . .[C]

I pause at the dogmatists' only strong point, which is that we cannot doubt natural principles if we speak sincerely and in all good faith.[D]

To which the sceptics reply, in a word, that uncertainty as to our origin entails uncertainty as to our nature. The dogmatists have been trying to answer that ever since the world began. . . .[E]

This means open war between men, in which everyone is obliged to take sides, either with the dogmatists or with the sceptics, because anyone who imagines he can stay neutral is a sceptic *par excellence*. This neutrality is the essence of their clique. Anyone who is not against them is their staunch supporter, and that is where their advantage appears. They are not even for themselves; they are neutral, indifferent, suspending judgment on everything, including themselves.[F]

What then is man to do in this state of affairs? Is he to doubt everything, to doubt whether he is awake, whether he is being pinched or burned? Is he to doubt whether he is doubting, to doubt whether he exists?

No one can go that far, and I maintain that a perfectly genuine sceptic has never existed. Nature backs up helpless reason and stops it going so wildly astray.[D]

Is he, on the other hand, to say that he is the certain possessor of truth, when at the slightest pressure he fails to prove his claim and is compelled to loose his grasp?[G]

What sort of freak then is man? How novel, how monstrous, how chaotic, how paradoxical, how prodigious! Judge of all things, feeble earthworm, repository of truth, sink of doubt and error, glory and refuse of the universe![H]

Who will unravel such a tangle? This is certainly beyond dogmatism and scepticism, beyond all human philosophy. Man transcends man. Let us then concede to the sceptics what they have so often proclaimed, that truth lies beyond our scope and in an unobtainable quarry, that it is no earthly denizen, but at home in heaven, lying in the lap of God. . . .

You cannot be a sceptic . . . without stifling nature, you cannot be a dogmatist without turning your back on reason. . . .[1]

Know then, proud man, what a paradox you are to yourself. Be humble, impotent reason! Be silent, feeble nature! Learn that man infinitely transcends man, hear from your master your true condition, which is unknown to you.

Listen to God.[J]

Is it not as clear as day that man's condition is dual? The point is that if man had never been corrupted, he would, in his innocence, confidently enjoy both truth and felicity,[K] and, if man had never been anything but corrupt, he would have no idea either of truth or bliss.[L] But unhappy as we are (and we should be less so if there were no element of greatness in our condition) we have an idea of happiness but we cannot attain it.[M] We perceive an image of the truth and possess nothing but falsehood, being equally incapable of absolute ignorance and certain knowledge; so obvious is it that we once enjoyed a degree of perfection from which we have unhappily fallen.

Let us then conceive that man's condition is dual. Let us conceive that man infinitely transcends man, and that without the aid of faith he would remain inconceivable to himself, for who cannot see that unless we realize the duality of human nature we remain invincibly ignorant of the truth about ourselves?

It is, however, an astounding thing that the mystery furthest from our ken, that of the transmission of sin, should be something without which we can have no knowledge of ourselves. . . .[N]   (434)

[131]

A

Innately known, self-evident propositions like "2 + 2 = 4",

"Effects have causes", "The whole is greater than the part", and even the law of noncontradiction itself ("x ≠ non-x").

B

Pascal means by "intuition", not something irrational, but direct, immediate intellectual understanding as distinct from proving, reasoning, calculating.

These principles are universally known. They are like software in all our human computers (brains). Pascal asks how we can be sure we can trust this software to be true.

The obvious answer is that we just see it, we "intuit" it. But this intuition itself can be questioned. Where did it come from?

There are three possible sources:

(1) a good and wise (nondeceiving and nondeceived) mind;

(2) a bad or foolish (deceiving or deceived) mind;

(3) no mind at all but blind chance.

The only candidate for (1) is God. The only candidate for (2) is the Devil (unless you want to throw in the possibility of extraterrestrials). (3) is modern scientific secularism (for example, mere "natural selection").

Pascal's point is that only if God designed our minds do we have the right to trust our minds.

But how do we know there is a God? By reason, that is, by using our computers? That begs the question and argues in a circle—as Descartes did when he appealed to innate "clear and distinct ideas" as the criterion of truth, including the truth about God, and then appealed to God as perfect and nondeceiving to prove the validity of our innate clear and distinct ideas. The fallacy is so famous that it has a name: "the Cartesian circle".

Pascal argues that only faith can cut this Gordian knot, this Cartesian circle. To reason is to rely on reason, and to rely on reason is an act of faith, not of reason. Therefore reason presupposes faith.

This is an extremely serious problem—probably an unsolvable problem—for the philosopher who accepts Descartes' and modernity's demand to prove everything, including a critical justification of human reason itself.

Indeed, how could reason itself be validated? There are only three possibilities: (1) by something subrational, like animal instinct (which is obviously absurd: How can the inferior validate the superior?); or (2) by something rational, by a piece of reasoning (which is also absurd: How can the part justify the whole? All reason is on trial; how dare the one piece of reasoning you use to justify all reasoning be exempt from trial?); or (3) by something superrational, by faith in God (which is the only possibility left).

C

Having resuscitated Descartes' famous "universal doubt" in the figure of his evil demon (see *Meditations* I), Pascal now does the same with Descartes' "dream" doubt. How *do* we know with certainty that we are not dreaming now? Pascal implies that Descartes did not answer either question; that reason has not refuted these two skeptical doubts against itself.

D

You can think skepticism, but you can't live it. Aristotle refuted the Sophist skeptic Protagoras this way (*Metaphysics* Γ, 4–6): by an *ad hominem* argument, by showing a lived contradiction between the skeptic's theory and his practice. Universal doubt is psychologically impossible. No one can *do* it. For example, to choose to doubt is not to doubt that there is a difference between doubting and not-doubting.

E

The skeptic's reply is that these undoubtable principles like the law of noncontradiction are dependent on our origin, our programmer; and if this is not God, there is no reason to trust them. Thus the argument between the dogmatist (who believes in certainty) and the skeptic (who does not) goes on in a circle forever.

F

The consistent skeptic is skeptical of everything, including his own skepticism. If not, he is refuted: "My, how dogmatic you are about your skepticism!"

G

See *pensées* no. 33 (p. 106) and no. 34. As soon as there is a dogmatist, the skeptic wins—just as, as soon as there is a balloon, the pin wins.

H

Why does Pascal tie us in knots, circles and inescapable dilemmas like this? To show us this terrific truth about ourselves, a truth we hide from, the truth that we are two incredible paradoxical extremes: judge and worm, glory and garbage.

And to show us that no human philosophy can unravel this riddle (next paragraph); to put us in the market for *listening* to God, that is, destroying the pretensions of proud, chattering reason; to create silence. For only in silence can God's word be heard (see Job 31:40b; 38:1–4).

I

Here is the unsolvable dilemma. We cannot deny reason without contradicting ourselves and invalidating our very denial, and we cannot deny our nature because we *are* our nature. If we deny our reason, we must use our reason to do so, and if we deny our nature, we must use our nature to do so. Yet our reason and our nature contradict each other! Our reason insists on doubt, our nature insists on certainty. Our reason is a skeptic, our nature is a dogmatist. Our reason insists on assuming nothing, our nature insists on assuming innate principles.

The point, the lesson, now follows. Both nature and reason must learn faith, silence, humility, *listening* (to God). Without this, there is no fulfillment of our reason *or* our nature, and no solution to the dilemma between them.

J

The most important step in the whole apologetic strategy is this. Good apologists are not teachers but pointers to The Teacher. Unless they can get their listeners to listen to God, it will do no good at all to get their listeners to listen to them; and if they do get them to listen to God, it will soon be unnecessary to get them to listen to them any more; so in either case they are disposable, like tissues, once they have done their work.

"Listen to God"—perhaps the three most important words in the whole book.

K, L

This is a tight, valid syllogism:

If man had never been uncorrupted, he would have no idea (or desire or memory) of perfect truth or bliss.

But man does have an idea and a desire (and, it seems, a memory) of perfect truth and bliss.

Therefore man has once been uncorrupted.

Here is logical and empirical evidence for the Fall, of the distinctively Christian claim in anthropology: that man's present state is abnormal, not normal.

M

Data: we are unhappy.

If we had no idea of happiness, we would not feel unhappy, for we would have no standard with which to measure our present state and call it lacking.

Only Christian "abnormalism", only the Fall, explains these two primal truths: that we are unhappy and ignorant, and that we long to be happy and certain.

We cannot stop demanding our two foods, happiness and certainty. Nor can we attain them. They are the only two innate desires that are never satisfied, the only hungers for foods not found here on earth and in time.

N

If you stare directly at the sun, you see a black spot. Yet only by the sun's light can you see everything else. Similarly, if you look at the dogmas of Christianity, especially the dogma of Original Sin, it seems dark and irrational. Yet only in light of this truth can we understand our whole existence (see the two preceding notes).

406

Instinct, reason. We have an incapacity for proving anything which no amount of dogmatism can overcome.

We have an idea of truth which no amount of scepticism can overcome. (395)

[406]

Our unavoidable and unsolvable dilemma: we cannot rest in either Dogmatism or Skepticism (above, notes D, E and F). Where are we left? In defeat (note H), ready at last for faith (notes I and J), ready to say to God the puzzle-Master, "I give up. What's *your* solution?"

9. Vanity of the Philosophers

This point follows hard upon, and is closely linked to, the previous one about the vanity of dogmatism, for most philosophers are prime examples of just this vanity, notably Descartes, the guru of Pascal's age and of secular rationalist "enlightenment", the new religion that has been Christianity's chief rival among "educated" people for the last 300 years.

84

Descartes. **In general terms one must say: . . . Pointless, uncertain, and arduous.**[A] **Even if it were true we do not think that the whole of philosophy would be worth an hour's effort.**[B]   (79)

[84]

A

The three things Descartes longs for the most: certainty, utility and ease. His chief critique of the ancients was that they lacked certainty, or "a sufficient *criterion*". Certainty, in turn, was his means to the end of utility, or efficiency, or "the conquest of nature" (see the last three pages of the *Discourse on Method*). This technological conquest, in turn, was a means to "the relief of man's estate", that is, ease, comfort, the abolition of suffering.

Yet these are precisely the three things his philosophy, and the civilization that has been seduced by it, not only fails to deliver but destroys. Life has never been so full of confusion and uncertainty; the average person has never felt so weak and helpless; and all social indicators show we feel exactly the opposite of ease and comfort. This is proved both by the statistics on violence, rape, child abuse, incest, depression and divorce (a form of violence, the suicide of the "one flesh"), and also by the plethora of peace-of-mind, how-to-cope self-help books we buy.

Pascal is a prophet. Descartes is a false prophet.

B

Gilson said he loved to be told that philosophy, his life's work, is not worth an hour's effort when it is Pascal who tells him, for "a man always has the right to disdain what he surpasses." But let no mere student, or second-rate philosopher, tell us such a thing.

Aquinas declared all his writings mere "straw" and would not finish the *Summa*—not out of laziness but in light of God's face seen in graced mystical vision. Job, too, put his finger to his lips when he saw God (Job 42:1–6). This is the chief use of reasoning, questioning and genius: that we may have something to quiet. The chief use of philosophy is to have something to immolate on the altar. The ultimate purpose of speech is to frame the great mystical silence.

Philosophy is, after all, the love of wisdom; and wisdom is *alive*, like a woman. So how could we think our courtship of her is a one-way activity? This is true only for the pursuit of things and abstract ideas, but never for persons, not even human persons, and much less the divine Person who *is* Wisdom (1 Cor 1:30). He spoke and we were created. He speaks (in Christ, in Scripture) and we listen.

140

Even if Epictetus did see the way quite clearly, he only told men: 'You are on the wrong track.' He shows that there is another, but he does not lead us there. The right way is to want what God wants. Christ alone leads to it.   (466)

[140]

Many philosophers can do the first thing: tell us we are on the wrong track. Even Marx can do that. Some can go farther and tell us what the right track is: for example, moralists like Plato, Epictetus and the Stoics. But only Christ can get us there.

Philosophers of the first type (1) observe our symptoms and sometimes even (2) diagnose our diseases. Philosophers of the second type go farther and (3) give us a prognosis of

our healing. But only Christ gives us our actual, real
(4) prescription and treatment, the medicine (grace) and the
surgery (salvation). Only "the Wounded Surgeon" can "ply
the steel" (T. S. Eliot).

141

Philosophers. **All very well to cry out to a man who does
not know himself that he should make his own way to
God!** (509)

[141]

If you do not know yourself, whom you have seen, how can
you know God, whom you have not seen? And if you do not
know him, how can you reach him? Even if you *do* know
him, how can you reach him? Having a photo of Everest is not
attaining the summit.

142

(Against the philosophers who have God without Christ.)
Philosophers. **They believe that God alone is worthy of
love and admiration; they too wanted to be loved and admired by men and do not realize their own corruption.**
(463)

[142]

Philosophers and theologians do not practice what they preach
any better than the rest of us—less, if they preach better than
the rest of us.

The kind of philosopher Pascal castigates here is the idealist
who does not believe in sin—for example, Plato, Rousseau
and secular humanists.

Pascal castigates even himself in no. 627 (pp. 80–81).

143

Philosophers. **We are full of things that impel us outwards.
Our instinct makes us feel that our happiness must be**

sought outside ourselves. Our passions drive us outwards, even without objects to excite them. External objects tempt us in themselves and entice us even when we do not think about them. Thus it is no good philosophers telling us: Withdraw into yourselves and there you will find your good. We do not believe them, and those who do believe them are the most empty and silly of all.

(464)

[143]

"Our happiness must be sought outside ourselves"—this is materialism.

"Withdraw into yourselves and there you will find your good"—this is subjectivism.

Both are foolish, yet it seems we cannot avoid one or the other, just as with the dilemma of Dogmatism and Skepticism.

Materialism and externalism are vanity, but so are subjectivism and internalism. For we are no more our own God, our own end, than the material world is.

In fact, the worshiper of matter is closer to God than the worshiper of self, even though the self is God's image and matter is not. For the worship of self is far worse than the worship of sun or moon. The first is devilish, the second is only animalish. As Chesterton says,

> That Jones shall worship the god within him turns out ultimately to mean that Jones shall worship Jones. Let Jones worship the sun or moon, anything rather than the Inner Light; let Jones worship cats or crocodiles, if he can find any in his street, but not the god within. Christianity came into the world firstly in order to assert with violence that a man had not only to look inwards, but to look outwards, to behold with astonishment and enthusiasm a divine company and a divine captain. The only fun of being a Christian was that a man was not left alone with the Inner Light, but definitely recognized an outer light, fair as the sun, clear as the moon, terrible as an army with banners. (*Orthodoxy*, chap. 5)

533

We always picture Plato and Aristotle wearing long academic gowns, but they were ordinary decent people like anyone else, who enjoyed a laugh with their friends.^A And when they amused themselves by composing their *Laws* and *Politics* they did it for fun. It was the least philosophical and least serious part of their lives: the most philosophical part was living simply without fuss.^B

If they wrote about politics it was as if to lay down rules for a madhouse.^C   (331)

[533]

A

Why do we find this a bold and unusual thought? Why do we remove great philosophers from ordinary humanity? Not even God in the flesh was removed from ordinary humanity; "he was like us in all things but sin" (Heb 4:15). He, too, must have enjoyed a good laugh with his friends. If the God who is not man laughs (Ps 2:4; 37:13) and if the man who is not God laughs (Qo 3:4; Ps 126:2), how can the One who is both God and man not laugh?

B

That is the wisest, highest, rarest and most precious wisdom. It also requires humility.

C

Unfortunately, Pascal is probably idealizing Plato and Aristotle here, who both seem to have taken themselves quite seriously, unlike Socrates.

10. Alienation: "Lost in the Cosmos"

This seems to be a wholly modern phenomenon. Although some of the ancients felt *detached* from the world, they didn't feel *alienated* from it, for their science had not yet reduced it to something out of all proportion and relation to the human spirit. The prescientific picture of nature was always anthropomorphic. The most popular and lasting image of nature was that of a mother; "Mother Nature" is a monomyth. When science seemed to show that nature was not a mother but a machine, not a womb but a Skinner box, her children became anxious.

(Of course, science proved no such thing. Reductionistic and materialistic *philosophies* are the villains here, not science; Bacon, Locke and Hobbes, not Galileo, Copernicus and Newton. Science no more proves that nature is not a mother but only matter than an X-ray proves that a woman is not a mother but only a bag of bones.)

199

Disproportion of man. . . . Before going on to a wider inquiry concerning nature, I want him to consider nature just once, seriously and at leisure, and to look at himself as well, and judge whether there is any proportion between himself and nature by comparing the two.[A]

Let man then contemplate the whole of nature[B] in her full and lofty majesty, let him turn his gaze away from the lowly objects around him; let him behold the dazzling light set like an eternal lamp to light up the universe, let him see the earth as a mere speck compared to the vast orbit described by this star, and let him marvel at finding this vast orbit itself to be no more than the tiniest point compared to that described by the stars revolving in the firmament. But if our eyes stop there, let our imagination proceed further; it will grow weary of conceiving things before nature tires of producing them. The whole visible world is only an imperceptible dot in nature's ample bosom. No idea comes near it; it is no good inflating our conceptions beyond imaginable space, we only bring forth atoms compared to the reality of things.^{C} Nature is an infinite sphere whose centre is everywhere and circumference is nowhere.^{D} In short it is the greatest perceptible mark of God's omnipotence that our imagination should lose itself in that thought.^{E}

Let man, returning to himself, consider what he is in comparison with what exists; let him regard himself as lost, and from this little dungeon, in which he finds himself lodged, I mean the universe, let him learn to take the earth, its realms, its cities, its houses and himself at their proper value.

What is a man in the infinite?^{F}

But, to offer him another prodigy equally astounding, let him look into the tiniest things he knows. Let a mite^G show him in its minute body incomparably more minute parts, legs with joints, veins in its legs, blood in the veins, humours in the blood, drops in the humours, vapours in the drops:^{H} let him divide these things still further until he has exhausted his powers of imagination, and let the last thing he comes down to now be the subject of our discourse.^{I} He will perhaps think that this is the ultimate of minuteness in nature.

I want to show him a new abyss.^{J} I want to depict to him not only the visible universe, but all the conceivable immensity of nature enclosed in this miniature atom. Let him see there an infinity of universes, each with its firmament, its planets, its earth, in the same proportions as in the visible world, and on that earth animals, and finally mites, in which he will find again the same results as in the first; and finding the same thing yet again in the others without end or respite, he will be lost in such wonders, as astounding in their minuteness as the others in their amplitude.[K] For who will not marvel that our body, a moment ago imperceptible in a universe, itself imperceptible in the bosom of the whole, should now be a colossus, a world, or rather a whole, compared to the nothingness beyond our reach? Anyone who considers himself in this way will be terrified at himself, and, seeing his mass, as given him by nature, supporting him between these two abysses of infinity and nothingness, will tremble at these marvels. I believe that with his curiosity changing into wonder he will be more disposed to contemplate them in silence than investigate them with presumption.[L]

For, after all, what is man in nature? A nothing compared to the infinite, a whole compared to the nothing, a middle point between all and nothing, infinitely remote from an understanding of the extremes; the end of things and their principles are unattainably hidden from him in impenetrable secrecy.[M]

Equally incapable of seeing the nothingness from which he emerges and the infinity in which he is engulfed.

What else can he do, then, but perceive some semblance of the middle of things, eternally hopeless of knowing either their principles or their end? All things have come out of nothingness and are carried onwards to infinity. Who can follow these astonishing processes? The author of these wonders understands them: no one else can.

Because they failed to contemplate these infinities, men have rashly undertaken to probe into nature as if there were some proportion between themselves and her.

Strangely enough they wanted to know the principles of things and go on from there to know everything, inspired by a presumption as infinite as their object. For there can be no doubt that such a plan could not be conceived without infinite presumption or a capacity as infinite as that of nature.

When we know better, we understand that, since nature has engraved her own image and that of her author on all things, they almost all share her double infinity. Thus we see that all the sciences are infinite in the range of their researches, for who can doubt that mathematics, for instance, has an infinity of infinities of propositions to expound? They are infinite also in the multiplicity and subtlety of their principles, for anyone can see that those which are supposed to be ultimate do not stand by themselves, but depend on others, which depend on others again, and thus never allow of any finality.

But we treat as ultimate those which seem so to our reason, as in material things we call a point indivisible when our senses can perceive nothing beyond it, although by its nature it is infinitely divisible.

Of these two infinites of science, that of greatness is much more obvious, and that is why it has occurred to few people to claim that they know everything. 'I am going to speak about everything,' Democritus used to say.[N]

But the infinitely small is much harder to see. The philosophers have much more readily claimed to have reached it, and that is where they have all tripped up. This is the origin of such familiar titles as *Of the principles of things*, *Of the principles of philosophy*,[1] and the like, which are really as pretentious, though they do not look it, as this blatant one: *Of all that can be known*.[2]

We naturally believe we are more capable of reaching the centre of things than of embracing their circumference, and the visible extent of the world is visibly greater than we. But since we in our turn are greater than small things, we think we are more capable of mastering them, and yet it takes no less capacity to reach nothingness than the whole. In either case it takes an infinite capacity, and

[1] By Descartes (1644).   [2] By Pico della Mirandola (1486).

it seems to me that anyone who had understood the ultimate principles of things might also succeed in knowing
infinity. One depends on the other, and one leads to the
other. These extremes touch and join by going in opposite
directions, and they meet in God and God alone.º

Let us then realize our limitations. We are something
and we are not everything. Such being as we have conceals from us the knowledge of first principles, which arise
from nothingness, and the smallness of our being hides
infinity from our sight.

Our intelligence occupies the same rank in the order of
intellect as our body in the whole range of nature.

Limited in every respect, we find this intermediate state
between two extremes reflected in all our faculties. Our
senses can perceive nothing extreme; too much noise deaf-
ens us, too much light dazzles; when we are too far or too
close we cannot see properly; an argument is obscured by
being too long or too short; too much truth bewilders us.
I know people who cannot understand that 4 from 0
leaves 0. First principles are too obvious for us;P too much
pleasure causes discomfort; too much harmony in music is
displeasing; too much kindness annoys us. . . .

We feel neither extreme heat nor extreme cold. Qualities carried to excess are bad for us and cannot be perceived; we no longer feel them, we suffer them. Excessive
youth and excessive age impair thought; so do too much
and too little learning.

In a word, extremes are as if they did not exist for us
nor we for them; they escape us or we escape them.

Such is our true state. That is what makes us incapable
of certain knowledge or absolute ignorance.Q We are
floating in a medium of vast extent, always drifting uncer-
tainly, blown to and fro; whenever we think we have a
fixed point to which we can cling and make fast, it shifts
and leaves us behind; if we follow it, it eludes our grasp,
slips away, and flees eternally before us. Nothing stands

still for us.[R] This is our natural state and yet the state most contrary to our inclinations.[S] We burn with desire to find a firm footing, an ultimate, lasting base on which to build a tower rising up to infinity, but our whole foundation cracks and the earth opens up into the depth of the abyss.[T]

Let us then seek neither assurance nor stability [here]; our reason is always deceived by the inconsistency of appearances; nothing can fix the finite between the two infinites which enclose and evade it.

Once that is clearly understood, I think that each of us can stay quietly in the state in which nature has placed him.[U] Since the middle station allotted to us is always far from the extremes, what does it matter if someone else has a slightly better understanding of things? If he has, and if he takes them a little further, is he not still infinitely remote from the goal? Is not our span of life equally infinitesimal in eternity, even if it is extended by ten years? . . .

If man studied himself, he would see how incapable he is of going further. How could a part possibly know the whole? But perhaps he will aspire to know at least the parts to which he bears some proportion. But the parts of the world are all so related and linked together that I think it is impossible to know one without the other and without the whole. . . .[V]

And what makes our inability to know things absolute is that they are simple in themselves, while we are composed of two opposing natures of different kinds, soul and body. . . .[W]

That is why nearly all philosophers confuse their ideas of things, and speak spiritually of corporeal things and corporeally of spiritual ones, for they boldly assert that bodies tend to fall, that they aspire towards their centre, that they flee from destruction, that they fear a void, that they have inclinations, sympathies, antipathies, all things pertaining only to things spiritual. And when they speak of minds,

they consider them as being in a place, and attribute to
them movement from one place to another, which are
things pertaining only to bodies.

Instead of receiving ideas of these things in their purity,
we colour them with our qualities and stamp our own
composite being on all the simple things we contemplate.

Who would not think, to see us compounding everything of mind and matter, that such a mixture is perfectly
intelligible to us? Yet this is the thing we understand least;
man is to himself the greatest prodigy in nature, for he
cannot conceive what body is, and still less what mind is,
and least of all how a body can be joined to a mind. This
is his supreme difficulty, and yet it is his very being. *The
way in which minds are attached to bodies is beyond man's
understanding, and yet this is what man is.*[3] W   (72)

[199]
A

The typical modern, in a hurry to be off and running with his
science, forgets his philosophical perspective. "Inchworm,
inchworm, measuring the marigolds" ignores the philosophical
question of the fundamental relation between the mind of man
the measurer and the material (marigolds; nature) measured.

The modern mind was born when Bacon trumpeted "man's
conquest of nature" as the new *summum bonum*. Nearly everyone hopped on his bandwagon, but not Pascal. Today nearly
everyone can plainly see that Pascal was right and Bacon
wrong; that man's conquest of nature by science and technology, despite its spectacular success, has not made us happier,
has not made us wiser and has not made us holier. It has not
even made us more powerful; the individual feels a far greater
sense of impotence today than ever before.

The question Pascal remembered and the founders of the
modern mind forgot is the question of whether there is any

[3] St. Augustine, *City of God*, XXI. 10.

proportion between the new, modernly conceived human mind and the new, modernly conceived material universe. The new mind is a calculator rather than a poet and prophet, a technocrat rather than a contemplator. And the universe is a lifeless, mindless, purposeless machine.

There are two answers to the question of the proportion between these two new actors in the modern drama. Both are contained in no. 113 (p. 57). (1) Man is utterly dwarfed by the universe materially; and (2) the universe is utterly dwarfed by man mentally. But what is forgotten in both these calculations (as will emerge only later in this *pensée*) is the most important thing of all, the "heart".

B

"Nature" = the universe. "The world" = the planet Earth.

C

It was well known throughout the Middle Ages that the universe was unimaginably vast. Ptolemy had already taught that in his *Almagest*, which was *the* authoritative astronomy text before Copernicus; and Boethius had popularized this teaching in *The Consolation of Philosophy*, which was more widely read than anything except the Bible and Augustine's *Confessions* and *City of God*. The notion that the medieval universe was small, cozy and not awesomely vast is simply false. This false idea has become enormously popular and embedded in the contemporary mind, which repeats secondary sources as "authoritative" without knowing or respecting the primary sources, much more "authoritarianly" than the Middle Ages did.

D

This famous description was well known to the Middle Ages. It comes from Pseudo-Dionysius the Areopagite and describes *God*, not nature. The fact that Pascal now applies it to nature is a shocking and fascinating change. Nature now elicits the religious awe that only God had elicited in the Middle Ages.

There seems to be an obvious connection between modernity's divinizing nature and its naturalizing God. Both these things happen when you stand upside down.

E

In Pascal, as in the Middle Ages, the vast size of the universe is used to show forth the vastness of God's power. The very same fact is commonly used by the modern mind (which ignorantly thinks it is the first to discover the fact) as evidence for a-theism! "How could you believe in a God when Man is but a lost speck in an infinite abyss?" Why the size of the universe should count against theism is never argued for, only assumed. For the *argument* is worthless or nonexistent, but the *feeling* is strong. That's where the change takes place: in feeling, in sensibility. It is a change from feeling at home to feeling lost, and from a universe full of signs that point beyond themselves to their Author to a universe that is empty and silent (see no. 201, p. 135).

F

The clear medieval distinction between the infinity of God and the finitude of the universe is breaking down. Even as orthodox a Christian as Pascal now speaks of the universe as infinite (see note D), though not yet of God as finite.

G

A tiny flea.

H

The substitution of modern for medieval chemical terminology does not change the essential point.

I

The atom. The word (*a-tomos* in Greek) literally means "not divisible", "not splittable", that is, a unit. Pascal was prophetic in supposing that atoms were not in fact unsplittable. Perhaps the only thing in nature that is truly unsplittable, or a true unit, is a person, a self, an "I". (At least by natural power, discounting demonic possession and literal "split personalities" in Hell.)

J

The very same abyss of unendingness and unboundedness that we discovered in the universe outside us, we now discover in the universe inside us. The microcosm is as much an infinite abyss as the macrocosm. The essential point here is not the scientific speculation but the human consequence, the abyss, the bottomless hole into which our thought falls when contemplating these wonders.

K

Pascal's physics is crude but prophetic—far less crude and more prophetic than that of Democritus and the classical atomists. Our present-day particle physics is as crude as Columbus' maps—we have barely landed on the beach of this new world—and it is quite possible that each atom is not only a very mysterious and complex structure but an entire universe. It is equally possible that our entire astronomical universe is but an atom in a larger universe. Finally, it is possible that this process goes on for "astronomical" numbers.

In that case, perhaps we should think twice before we split an atom; we may be destroying a universe. And if this were so—since cosmic justice is not limited temporally or spatially and applies to all universes—we will surely reap what we sow; perhaps our universe will be destroyed by some atom-splitting scientist who is living in that larger universe in which ours is one atom.

Neither Pascal nor any contemporary scientist is claiming that this is in fact exactly the case; but such "fantasy" scenarios are truer to the fundamental facts, the human situation vis-à-vis the universe, the disproportion and the consequent stammering terror, than any other, cozier picture. The point of Pascal's picture is not scientific but philosophical (note L); if it is not scientifically true (and we are not sure of that, are we?), it is nevertheless a true myth, as Tolkien's *Lord of the Rings* is a far truer tale of the way things really are than libraries of statistics.

L

Here is the "bottom line", the point and purpose of this spectacular *pensée*. It is not a spectacle but a moral, not speculative but practical, not about nature but about man. It is a slap in the face, to teach us the wisdom of wonder, silence and humility. It is not designed to fill our heads but to bow them.

For over three centuries, since Pascal wrote these words, our arrogance has become larger than the universe and our awe smaller and harder to find than an atom. Even the Nazi-inflicted Holocaust, the fear of a worldwide nuclear and/or ecological holocaust and the ghastly breakdown of social morality and the family have hardly dented our arrogance. The "wonder", "contemplation" and "silence" Pascal calls for are still largely the province of socially marginal ("flake") groups. The "bottom line" of Pascal's three-century-old "fantasy" is far more, not less, relevant in our day than it was in his.

We have been living in an unstable and temporary situation for three centuries, as if in an airlock or a bridge or a time warp. And Pascal is the first to see it. He is suspended between two worlds: the premodern, prescientific world in which we have a cosmic place, meaning and harmony with nature; and the scientific, or rather scientistic, world view according to which the universe (whether it is a clockwork machine, a drama of the blind Will to Power or Life Force, or a mathematical equation) is inhuman, alien, unfit for habitation, not a *home*.

Homelessness is an unstable condition. The homeless have short life expectancies. We cannot live for long with one foot on the medieval, stable land and one foot in the modern, relativistic boat. We must either find our way back to a home or turn ourselves into machines or equations to fit our new universe, like Bauhaus and Nazi architecture or Le Corbusier, who redefined a house as "a machine to live in".

Pascal does not guide us into either answer, because he is not an anthropologist but an apologist. His eyes are on God, not man, as the standard. He uses our modern alienation from the cosmos, not to lead us back to a more human world, nor forward to a "brave new world", but to goad us *away* from the world into the arms of God, who alone can save us. It is the same strategy as Augustine's in book 19 of *The City of God*. Its point is precisely that "this world is *not* my home."

This is not to say that burning social questions are not burning, only that Pascal deals with roots, not fruits. Unlike Aquinas and Aristotle, and like Augustine and Plato, he is impatient with second causes and runs immediately to first, ultimate causes. We obviously need both kinds of thinkers.

M

The same is true of *time's* beginning and end as of *space's* infinite enormity and infinite tininess. We are disproportionate. We cannot relate. "It does not compute."

Augustine has a terrifying and wonderful image of time as a mighty, rushing river, carrying down it all the flotsam and jetsam of the universe—people, animals, plants, planets, nations, civilizations, everything. Its flow emerges out of a dark and unexplorable cave called Beginnings, or Births. And it flows in one direction—down—unstoppably into an equally dark and unexplorable cavern called Death, or The End. Everything that exists bobs for a bit on its rapids and rapidly disappears. (Commentary on Psalm 90.)

Surprisingly, modern physics seems to be helping us back to a physical absolute by Big Bang cosmology, which gives our universe a finite time. All time came into existence fifteen to twenty billion years ago. We also know that the universe's space and matter are finite—"only" fifteen to twenty billion light years in diameter.

But before the Big Bang? Science is prevented in principle

from answering that question, since all time came into existence with matter in the Bang. There can be no Before "before" time itself.

Nor does science tell us about God or of his ultimate purpose and end and design and will for us and our universe. Salvation is not written in the sands but in the soul.

So Pascal's bottom line still holds: "The end of things and their principles [beginnings] are unattainably hidden in impenetrable secrecy." That's just what God told Job. It's still the hardest lesson to learn, Socrates' Lesson One, the wisdom of ignorance. "The author of these wonders understands them; no one else can."

N

Hilaire Belloc wrote a book entitled *On Everything* in this century, but the title was meant and known to be a joke, unlike the titles of works by Democritus, Pico and Descartes.

Pascal here excoriates both (1) the theoretical rashness of Descartes, who thought he could deduce all the truths of nature from the principles of his philosophy (*Discourse on Method*, 1) and (2) the practical rashness of technologists like Bacon, who thought that his "knowledge for power" and "man's conquest of nature" by the "new organon [tool]" of inductive logic and scientific method would create a "new Atlantis", a Utopia of wisdom, goodness, happiness, prosperity and peace.

One name refutes Bacon: "Los Angeles".

O

God is infinitely great *and* infinitely small: greater than the universe and smaller than the atom, containing the universe and contained by each atom, transcendent and immanent, outside and inside, the circumference that is nowhere and the center that is everywhere. (Pascal probably got this point from Nicholas of Cusa.)

P

I have had A students in logic who could understand everything except the indubitability of the Law of Noncontradiction.

Q

The dilemma of skepticism and dogmatism (point 8) is now
better understood in the more universal perspective of our
magnetic repulsion from extremes.

R

Perhaps this is one of the many deep reasons why we are so
rapt and arrested by the sea, especially its restless waves: in it
we meet ourselves.

We are land creatures in a world that seems all sea. We are
the dove that Noah let out of his ark; it found no land to rest
on and came flying back. We have feet but no place to put
them down. We are like foxes living among fish, finding no
lair.

We need land. We need a stable center, an absolute by
which we can measure the relative. But in this universe, we
have found, everything is relative. Copernicus told us we were
not at the center. Pascal tells us the universe's circumference is
everywhere and center is nowhere (note D). Soon Einstein
would tell us that space and time itself were relative.

Ancient tribes often drove their holy temple tent-pole into a
hole they labeled "the navel of the earth" and declared, like
Bostonians, that this was "the Hub of the universe". We have
lost that hole.

If our spiritual tent-pole had remained stuck into God,
Copernicus' physical decentrification would not have mattered
much. Nor would anyone have made the foolish but common
mistake of confusing Einstein's physical relativity with moral
and spiritual relativity. Space and time are indeed relative, but
truth is not. Indeed, if truth were relative, we could not truly
say that space and time were relative!

S

Here are two facts, two pieces of crucial data. Both are equally solid. First, that no thing in this universe is solid, stable, absolute and unchanging, least of all ourselves. Second, that we scream for that solidity. We yearn, we demand, we act like babies deprived of milk, fish of water, birds of air. We act like land creatures sucked from their home by a tidal wave in a past so remote and forgotten that we seem to have been drifting always. But all driftwood originally came from a tree, with roots. The deep inner wisdom of our "inclinations", our innate desire for eternity and absoluteness, leads us back to God, our true home, "the fixed point of the turning world".

Pascal's apologetic strategy is a long footnote to Augustine's "restless heart".

T

All our Towers of Babel fall because they are erected not on the foundation of the Rock but on our restless, shifting sands, our relative Earth and our understanding of it, our science. It is the Babel story repeated. There, the Tower fell because God confused its builders' *language*. To the ancients, language was identified with thought; a concept was an unspoken *word*. So the foundation was human knowledge, reason, science. This is the foundation of all human Towers of Babel, including anti-intellectual ones (we must *know* even to scorn knowledge). That is why they all fall, like sand castles.

What is the alternative? There is indeed a Rock (see Mt 7:24–29), and it is not knowledge. The beginning of wisdom is "the fear of the Lord". Knowledge of him and of ourselves comes from obedience, from love. If our will is to do his will, we will understand his teaching (Jn 7:17), not otherwise. (See point 16.)

U

How much of our civilization's restlessness and "progressivism" comes from our inability to be quiet and happy at home and mind our own business? All of it, according to Pascal (see no. 136, p. 172).

It seems exaggerated, but it is true. Staggeringly enormous miseries have been the fruit of modernity's five great revolutions: the Industrial Revolution, the French Revolution, the Bolshevik Revolution, the National Socialist Revolution and the Sexual Revolution.

These five revolutions are one revolution: five visible outcroppings of the same invisible undersea continent. Each stems from the same root: the idolatrous search for a new absolute, the divinization of power or freedom or equality or pride or pleasure, respectively.

Our civilization has the fidgets.

V

Cf. Tennyson's "Flower in the Crannied Wall":

> Flower in the crannied wall,
> I pluck you out of the crannies,
> I hold you here, root and all, in my hand,
> Little flower—but if I could understand
> What you are, root and all, and all in all,
> I should know what God and man is.

W

Pascal seems to accept Descartes' mind-body dualism here (and in point 15). If we do this, we are as alienated from our own being as from nature. We are, in fact, no longer nature at all, only spirit plus artifice, ghost plus machine, an angel in a box.

But Pascal, like a French cook, can use even this rotten spice in his cooking. He concludes from it that we cannot understand or master ourselves any more than nature. "Know thyself" is our unsolvable *koan*.

201

The eternal silence of these infinite spaces fills me with dread.   **(206)**

[201]

This miniscule *pensée* contains within it a cosmic earthquake. It manifests a radically new relationship between Man and Nature, one that sets off the mind of modern Western civilization from every other civilization in history; and it is about something that is omnipresent and all-embracing.

The usual way of describing this change is to say that scientific knowledge of nature and technological control of it have progressed enormously; that man now has a radically greater knowledge of nature. This is exactly the opposite of the truth. Our knowledge of nature has *shrunk*. For nature now appears empty, purposeless, meaningless. This is a minus, not a plus. If the old meanings that every premodern civilization saw in nature were really there, then modernity is not demythologized but orphaned, delivered not from superstition but from home.

No premodern writer ever used the word "space" as Pascal does here, and as we all do today. What we call "space", the ancients and medievals called "the heavens". The linguistic change is not accidental; the whole cosmos has been *emptied*. An "emptiness" word ("space") has replaced a "fullness" word ("heavens").

Exactly parallel to this is the change in the auditory metaphor: where we used to hear music ("the music of the spheres" of Pythagoras), we now hear silence. That is why where we once felt wonder we now feel dread, an inner emptiness reflecting the outer emptiness. We are alienated from our cosmic mother; we are "the cosmic orphan" (William Craig, *The Son Rises*); we are "lost in the cosmos" (Walker Percy).

When we go out into our back yard at night and look up at the stars (if we are still fortunate enough to be able to see any through the smog of our pollution—what a perfect symbol!), we spontaneously feel we are looking *out* into darkness, emptiness and silence, like Viking hunters huddling round a tiny campfire (this "civilized" planet), surrounded by the howling darkness of a stormy winter night. But the ancients did not see the stars this way at all! They felt they were looking *in*, like children sneaking halfway downstairs from their bedroom to eavesdrop on their parents' New Year's party in the living room. Some of the ancient Greeks even thought that the night sky was a dark curtain, and that the stars were holes in this curtain through which one could see thousands of tiny, precious glimpses of the campfires of the gods or the very light of Heaven.

Where did the cosmic fullness go? What has it emptied out into? Into our own minds. We are like King Midas—swollen with riches and power, but everything we touch, we kill, as Midas' daughter turned dead and cold as gold when he touched her. What Midas did to his daughter, we have done to our Mother.

Very few changes in history have been as catastrophic as this, for this affects everything, and the difference it makes is the difference between everything being living or dead, full or empty, Mother or machine.

Of course Newton's simple clockwork universe is now passé (except in the popular imagination), and modern physics has discovered something incredibly more mysterious at the heart of the matter. But for the most part the machine has been replaced by something *less* than a machine—a set of mental constructs, myths or paradigms; or mathematical equations; or Nothing producing Something. But not anything like a Mother, not anything with design and teleology, mind and purpose, intelligence and value.

There is surely a close connection between this linguistic change in the meaning of the word "space" and a second radical linguistic change, which we will explore in point 13: the emergence of a totally new word (and experience), "boredom". Children naturally get bored with machines or equations, but not with real mothers or live pets or angels and demons, if they meet any. (Some still do.)

Can we orphans find our Mother again? No one knows. But we can find our Father again, and that's what the *Pensées* helps us to do. The death of Mother can send us to despair, or it can drive us back to Daddy's arms.

Modern alienation is an echo from the Big Thud in Eden, the Fall; it is the latest stumble in a series of downhill bumps. What began with nature becoming "thorns and thistles" and "the sweat of thy brow" and pain in childbirth now continues in the same direction, the direction from garden to wilderness. The technological rape of our planet is its natural extension. It is cosmic incest. It is the collective Oedipus Complex in which we kill God the Father and rape Mother Earth, forcing *our* life and will upon her. The Left has totally ignored the first half of this cosmic crime (since they have *committed* it), and the Right has largely ignored the second (for they have largely committed that).

68

When I consider the brief span of my life absorbed into the eternity which comes before and after—*as the remembrance of a guest that tarrieth but a day*[4]—the small space I occupy and which I see swallowed up in the infinite immensity of spaces of which I know nothing and which know nothing of me, I take fright and am amazed to see myself here rather than there: there is no reason for me to be here rather than there, now rather than then. Who put me here? By whose command and act were this time and place allotted to me? (205)

[68]

The "who" questions Pascal asks here stem from the old way of looking at nature: as a Between, a word, a sign. Who wrote it? Who wrote the script of the play I find myself in? To a Christian, everything that exists is a Between, is something between God and me, something God uses to get at my soul and something I can use (like a road) to run to him or from

---

[4] Wisdom 5:15.

him. To the modern, material nature is the absolute, and God is questioned as to his place relative to it: Is he in it? Outside it? In me or outside me? To a Christian, these are all wrong-headed questions, with wrong premises.

Modern man's heart, which questions, is still more Christian than his head, which answers; for his heart still asks questions like these that Pascal formulates here; questions that look for the Designer, the Playwright. Paradoxically, the very emptiness and meaninglessness of nature drive him more effectively, through desperation, than its old fullness, through fascination. Fear makes us run faster sometimes than love.

"Why am I here and now rather than there and then?" No primitive ever asked this question. Why not? Because his standard of reference, his center, his absolute, was not the formless, empty and meaningless "space" and "time" that are our universal frame but rather his concrete, specific, personal *place* and *life*time. As C. S. Lewis put it, where ancient man felt himself guided through an immense cathedral, modern man feels adrift on a shoreless sea.

There are only three possible roads we can take from here.

1. We can continue down the path of infinite abstraction to further dehumanization and destruction, to "the abolition of man", as C. S. Lewis prophesies and as our century has increasingly fulfilled. Every detail of *Brave New World*—literally and specifically—is just around the next few corners.

2. We are also free to turn back, that is, to repent, to rise up and kill our new god "Progress". We are quite able to Turn Back the Clock. (Try it sometime. You can do it! Both literally and figuratively.) If we return to either Mother Nature or Father God, either one will likely reintroduce us to the other. For they love each other, like parents.

(I am aware of the theological inadequacy of the "Mother Earth" metaphor for Judaeo-Christian theism; no father *creates* his wife. But God created his own Son's Mother. Yet the metaphor has the validity of immediate intuitive experience.)

3. Or we can take the way Pascal opens for us—not out of

modernity to God but through modernity to God. Our very
alienation from nature may drive us to God in desperation.

Two chances out of three. Not bad.

But there is no fourth option.

400

**Man does not know the place he should occupy. He has
obviously gone astray; he has fallen from his true place
and cannot find it again. He searches everywhere, anxiously but in vain, in the midst of impenetrable darkness.**

(427)

[400]

The "true place" we have fallen from is first of all God and
our Edenic relation with him. Secondly, it is nature as God's
design, his rendezvous place to meet us.

The second fall, from nature, happened only recently, in
Pascal's time. It is the fall from *place* to *space*, and from *kairos*
(lived time, life-time, human time) to *chronos* (material time).
Both are implied in the fall from the universe as Mother to the
universe as machine.

Thus we are "lost in space", but we are never "lost in
place". For to be in our place is precisely *not* to be lost.

We can recognize our place relative to our home or our
Mother. Thus ancient men never felt lost.

Jewish, Christian and Muslim man was never lost, either,
because he had the script, the Book written by Father. The
script tells us our place, too, our place in the play. (Nature is
like the setting of the play, part of the play; so theistic man did
not feel lost in nature either.)

Modern science, however, does not give us the script of the
play that is the history of the cosmos. Nor does it give us the
script of the play that is our lives. It only scrutinizes the sylla-
bles.

The Bible is to astrophysics what astrophysics is to geology:
the larger frame.

11. Death

Of all the proofs that man is wretched (the first of Pascal's two main points, remember), death is surely the surest, simply the simplest and most obviously the most obvious. It is the most certain fact of life, the *only* certain fact in life. Augustine remarks that parents and relatives always wonder about a new baby whether he will be happy, healthy, wealthy, wise, virtuous or long-lived, but never wonder whether he will die.

Death is the most unsentimental of facts: simple, decisive, businesslike. Therefore Pascal's *pensées* on death are also unsentimental, simple, decisive and businesslike. There is no nonsense, no evasion, no "nuancing", no little mental two-step about death.

Pascal classified most of his *pensées* about death under the heading "Beginning". Death is an excellent beginning for his apologetic, for three reasons: it is a great attention-grabber; it is a solid, sound, secure and indisputable fact; and it slaps us in the face with our own wretchedness, our utter helplessness before the loss of *everything*. It is our obvious problem, and Christ claims to be the answer.

If there were no death, there would probably be no religion. As long as there is death, there will be religion—unless our pop psychologists can make us all insane enough to "accept death" calmly and blandly as something natural, as our friend, as "a stage of growth". That's like telling a quadriplegic that paralysis is a stage of exercise, or a divorcée that divorce is a stage of marriage. It's the kind of joke only a moron or a sadist would tell.

326
Anyone with only a week to live will not find it in his interest to believe that all this is just a matter of chance.

Now, if we were not bound by our passions, a week and a hundred years would come to the same thing. (694)

[326]

There are no atheists on deathbeds. Or, rather, the only atheists on deathbeds are fools.

But if we only judged things truly, calmly, sanely, objectively and rationally, we would realize the truth of life's one absolutely unquestionable certainty: that we are all on our deathbeds. The birthbed is a deathbed. The bed on which your mother lay when you were born is her deathbed and yours. "We give birth astride a grave" (Samuel Beckett).

These two paragraphs form two premises. Can you draw the conclusion?

152

Between us and heaven or hell there is only life half-way, the most fragile thing in the world. (213)

[152]

Life is a thin membrane, eminently puncturable. On the other side lies Heaven or Hell. Earth is only the porch of one or the other. "All that seems earth is [the beginning of] Hell or Heaven" (C. S. Lewis).

We usually live with an unconscious image of earth as a large, stable, secure place, the absolute, the center, with Heaven and Hell as barely visible points in the sky, shimmering and remote fantasies, tiny and uncertain. In fact, it is *Earth* that is tiny and uncertain.

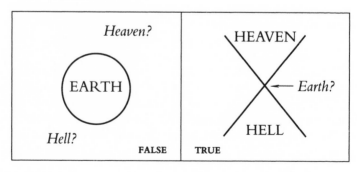

This is sanity. *This* is the cold light of day, "the way it is" In order for us to be sane, to live in the real world, this vision would have to become habitual. We may gauge our sanity level by how habitual it is.

434

Imagine a number of men in chains, all under sentence of death, some of whom are each day butchered in the sight of the others; those remaining see their own condition in that of their fellows, and looking at each other with grief and despair await their turn. This is an image of the human condition. **(199)**

[434]

Not only words and sentences but also pictures, images, symbols and myths can be true or false. This one is true. It is us.

Note Pascal's effective literary style, holding back until the last sentence the revelation that this terrible picture, which naturally elicits a gasp of horror and pity from us, is our own life. Compare Plato's similar technique in the "parable of the cave" in the *Republic* 515c:

> "What a strange image you speak," he said, "and what strange prisoners!" "Like ourselves", I said.

Pictures are more powerful than words to jolt us into sudden realization of the truth, especially a truth we know deep down but fight to forget. Thus Christ used parables, not theology. Our subconscious strategy of self-shielding is the hidden cause for our creating a society of diversion through social and technological complexities. It is the strange key that unlocks the strangely shaped lock, namely, the puzzle that we who seek happiness create a society that makes us unhappy. It is to divert us from the deeper terror of death and the despair that comes from facing this without God.

(These terrible truths will be worked out more carefully in point 13.)

164

I agree that Copernicus' opinion need not be more closely examined. But this:

It affects our whole life to know whether the soul is mortal or immortal.   (218)

[164]

How relatively trivial are the most revolutionary discoveries in our science of the external world, compared to the least pieces of progress in the sciences of life—that is, morality and religion.

Death is the touchstone, the criterion of true human importance. As we lie dying, knowledge of how to live will compensate us for ignorance of worldly science, but knowledge of science will not compensate us for ignorance of how to live. What does it profit a man to get A's in all his courses but flunk life?

Voltaire joked that medieval French peasants knew more about the geography of Heaven than about the geography of France. Pascal would not see this as a joke but as a privilege, and eminently reasonable. Why should we pay more attention to our cars than to our homes, to the road than to the destination?

165

The last act is bloody, however fine the rest of the play. They throw earth over your head and it is finished for ever.   (210)

[165]

A story, like a syllogism, gets its unity and point from its conclusion, its end. Life seems wretched and vain because its end, and hence its point, seems to be death, and death seems to be nothingness.

Therefore the question of immortality is existentially crucial. As Pascal has said in no. 164, "It affects our whole life to know whether the soul is mortal or immortal." Therefore the

absolute nadir of insanity is indifference to this question (point
14, especially no. 427)—which is essentially the attitude of
modern man and his prophets, pop psychologists and secular
humanists. Even Satanists and neo-Nazi skinheads are in a
sense closer to the truth: they at least *care* about something
more than "caring"!

166
**We run heedlessly into the abyss after putting something
in front of us to stop us seeing it.**   (183)

[166]

Here is another image of the human situation.

We are locked in a car (our body), rushing furiously down a
hill (time), through fog (ignorance), unable to see ahead, over
rocks and pits (wretchedness). The doors are welded shut, the
steering works only a little, and the brakes are nonexistent.
Our only certainty is that all the cars sooner or later fall over
the edge of the cliff (death).

So what do we do? We erect billboards at the edge of the
cliff, so that we do not have to look at the abyss. The billboards are called "civilization".

Our "solution" is the biggest part of our problem.

Conclusions about Death

There are only five solutions to our most crudely obvious
problem, death:

1. Don't look at it. Look the other way. Be an ostrich; hide
your head in the sand, your mind in worldliness. Stay diverted
(point 13).

2. Look at it with a heart dulled by pop psychology.
"Accept" it. Be bland and indifferent to it (point 14). Do go
gentle into that good-night; do not rage against the dying of
the light.

3. Look at it and despair. This is the admirable but unlivable honesty of nihilism; of Sartre, and Camus, and Jons in *The Seventh Seal*.

4. Look at it and put your hope and faith in science to conquer death by technology, by cryogenics or by artificial immortality by genetic engineering. This is a faith as old as Renaissance alchemy and occultism. There has never been anything whatever to verify this faith, and if it *were* verified, it would create not Heaven on Earth but Hell.

5. Put your faith in God, in Christ, in Resurrection.

Pascal eliminates all other contenders. The problem itself eliminates all other contenders. Death kayos all the philosophies; only Christ kayos death.

12. Sin, Selfishness, Self-Love

Is there anything worse than death? Yes. Sin. For sin is spiritual death.

This is not just a metaphor. Sin kills the life of the soul.

The *essence* of sin is self-love, or selfishness. The *forms* of sin are what Christian theology calls "Original Sin" and "actual sin". These two basic points must be made clear first so that we understand what Pascal is doing in trying to convince us "of sin, of righteousness and of judgment" (Jn 16:8).

The Essence of Sin

The essence of sin is selfishness, "me first", self-love or pride.

Pride is essentially competitive. "Me first" necessarily means "you second". Pascal would like Rodney Dangerfield's line about this: "When you're looking out for Number One, you're going to step on some Number Two."

Self-love, or pride, is not the same as self-respect. Self-respect means treating yourself, like all selves, as valuable. This is true, because the self is (1) made in God's image, (2) has reason and free will, (3) is spirit, not just animal, (4) is immortal and (5) is loved by God, offered adoption into his family and destined for spiritual marriage to him in eternal righteousness, truth and joy.

Self-love, on the other hand, means making yourself your own God: that is, your own end, good and goal; seeking your happiness and purpose and destiny and meaning in yourself rather than in God. It means Hamlet thinking he's Shakespeare.

Christianity teaches that we ought to have more self-respect and less self-love. As Chesterton puts it, "a man cannot think too little of his self, or too much of his soul." Christianity tells us to be soulish but not selfish; modernity tells us to be selfish but not soulish.

147

The Forms of Sin

Actual sin is simple: it means the sins we commit. Original Sin is more problematic: it is the sin we are.

A Chinese proverb says: "When the wrong man uses the right means, the right means work in the wrong way." My fundamental problem is that I am the wrong man. I sin because I am a sinner, just as I sing because I am a singer. Original Sin is like spiritual cancer. It lodges in my nature, in my proclivities. It is the slippery slope I fall down every time I try to pray or sacrifice. It is a disease we catch from our environment only because we first catch it from our heredity. It cannot be dealt with by fine tuning, by good advice (as Plato thought) or social engineering (as Liberalism thinks).

Original Sin is the radically unpopular doctrine. Yet it is very similar to one of the most popular doctrines of Freud, one of Christianity's most powerful enemies: namely, the doctrine of the "pleasure principle". Both teach essentially the same thing: that we are all born into the world as selfish little pigs; that (as Augustine puts it) "the innocence of babies is in the helplessness of their bodies, not in the virtue in their souls"; that our original working philosophy is always "I want what I want when I want it"; and that even when we later learn to cover up and compromise this demand, it remains down at the bottom of our heart.

The difference between Freud and Christ is not about this *fact* but about whether it is to be judged and whether it can be cured. For the secularist, it is just human nature, and all we can do is live with it, compromise, "cope". For Christianity, it is our disease, not our design, and it must and can be destroyed. In other words, Christianity, with its dogma of Original Sin, is wildly more optimistic.

Secular morality is a plan for the fulfillment of selfishness, Christianity is a plan for its destruction. It cuts to the heart. In fact, it is heart surgery.

Clearly, this is going to appear optimistic only to one who knows he has heart disease. No one who thinks he is healthy is going to be happy to be offered a free heart transplant. Pascal now has the unenviable task of convincing us of this Bad News so that we will be open to the Good News.

978

Self-love. The nature of self-love and of this human self is to love only self and consider only self.[A] But what is it to do?[B] It cannot prevent the object of its love from being full of faults and wretchedness: it wants to be great and sees that it is small; it wants to be happy and sees that it is wretched; it wants to be perfect and sees that it is full of imperfections; it wants to be the object of men's love and esteem and sees that its faults deserve only their dislike and contempt. The predicament in which it thus finds itself arouses in it the most unjust and criminal passion that could possibly be imagined, for it conceives a deadly hatred for the truth which rebukes it and convinces it of its faults.[C] It would like to do away with this truth, and not being able to destroy it as such, it destroys it, as best it can, in the consciousness of itself and others; that is, it takes every care to hide its faults both from itself and others, and cannot bear to have them pointed out or noticed.[D]

It is no doubt an evil to be full of faults, but it is a still greater evil to be full of them and unwilling to recognize them, since this entails the further evil of deliberate self-delusion.[E] We do not want others to deceive us; we do not think it right for them to want us to esteem them more than they deserve; it is therefore not right either that we should deceive them and want them to esteem us more than we deserve.[F]

Thus, when they merely reveal vices and imperfections which we actually possess, it is obvious that they do us no wrong, since they are not responsible for them, but are really doing us good, by helping us to escape from an evil, namely our ignorance of these imperfections. We ought not to be annoyed that they know them and despise us, because it is right that they should know us for what we are and despise us if we are despicable.

These are the feelings which would spring from a heart full of equity and justice. What then should we say of ours, seeing it quite differently disposed?[G] For is it not true that we hate the truth and those who tell it to us, and we like them to be deceived to our advantage, and want to be esteemed by them as other than we actually are?

Here is a proof of it which appals me. The Catholic religion does not oblige us to reveal our sins indiscriminately to everyone; it allows us to remain hidden from all other men, with one single exception, to whom it bids us reveal our innermost heart and show ourselves for what we are. There is only this one man in the world whom it orders us to disillusion, and it lays on him the obligation of inviolable secrecy, which means that he might as well not possess the knowledge of us that he has. Can anything milder and more charitable be imagined? And yet, such is man's corruption that he finds even this law harsh, and this is one of the main reasons why a large part of Europe has revolted against the Church.[H]

How unjust and unreasonable the heart of man is, that he should resent the obligation to behave towards one man as it would be right, in some ways, to behave towards all! For is it right that we should deceive them?

This aversion for the truth exists in differing degrees, but it may be said that it exists in everyone to some degree, because it is inseparable from self-love. . . .[I]

The result is that anyone who has an interest in winning our affection avoids rendering us a service which he knows to be unwelcome; we are treated as we want to be treated; we hate the truth and it is kept from us; we desire to be flattered and we are flattered; we like being deceived and we are deceived.[J]

This is why each rung of fortune's ladder which brings us up in the world takes us further from the truth,^K because people are more wary of offending those whose friendship is most useful and enmity most dangerous. A prince can be the laughingstock of Europe and the only one to know nothing about it. This does not surprise me: telling the truth is useful to the hearer but harmful to those who tell it, because they incur such odium.^L Now those who live with princes prefer their own interests to that of the prince they serve, and so they have no wish to benefit him by harming themselves.^M

This misfortune is no doubt greater and more common among those most favoured by fortune, but more modest people are not exempt, because we always have some interest in being popular.^N Thus human life is nothing but a perpetual illusion; there is nothing but^O mutual deception and flattery. No one talks about us in our presence as he would in our absence. Human relations are only based on this mutual deception; and few friendships would survive if everyone knew what his friend said about him behind his back, even though he spoke sincerely and dispassionately.

Man is therefore nothing but^O disguise, falsehood and hypocrisy, both in himself and with regard to others. He does not want to be told the truth. He avoids telling it to others, and all these tendencies, so remote from justice and reason, are naturally rooted in his heart.   (100)

[978]

A

The key word is "only". Pride isolates. There can be only one absolute; the question is: Is it me or is it God? If God, others can be equal to me. If me, others can never be equal to me.

B

There is a built-in failure mechanism, an inescapable "pain principle", in the "pleasure principle". For our natural, selfish love (*eros*) loves only what is lovable, what is worthy of love, what is perfect; but our motive for loving is that we are needy and imperfect, and thus *not* lovable. But if there is no God, we have nothing but these imperfect selves. We are a circle of emotional cannibals, eating each other round and round, for there is nothing better than ourselves, and all loving is eating.

The next sentences in Pascal show the inevitable failure of humanism, that is, "the wretchedness of man without God". We cannot alter either of the two data of the problem, either our need for happiness, perfection, lovability and certainty, or our inability to attain them. Our *demand* to be more and our *inability* to be more are both in our nature. In other words, built into our nature is a practical self-contradiction.

Stoics, Buddhists and "peace of mind" psychologists try to change the first of these two data, our desires. Modern technology and politics try to change the second datum, the imperfections in our world.

Neither works. Never has, never will.

That truth is so awful that we are tempted to hate truth itself. It tempts us to the moral dishonesty Pascal diagnoses in the next few sentences: a cure that is worse than the disease.

C

If Pascal's words seem exaggerated here, consider this: to hate the truth is even more horrible than to hate a person. For if we love the truth but hate a person, the truth will tell us that persons are not to be hated. But if we hate the truth, there is no more hope for us to find the true way, the way of love, than there is for a man with a deadly disease operating on himself after he has just thrown a brick at the unflattering lights in the operating room.

D

The result, as Augustine says in the *Confessions*, is that

> They love truth when it enlightens them, they hate truth when it accuses them. Because they do not wish to be deceived and

do wish to deceive, they love truth when it reveals itself, and hate it when it reveals them. Thus it shall reward them as they deserve: those who do not wish to be revealed by truth, truth will unmask against their will, but it will not reveal itself to them. Thus, thus, even thus does the human mind, blind and inert, vile and ill-behaved, desire to keep itself concealed, yet desire that nothing should be concealed from it. But the contrary happens to it—it cannot be hidden from truth, but only truth from it. (X, 23)

E

Deliberate self-delusion may even be "the unforgivable sin", for once we shut our souls to the light, we shut them to God, for God is light. We can repent of any sin if only we see the light; refusing light (truth) makes repentance impossible.

The damned in Hell may be adamantly convincing themselves that they are in Heaven. And if you say "What does it matter, then, as long as they are satisfied?", you are infected with the same Hellish disease that sent them there: indifference to Truth, that is, to God.

F

That is, we ourselves testify to our own injustice by how we always expect others to behave to us. The greatest liar in the world is still outraged by being lied to. No one is a moral relativist, subjectivist or minimalist when it comes to others' behavior to him, only his to others.

G

How far we are from justice and sanity! How clearly appears Original Sin, innate selfishness! How natural and normal is our unnatural injustice! Of course we are annoyed at criticism, even true criticism. *Especially* true criticism. A man will forgive you for unjust criticism but not for just criticism. A bully will forgive you if you call him a coward but not if you call him a bully. A coward will forgive you if you call him a bully but not if you call him a coward.

Modern secularism, without the Fall, confuses the *natural* with the (statistically) *normal*. Sin is the most unnatural and the most normal thing in the world.

H

In our day the sacrament of confession has suffered a radical decline. In one large Dutch diocese during a twelve-month period there were *no* confessions. There is no place on earth the Devil fears more than the confessional. His desperate propaganda has been incredibly successful even within the Church.

I

Notice the deep connection between our two worst diseases: self-love instead of God-love and love of falsehood instead of love of truth. Truth and love are the two absolutes because they are what God is.

J

Nearly all our social conventions and interactions are based on this deception. We cannot function in society without deception. Imagine entertainment, imagine advertising, without deception! We contract to be deceived, we demand to be deceived, we pay to be deceived, we pant to be deceived.

K

Therefore poverty is blessed. Perhaps we should deliberately vote for a political candidate whose economic policies we think would precipitate a depression. We should certainly treat wealth like a live grenade (unless Jesus was exaggerating, which he never did).

L

This is why we murder our prophets and saints—for the same reason we lower the lights when our face is full of wrinkles.

M

Therefore flattery is the principle of survival in politics—in democracy just as much as with a monarch. If a candidate does not flatter his constituents, he will not be a candidate for long.

N

Much more so in our society than in any previous society this is true; see David Riesman and Nathan Glazer, *The Lonely Crowd*. Perhaps this is the origin of theological liberalism and modernism, with its eagerness to negotiate away all *unpopular* dogmas.

O

"Nothing but", not in quantity, of course, but in quality. If life were 100 percent deception, we could not even know that fact, for we would know no true light by which to judge the deception. But all of life is *infected* with deception. The image of God, the Father of Truth, is universally infected with the germs of the Father of Lies.

No one who sees this can ever believe in secular humanism again.

211

We have established and developed out of concupiscence admirable rules of polity, ethics and justice, but at root, the evil root of man, this evil stuff of which we are made is only concealed; it is not pulled up.   **(453)**

[211]

Even our systems of social justice are rooted in our Original Sin, the injustice in our nature. We can build well-designed buildings, but only out of broken bricks. The problem is not in our systems but in our selves. This is the reason all societies collapse, why the dams of goodness never hold out long against the floods of evil, why the bad people always somehow seem to come to the top. Society is only *us*. There *is* no "them".

If there were no such thing as Original Sin, why else couldn't we ever attain the goodness and justice and joy and peace that the majority of sane people always want and have always wanted? Original Sin is the only key that opens the mystery of history.

395
When we wish to think of God, is there not something which distracts us and tempts us to think of something else? All this is evil and innate in us. (478)

[395]
Why do we feel such a reluctance to pray? Why does it seem as if we are constantly sliding down a slippery slope away from God, as if God were a glass mountain and we had oil on our hands and feet?

We know from endlessly repeated experience that whenever we place ourselves in his presence, the result is joy and peace, and whenever we flee it, the result is restless unhappiness, a muffled undertone of anxiety and guilt, shiftiness and evasion throughout the day. Yet despite this experimental proof, we run from prayer, from his presence, as from a plague. We give any excuse to avoid it.

God could not have created us in such a state.

Our innate need for God and our innate fear of God form a double datum that only Christianity explains, with its twin dogmas of Creation and Fall. We need God because he is our Father, and we fear him because we have made ourselves his enemies through sin.

421
It is untrue that we are worthy to be loved [preferentially] by others. It is unfair that we should want such a thing. If we were born reasonable and impartial, with a knowledge of ourselves and others, we should not give our wills this

bias. However, we are born with it, and so we are born unfair. . . .

The bias towards self is the beginning of all disorder, in war, politics, economics. . . .

The will is therefore depraved. We are born unfair. . . . (477)

No religion except our own has taught that man is born sinful, no philosophical sect has said so, so none has told the truth. (606)

[421]

Here is *pensée* no. 978 in miniature. (See p. 149.)

The two distinctive doctrines of Christianity are Original Sin and Salvation, the very bad news that no one else dares tell us and the very good news that no one else has a right to tell us. The very good news makes sense only on the presupposition of the very bad news. A piece of wood is not a matter of life and death unless you know you are drowning and nothing else will save you, only the splintered Cross.

431

We cannot conceive Adam's state of glory, or the nature of his sin, or the way it has been transmitted to us. These are things which took place in a state of nature quite different from our own and which pass our present understanding.

Knowing all this does not help us to escape. All that it is important for us to know is that we are wretched, corrupt, separated from God but redeemed by Christ; and that is what is wonderfully proved to us on earth. (560)

[431]

We need to know only the two great truths about our present state (sin and salvation), not the two great truths about our past state in Paradise (innocence and Fall). We need to know the "before-and-after" difference faith makes, not the details of the "before-and-after" difference the Fall made. We need to know what happens when we are baptized, not what happened when Adam ate the apple. We need not know how our Titanic sank, only how we can be saved. Therefore God tells us about the first only in myth and mystery and symbol, but about the second in clear repetitions and exhortations. No one who reads the New Testament with an awake and open mind can miss it. John 3:16 and Romans 6:23 are so simple that anyone except a theologian can understand them.

562

There are only two kinds of men: the righteous who think they are sinners and the sinners who think they are righteous. (534)

[562]

The only choice, then, is between being sinners who know they are sinners and repent; or sinners who don't. Saints are not the opposite of sinners; saints are sorry sinners, saved sinners.

Socrates, the greatest of philosophers, made the same point on the level of mind and wisdom and philosophy that Pascal makes here on the level of will and righteousness and religion: that there are only two kinds of people, the wise who (like Socrates) think they are fools and the fools who think they are wise.

For both Socrates and Pascal, humility is Lesson One. Both the mind and the will are aspects of the image of God in us, prophets of God in our soul. We touch what God is when we touch wisdom and righteousness, truth and goodness. In both, humility is the first requirement because we can approach God only on our knees. St. Bernard, asked to name the four cardinal virtues, replied: "humility, humility, humility and humility."

Humility is not dishonest, cowardly, wormy smarmy; humility is the open and clear light of day. Humility is realism.

We are, *in fact*, sinners! The saints all say they are great sinners—do saints see less deeply into the soul than anyone else?
We who think so highly and comfortably of ourselves are not
more realistic, more in touch with reality, than the saints. How
could *we* be *less* full of sin than the saints, who say they are
crawling, sprawling masses of sins?

If the saints are wrong in calling themselves great sinners,
then sanctity and wisdom, sanctity and sanity, sanctity and
truth are enemies; and the holier and closer to God you are,
the *farther* away from truth and reality you are. Reduction to
absurdity!

If this cannot be, then the saints are wise. And if they are
wise, then they are right to call themselves sinners. And if they
are great sinners, we are greater sinners. Therefore our culture,
which scorns, sneers, fears, jeers, gibes and jokes at sin, is radically sick and spiritually insane.

Why would you want to trust an insane culture instead of
the saints and their Master?

597

'The self is hateful. You cover it up, Mitton,[1] but that
does not mean that you take it away. So you are still hateful.'

'Not so, because by being obliging to everyone as we
are, we give them no more cause to hate us.'

'True enough if the only hateful thing about the self
were the unpleasantness it caused us.

'But if I hate it because it is unjust that it should make
itself the centre of everything, I shall go on hating it.

'In a word the self has two characteristics. It is unjust in
itself for making itself centre of everything: it is a nuisance
to others in that it tries to subjugate them, for each self is
the enemy of all the others and would like to tyrannize
them. You take away the nuisance, but not the injustice.

---

[1] Daniel Mitton, a worldly gambler and friend of Pascal.

'And thus, you do not make it pleasing to those who hate it for being unjust; you only make it pleasing to unjust people who no longer see it as their enemy. Thus you remain unjust, and can only please unjust people.'

(455)

[597]

Mitton here is the nice, socially respectable man who makes other people happy. This is modernity's definition of a good man: one who makes others happy. Pascal's shocking point here is that it is not enough just to make others happy. Bad people can make other bad people happy, and good people can make other good people unhappy, and often must do so, in a bad world. (Are dentists *bad*?)

Love of neighbor is not enough. Kindness is not enough. Compassion is not enough. We also need righteousness, justice, holiness. Tender virtue without tough virtue is not enough; sincerity without road maps is not enough. (Is it enough for a travel agent?)

Most moderns already know that tough, private, character-building virtue without tender, public, social virtue is not enough; but they do not know the other, correlative truth.

Ann Landers defined Personality as the ability to say Yes and Character as the ability to say No. We need both. Personality without character (Pascal's friend Mitton) is like soft skin without a skeleton. It is a moral jellyfish. Character without personality is like hard bones without soft skin. It is a moral skeleton. Our ancestors tended to a too-skeletal morality, perhaps; but we certainly tend to a jellyfish morality.

We are more concerned with what Mitton *does* than what he *is*. The first question we ask about a man (and, increasingly, about a woman) is: What does he "do"? We really mean: Is he interesting? Can he make me happy by relieving my boredom a little?

616

Concupiscence has become natural for us and has become second nature. Thus there are two natures in us, one good, the other bad. (660)

[616]

"Concupiscence" means the innate and universal habit of selfishness, the demand to gratify all our desires for pleasure.

"Habit" is "second nature". We acquire habits by repeated acts, just as we acquire muscles by exercise, or cancer by smoking.

Original Sin is the "second nature" habit of sin and selfishness that we acquired by sinning.

Contrary to Calvinism, Catholicism teaches that our first nature, which God created in his image, remains good beneath our second nature, or sin nature. Original Sin is a shocking doctrine because it means we are spiritual schizophrenics. Yet this shocking truth is easily verifiable in experience. (Cf. Rom 7:15–25; Augustine's *Confessions* VIII, 7–9.)

617

Anyone who does not hate[A] the self-love within him and the instinct which leads him to make himself into a God[B] must be really blind. Who can fail to see that there is nothing so contrary to justice and truth? For it is false that we deserve this position and unjust and impossible to attain it, because everyone demands the same thing.[C] We are thus born into an obviously unjust situation from which we cannot escape but from which we must escape.[D]

However, no [other] religion has observed [1] that this is a sin, [2] that it is innate in us, or [3] that we are obliged to resist it, let alone [4] thought of providing a cure.[E] (492)

[617]

A

"Hate" does not mean here "fixate on, resent, grind your teeth at, froth at the mouth at, and wish ill to." It means "refuse, reject, turn your back on, turn away from, say No to"—as in Luke 14:26.

B

God's will is always done. One whose philosophy of life is "My will be done" is really playing God. Few think they are God in theory, but all do in practice.

C

There can be only one "I"; all others are "yous" or "its". There can be only one Absolute. All objects are relative to the subject, the I AM. The fundamental question of human existence is whether I will let God be I AM and consent to be his "you", or whether I will be I AM and make God into *my* "you", relative to me, "you, over there".

Playing God is the world's most competitive game. There can be at most one winner.

D

Here is the *koan*, the puzzle that *cannot* be solved yet *must* be solved. From this we can understand why the doctrine of Original Sin is so obstinately resisted.

E

Four remarkable and unique announcements. The fourth, the Good News, presupposes the first three, the Bad News.

The closest thing in depth to the Christian doctrine of Original Sin is perhaps Buddha's First Two Noble Truths: that all of life is *dukkha*, out-of-joint-ness, wretchedness, suffering; and that the cause of all of this is *tanha*: grasping, greed, selfishness, egotistic desire. But *tanha* is not *sin*, for, according to Buddha, (1) it does not proceed from a real individuality and free will, (2) it is not a personal offense against a personal God, a breaking of a marriage covenant, and (3) Buddha knows nothing of *agapē* (unselfish love) as the alternative to *eros* or *tanha* (selfish love); therefore he counsels impersonal "compassion" (*karuna, jihi*) instead of love. He knows no way of separating the patient (individual ego) from the disease (egotism) and so counsels a kind of spiritual euthanasia: cure the disease by killing the patient (or rather, seeing through the illusion that there is a patient, an individual ego, in the first place).

668

Each man is everything to himself, for with his death everything is dead for him. That is why each of us thinks he is everything to everyone. **(457)**

[668]

This is the psychological basis for moral egotism. We carry around with us our own false perspective, our own human ego as the center, the absolute, so that everything else, even God, must become "mine". To me, you are my "you", and not what you are to yourself; for you do not call yourself "you" but "I". To me, you are a character in my play; to you, I am a character in yours. (See Gabriel Marcel, *The Philosophy of Existentialism*, chap. 2).

Reality is theocentric, not anthropocentric. God announces the truth when he announces his own name to Moses: "I AM WHO AM" (Ex 3:14). The fact that we naturally begin our sentences with the word "I" shows whose place we instinctively usurp.

When I die, it seems the whole world dies with me, for "the" world has become "my" world. This is simply not true. It is true only to God! Another piece of evidence for our usurpation, our innate fallenness from the truth into falsehood.

869

**To make a man a saint, grace is certainly needed, and any-
one who doubts this does not know what a saint, or a
man, really is.**   (508)

[869]

It takes infinite power for God to create the universe out of
nothing. But it takes even greater power to make saints out of
sinners. For the nothingness out of which God created the universe did not resist him; but sinners do.

David prays: "Create in me a clean heart", and uses the
word "*bara'*" for "create". It is something only God can do.
The verb is never used with any other subject except God.

Do-it-yourself sanctity is an oxymoron. Albert Camus, the
great, honest atheist, saw this truth and agonized over it in *The
Plague*. His humanist hero and mouthpiece, the good Doctor
Rieux, knows he must be a saint but worries and wonders:
"How can one be a saint without God?" A haunting question.

Utopian humanists may know "what a saint is" but they do
not know "what a man is"; they see the good that we must be
but fail to see the evil we inevitably are without divine grace.
Cynical pragmatists, on the other hand, know "what a man is"
but not "what a saint is". For neither of these two philosophies
knows what grace is, or how gracious God is.

That is because neither knows Christ. As Pascal will later
show us (point 26, especially no. 417, p. 313), Christ alone
teaches us both of these two essential truths: our wretchedness
without God and our happiness with God, our sin and our salvation, our evil and our good. That is why Pascal will make
the bold claim that without Christ we cannot know ourselves
or the nature of God or the meaning of our lives or of our
death.

III

TWO POPULAR
PSEUDO-SOLUTIONS

13. Diversion

We now turn from the problem (points 3–12) to modernity's two most popular pseudo-solutions, Diversion and Indifference (points 13 and 14). Pascal diagnoses them as worse than total failures; as adding immeasurably to the problem; as two "cures" that are worse than the disease—like curing a migraine with cancer, or cancer with AIDS.

In his jeremiads against diversion and indifference, Pascal is at his most terrifyingly incisive, unendurably intimate and devastatingly unanswerable. My students are always stunned and shamed to silence as Pascal shows them in these *pensées* their own lives in all their shallowness, cowardice and dishonesty. He keeps doing the same to me all the time. Like the Holy Spirit.

*

For many years I used to bother people with a simple question that was never answered adequately until I read Pascal (the *pensées* in this section). It was a simple child's question, and I asked it of philosophers, theologians, psychologists, sociologists, anthropologists, historians, economists, and even ordinary, sane, real people; yet no one could give me a simple, straight answer. The question is: Why doesn't anybody have any time today? Where did all the time go?

I think the best answer I got was "Cleveland". If the "experts" can't answer a simple child's question, the world has come to a pretty sorry state.

The question is more puzzling than it seems. We ought to have much more time, more leisure, than our ancestors did, because technology, which is the most obvious and radical difference between their lives and ours, is essentially a series of time-saving devices. In ancient societies, if you were rich you had slaves to do the menial work so that you could be freed to enjoy your leisure time. Life was like a vacation for the rich because the poor slaves were their machines. We now no

longer have slaves for two reasons: moral and religious principles, and the Industrial Revolution. The first made us feel
guilty about slavery, and the second made slavery unnecessary.
So now that everyone has many slave-substitutes (machines),
why doesn't everyone enjoy the leisurely, vacationy lifestyle of
the ancient rich? Why have we killed time instead of saving it?

Your great-grandmother scrubbed clothes on a scrubbing
board and cooked on a coal stove. You push buttons on wash-
ing machines and microwave ovens full of prepared food. Yet
your great-grandmother had more time to talk to her daughter
than you do. Why?

A simple question. Once the true answer came, I knew I'd
know it. It didn't come until I read Pascal, and then it hit me
like an arrow, splitting the air and thudding into a bull's-eye—
like that scene in the movie *Moonstruck* where Cher asks a
middle-aged man why middle-aged men chase after young
women, and he answers, offhandedly and only half-seriously,
"Maybe it's the fear of death", and Cher stops dead in her
tracks and says "That's it!"

If the *pensées* in this section don't show you yourself, you
probably don't need to read any farther. You're either very
wise or very foolish. The masses in the middle—typically
modern harried and hassled people like me and most of the
people I know—will read on.

Since you are probably impatient, like most people today, I
will tell you Pascal's answer immediately. We *want* to complexify our lives. We don't *have* to, we *want* to. We want to be
harried and hassled and busy. Unconsciously, we want the very
thing we complain about. For if we had leisure, we would
look at ourselves and listen to our hearts and see the great gap-
ing hole in our hearts and be terrified, because that hole is so
big that nothing but God can fill it.

So we run around like conscientious little bugs, scared rabbits, dancing attendance on our machines, our slaves, and making them our masters. We think we want peace and silence
and freedom and leisure, but deep down we know that this

would be unendurable to us, like a dark and empty room without distractions where we would be forced to confront ourselves, the one person (next to God) whom we fear the most, yet need the most, and the only person (next to God) whom we are constantly trying to escape, yet the only person (next to God) whom we can never escape, to all eternity.

If you are typically modern, your life is like a rich mansion with a terrifying hole right in the middle of the living-room floor. So you paper over the hole with a very busy wallpaper pattern to distract yourself. You find a rhinoceros in the middle of your house. The rhinoceros is wretchedness and death. How in the world can you hide a rhinoceros? Easy: cover it with a million mice. Multiply diversions.

70

If our condition were truly happy we should not need to divert ourselves from thinking about it. (165b)

[70]

Therefore the society or individual which has the most diversions and amusements is not the happiest but the unhappiest.

Therefore our society is the unhappiest. All the social indicators bear out this conclusion: depression, divorce, suicide, drugs, violence—you name it.

The point is simple: we never want to divert ourselves from *happiness*, only from unhappiness. If life felt like a holiday, we would not want holidays from it.

Freud, in *Civilization and Its Discontents*, asks why we are not happier than our ancestors, since our technology has made us like gods and fulfilled nearly every fairy-tale wish and wishful thinking that invented the gods in the first place. He simply can't find out why we wielders of godlike knowledge and power are not happier than our ignorant and impotent ancestors.

Freud, unlike Pascal, cannot find the answer to this question because he does not believe in the Fall. He judges the healthy by the diseased instead of vice versa; judges faith and hope and love by atheism and cynicism and egotism rather than vice versa; judges Heaven by earth, gods by men, and innocence by guilt rather than vice versa. It is the fundamental falsehood of perspective that vitiates all secular sociologies and solutions.

132

Diversion. If man were happy, the less he were diverted the happier he would be, like the saints and God. Yes: but is a man not happy who can find delight in diversion?

No: because it comes from somewhere else, from outside; so he is dependent, and always liable to be disturbed by a thousand and one accidents, which inevitably cause distress.   (170)

[132]

After reading this argument, the reader may object: But though the *cause* of diversions is unhappiness, their *effects* can still be happiness, can't they?

The answer is No. Even Buddha clearly saw that selfish desire, even when gratified, produces fear—fear of the future, fear of losing the desired and attained toys. (What are all *things* but grown-ups' toys?) We make our souls hostage to fortune by pinning our happiness on external things, and we do this to divert ourselves from ourselves. George Macdonald says: "A man is a slave to whatever he cannot part with that is less than himself."

Experience as well as the above reasoning tells us that diversions, such as riches, power, pleasure and just plain keeping busy, have not in fact made us happy; that when we are the happiest we have the *least* diversions and want none.

133

Diversion. Being unable to cure death, wretchedness and ignorance, men have decided, in order to be happy, not to think about such things.   (169)

134

Despite these afflictions man wants to be happy, only wants to be happy, and cannot help wanting to be happy.

But how shall he go about it? The best thing would be to make himself immortal, but as he cannot do that, he has decided to stop himself thinking about it.   (168)

[133, 134]

This "solution" is brilliantly simple. Here's how it works.

It implicitly analyzes the problem this way: We are wretched and unhappy only when all three of the following conditions are fulfilled:

1. We are doomed to death, wretchedness and uncertainty.

2. We cannot cure death, wretchedness or uncertainty.

3. We *think* about death, wretchedness and uncertainty and our inability to cure them.

We cannot change conditions 1 or 2. We cannot change the truth. But we can change condition 3. We can change our awareness. The ostrich cannot defeat the tiger, but he can hide his head in the sand. The "solution" is ostrich epistemology.

But even that is not easy to do. We cannot just *stop thinking* about our afflictions; we have to "*stop ourselves* (from) thinking" about them by diversions. Just as a passion can be overcome only by a stronger passion, an unwelcome thought can be avoided only by a more welcome thought.

Thus the thousand mice hiding the rhinoceros. Thus the busy pattern of wallpaper over the hole. Thus the billboard at the edge of the cliff. We need diversions because in order *not* to think about one thing, we have to have other things to think about. We cannot simply obey a command like "Do *not* think of a blue monkey"—unless we obey the other command to think of a red crocodile.

The most effective diversion of all has always been the red crocodile of war. Nothing relieves boredom more effectively.

Diversion is the deepest reason, down in human hearts and motives, for most of our society's so-called "progress"—its complexification, its technology, its busyness. All this thinking keeps us from *thinking*.

136

Diversion. Sometimes, when I set to thinking about the various activities of men, the dangers and troubles which they face at Court, or in war, giving rise to so many quarrels and passions, daring and often wicked enterprises and so on;[A] I have often said that the sole cause of man's unhappiness is[B] that he does not know how to stay quietly in his room.[C] A man wealthy enough for life's needs would never leave home to go to sea or besiege some fortress if he knew how to stay at home and enjoy it.[D] Men would never spend so much on a commission in the army if they could bear living in town all their lives, and they only seek after the company and diversion of gambling because they do not enjoy staying at home. . . .

Imagine any situation you like, add up all the blessings with which you could be endowed, to be king is still the finest thing in the world; yet if you imagine one with all the advantages of his rank, but no means of diversion, left to ponder and reflect on what he is, this limp felicity will not keep him going; he is bound to start thinking of all the threats facing him, of possible revolts, finally of inescapable death and disease, with the result that if he is deprived of so-called diversion he is unhappy, indeed more unhappy than the humblest of his subjects who can enjoy sport and diversion.[E]

The only good thing for men[F] therefore is to be diverted from thinking of what they are, either by some occupation which takes their mind off it, or by some novel and agreeable passion which keeps them busy, like gambling, hunting, some absorbing show, in short by what is called diversion.

That is why gaming and feminine society, war and high office are so popular.[G] It is not that they really bring happiness, nor that anyone imagines that true bliss comes from possessing the money to be won at gaming or the hare that is hunted: no one would take it as a gift. What people want is not the easy peaceful life that allows us to think of our unhappy condition, nor the dangers of war, nor the burdens of office, but the agitation that takes our mind off it and diverts us. That is why we prefer the hunt to the capture.[H]

That is why men are so fond of hustle and bustle; that is why prison is such a fearful punishment; that is why the pleasures of solitude are so incomprehensible.[I] That, in fact, is the main joy of being a king, because people are continually trying to divert him and procure him every kind of pleasure. A king is surrounded by people whose only thought is to divert him and stop him thinking about himself, because, king though he is, he becomes unhappy as soon as he thinks about himself.[J]

That is all that men have been able to devise for attaining happiness; those who philosophize about it, holding that people are quite unreasonable to spend all day chasing a hare that they would not have wanted to buy, have little knowledge of our nature. The hare itself would not save us from thinking about death and the miseries distracting us, but hunting it does so. . . .[K]

It is wrong then to blame them; they are not wrong to want excitement—if they only wanted it for the sake of diversion. The trouble is that they want it as though, once they had the things they seek, they could not fail to be truly happy. That is what justifies calling their search a vain one.[L] All this shows that neither the critics nor the criticized understand man's real nature.[M]

When men are reproached for pursuing so eagerly something that could never satisfy them, their proper answer, if they really thought about it, ought to be that they simply want a violent and vigorous occupation to take their minds off themselves, and that is why they choose some attractive object to entice them in ardent pursuit. Their opponents could find no answer to that,

(Vanity, pleasure of showing off. Dancing, you must think where to put your feet.)[N]

But they do not answer like that because they do not know themselves. They do not know that all they want is the hunt and not the capture. The nobleman sincerely believes that hunting is a great sport, the sport of kings, but his huntsman does not feel like that. They imagine that if they secured a certain appointment they would enjoy resting afterwards, and they do not realize the insatiable nature of cupidity.[O] They think they genuinely want rest when all they really want is activity.

They have a secret instinct driving them to seek external diversion and occupation, and this is the result of their constant sense of wretchedness. They have another secret instinct, left over from the greatness of our original nature, telling them that the only true happiness lies in rest and not in excitement. These two contrary instincts give rise to a confused plan buried out of sight in the depths of their soul, which leads them to seek rest by way of activity and always to imagine that the satisfaction they miss will come to them once they overcome certain obvious difficulties and can open the door to welcome rest.[P]

All our life passes in this way: we seek rest by struggling against certain obstacles, and once they are overcome, rest proves intolerable because of the boredom it produces. We must get away from it and crave excitement. . . .[Q]

Man is so unhappy that he would be bored even if he had no cause for boredom, by the very nature of his temperament, and he is so vain that, though he has a thousand and one basic reasons for being bored, the slightest thing, like pushing a ball with a billiard cue, will be enough to divert him.[R]

'But,' you will say, 'what is his object in all this?' Just so that he can boast tomorrow to his friends that he played better than someone else. Likewise others sweat away in their studies to prove to scholars that they have solved some hitherto insoluble problem in algebra. Many others again, just as foolishly in my view, risk the greatest dangers so that they can boast afterwards of having captured some stronghold. Then there are others[S] who exhaust themselves observing all these things, not in order to become wiser, but just to show they know them, and these are the biggest fools of the lot, because they know what they are doing, while it is conceivable that the rest would stop being foolish if they knew too.

A given man lives a life free from boredom by gambling a small sum every day. Give him every morning the money he might win that day, but on condition that he does not gamble, and you will make him unhappy. It might be argued that what he wants is the entertainment of gaming and not the winnings. Make him play then for nothing; his interest will not be fired and he will become bored, so it is not just entertainment he wants. A half-hearted entertainment without excitement will bore him. He must have excitement, he must delude himself into imagining that he would be happy to win what he would not want as a gift if it meant giving up gambling.[T] He must create some target for his passions and then arouse his desire, anger, fear, for this object he has created, just like children taking fright at a face they have daubed themselves.[U]

That is why this man, who lost his only son a few months ago and was so troubled and oppressed this morning by lawsuits and quarrels, is not thinking about it any more. Do not be surprised; he is concentrating all his attention on which way the boar will go that his dogs have been so hotly pursuing for the past six hours. That is all he needs. However sad a man may be, if you can persuade him to take up some diversion he will be happy while it lasts, and however happy a man may be, if he lacks diversion and has no absorbing passion or entertainment to keep boredom away, he will soon be depressed and unhappy. Without diversion there is no joy; with diversion there is no sadness. That is what constitutes the happiness of persons of rank, for they have a number of people to divert them and the ability to keep themselves in this state.

Make no mistake about it. What else does it mean to be Superintendent, Chancellor, Chief Justice, but to enjoy a position in which a great number of people come every morning from all parts and do not leave them a single hour of the day to think about themselves? When they are in disgrace and sent off to their country houses, where they lack neither wealth nor servants to meet their needs, they infallibly become miserable and dejected because no one stops them thinking about themselves.[v]   (139)

[136]

This is, to my mind, the most powerful of all the *pensées*. Students never fidget or whisper through this sermon.

A

In other words, all of our history and all of our lives.

B

At this point I dare you to cover up Pascal's next words and guess what he will say. I did that the first time I read it, and my guess was nowhere near Pascal's answer and nowhere near his bull's-eye. My answers were all more abstract, invisible, ponderous and platitudinous. When I looked at Pascal's answer I was disarmed, then charmed by its simplicity. I remember a similar reaction when first reading in Plato's *Republic* his answer to another great question: What is Justice? He says it is "minding your own business"! (Each part of the soul and each part of the state, like each organ in the body, does its proper work and not another.) We expect something abstract, remote, profound-sounding and esoteric, and he gives us something as plain as the light of day.

C

Once I read this answer, I felt insulted and then challenged by Pascal. Am I really incapable of the simple deed of staying quietly in my own room? Could I endure my own company alone for one hour, or am I so bored with myself that I have to invent some trouble to divert myself? I resolved to refute Pascal's implied insult—and failed flat. I went into the smallest and darkest room in my house and turned off the lights. To drown out distracting noise, I turned on an electric fan to make "white noise". I set an alarm clock outside the room for one hour. I then prepared myself to have a good, instructive, happy time meeting myself.

After ten minutes, I checked the alarm and was surprised that the hour had not yet passed.

After another ten minutes, I woke up to find myself asleep.

I deliberately didn't think about anything outside the room. I didn't bring in other people or my relationships with them or my work or my plans for the future or my past. For all these things were not really there in that room with me then. Only I was. I thought I should be able to endure my own presence without running away from myself into something external, even relationships, good and important as these are; for I wanted to encounter *who* it was who *had* all these relationships. If I can't meet *him*, if everything I do is a diversion from the doer, I'm in big trouble.

I think I'm in big trouble.

This was not the end of the story. But I don't want to tell you what I found next, because I don't want to preprogram you. You must be free to find whatever is real and true there, in you. But let me reassure you that there can be a light at the end of the tunnel, a floor under the nothingness, a Somebody under all the masks and roles and relationships. I wouldn't be recommending this experiment to you if there was no good news beyond the bad news. But you must find it for yourself. It's not easy.

D

C. S. Lewis somewhere defines modern Progressivism as "the absurd notion that the chief business of life should be the progressive attainment of goods we do not yet have rather than the appreciation and enjoyment of goods we already have."

E

Even the rich and powerful need diversion—especially they— which proves that even they—especially they—are unhappy. "Blessed are the poor" is not only good morality, it is also good psychology.

F

That is, the only happiness that man in the natural order, without God, has been able to devise.

G

Here is a good part of the origin of war, as well as politics and sports. Most of politics is as unnecessary as sports, but more harmful. And sports are obviously warfare sublimated.

As for "feminine society", consider how dull is a party without women.

H

We want *neither* peace and leisure as such *nor* pain and danger as such, but the diversion of danger with the illusion that it is the road to a happy peace. That is why many say "It is better to travel hopefully than to arrive"—a bromide C. S. Lewis refutes conclusively at one stroke: "If that were true, and known to be true, how could anyone ever travel hopefully? There would be nothing to hope for."

I

Surely it is a development of spectacular social significance that the very thing ancient saints and sages loved and longed for is the thing we impose on our most desperate criminals as the cruelest torture our minds can devise—solitude.

J

Surely this is one of the reasons the suicide rate is always much higher among the rich than among the poor: the poor always have things to do. They have to work to survive.

K

Our whole complex civilization is mostly fox hunting.

L

It is vain because it is self-delusion. Self-delusion is worse than shallowness, because it excludes self-knowledge, thus repentance and hope.

M

"The critics" are the snobs, "the criticized" are the slobs.

"The critics" are the Stoics, "the criticized" are the Epicureans.

"The critics" are the preachers, "the criticized" are the congregation.

"The critics" are the philosophers, "the criticized" are the masses.

N

Another image for all our social life: thinking where to put your feet to play the artificial social games acceptably, conforming to the dance. The social dance has replaced the Cosmic Dance (the medieval image) as the pattern to conform to.

(N.B. Pascal was evidently a poor dancer if he had to *think* about where to put his feet.)

O

Cupidity, or greed, is not for natural wealth, like land or food, but for artificial wealth: money, prestige and power. These things have no natural limit, therefore the desire for them is infinite and infinitely addictive. We delude ourselves with the thought that the next million will make us happy, satisfy us and be "enough". It never is.

For we do not want the thing, which has limits, but the activity of getting more of it, which has none.

P

Pascal here psychoanalyzes our collective unconscious and finds two contradictory drives: the fallen instinct for diversions to escape our unhappiness, and the instinct remaining from Eden for peace and rest. The unconscious harmonizes these two contradictory drives by the self-deluding faith that they are compatible as means and end, that work and diversion will be an effective means to rest and happiness. "Thus we never are happy, but only hope to be happy" (no. 47, p. 74). Like tomorrow, happiness is always a day away.

I call this "the if-only syndrome": If only I work hard enough to retire with a yacht, I'll be happy; If only I get another wife, I'll be happy; If only I win this tournament, I'll be happy; and so on.

It is the world's most universally failed experiment—and the world's most universally repeated one. It is stupid, self-deluding, wasteful and self-destructive. And we all do it, we all think it.

Q

Thus individuals and societies are pendulums swinging between boredom and excitement—for example, from the boring, stable fifties to the exciting but destructive sixties and seventies, back to the boring eighties. Neither boredom nor excitement brings happiness, of course.

R

Very insulting, very "negative", very "misanthropic"—and very true.

S

The philosophers!

T

Pascal here uses gambling as an image of life. Later he will use it as an image of faith, in his famous "wager".

His penetrating question here is: What does the gambler (symbolically, all of us) *want*? (a) Not just the winnings, and (b) not just the playing, but (c) the *self-delusion* that comes from "the if-only syndrome"; the false faith that winning would make him happy.

If he *experiences* winning, he is not happy for long; but if he *plays* with the *hope* of winning, he can be happy for a long time by being both diverted (by playing) and deluded (believing he'd be truly happy if he won). Success is the sure spoiler. We are happy only climbing the mountain, not staying peacefully on the summit; only chasing the fox, not catching it; only courting, not marrying; only traveling, not arriving; only fighting wars, not keeping a boring peace.

U

What else is advertising than this? Here is its essential formula: create a target for passion, then arouse it.

And without advertising, our whole economy would collapse, and with it our whole economistic society.

The world's oldest profession is advertising. It was invented by the Devil in Eden: "See this apple? Eat it and you'll be like God."

We are all large children playing with Halloween faces painted with advertisements of desire and fear.

If (1) our lives are dependent on society (we are social conformists), and (2) our society is dependent on economy (we are consumerists), and (3) our economy is dependent on advertising, and (4) advertising is dependent on delusion, then (5) our lives are dependent on delusion.

V

This is why most depressions and suicides happen during summer or winter vacations.

773

Only the contest appeals to us, not the victory.

We like to watch animals fighting, but not the victor falling upon the vanquished. What did we want to see but the final victory? And once it has happened we have had enough. It is the same with gaming, with the pursuit of truth. We like to see the clash of opinions in debate, but do we want to contemplate the truth once it is found? Not at all. If we are to enjoy it, we must see it arising from the debate.[A] It is the same with passions; there is some pleasure in seeing the collision of two opposites, but when one asserts its mastery it becomes mere brutality.

We never go after things in themselves, but the pursuit of things. Thus in the theatre scenes of unclouded happiness are no good. . . .[B]   (135)

[773]
A
This is why we like Socratic dialogue better than monologue.

B
All the fairy tales fail in the last line. No one can ever *show* how "they all lived happily ever after." We can't *imagine* a Heaven that is not boring; we can only *believe* in it.

641
Our nature consists in movement; absolute rest is death.
                (129)

[641]

We are sharks.

137

Diversion. Is not the dignity of kingship sufficiently great in itself to make its possessor happy by simply seeing what he is? Does he need to be diverted from such thoughts like ordinary people? I can quite see that it makes a man happy to be diverted from contemplating his private miseries by making him care about nothing else but dancing well, but will it be the same with a king, and will he be happier absorbed in such vain amusements than in contemplating his own greatness? What more satisfying object could his mind be offered? Would it not therefore be spoiling his delight to occupy his mind with thoughts of how to fit his steps to the rhythm of a tune or how to place a bar skilfully, instead of leaving him in peace to enjoy the contemplation of the majestic glory surrounding him? Put it to the test; leave a king entirely alone, with nothing to satisfy his senses, no care to occupy his mind, with no one to keep him company and no diversion, with complete leisure to think about himself, and you will see that a king without diversion is a very wretched man. Therefore such a thing is carefully avoided, and the persons of kings are invariably attended by a great number of people concerned to see that diversion comes after affairs of state, watching over their leisure hours to provide pleasures and sport so that there should never be an empty moment. In other words they are surrounded by people who are incredibly careful to see that the king should never be alone and able to think about himself, because they know that, king though he is, he will be miserable if he does think about it.

In all this I am not speaking of Christian kings as Christian but merely as kings. (142)

[137]

Pascal distinguishes between necessary diversions (from misery) and unnecessary diversions, which are sought especially by the rich and powerful. Pascal is not condemning diversion as such—it is important not to misunderstand him as some kind of Puritan—but only wants to show us that we are more unhappy than we think. He shows this by noting that we seek diversion not only when we are poor and miserable but also (especially) when we are rich and powerful. This is simple and experimental proof that these things (riches, power, glory, kingship, worldly success) do not in fact make us happy.

The last sentence shows that everything changes when Christ enters. He can make even a king or a rich man happy. What Pascal means by a "Christian" is not merely one who holds a religious label or opinion or public membership, but one who is in real, live contact with the real, live Christ, the man who is God, and therefore infinite, and therefore not ever boring to all eternity. Therefore a Christian experiences no boredom and need for diversion in proportion as he experiences Christ.

139

Diversion. **From childhood on men are made responsible for the care of their honour, their property, their friends, and even of the property and honour of their friends; they are burdened with duties, language-training and exercises, and given to understand that they can never be happy unless their health, their honour, their fortune and those of their friends are in good shape, and that it needs only one thing to go wrong to make them unhappy. So they are given responsibilities and duties which harass them from the first moment of each day. You will say that is an odd way to make them happy: what better means could one devise to make them unhappy? What could one do? You would only have to take away all their cares, and then they would see themselves and think about what** they are, where they come from, and where they are going. That is why men cannot be too much occupied and distracted, and that is why, when they have been given so many things to do, if they have some time off they are advised to spend it on diversion and sport, and always to keep themselves fully occupied.

How hollow and foul is the heart of man! (143)

[139]

Thus, as we have seen earlier (pp. 172ff.), we secretly love the very hassles we complain about. We devised them, after all; they did not come from Heaven or from a tyrant. They are our diversions.

Unless we transcend our instinctive negative knee-jerk reaction to the conclusion of this *pensée* in the last sentence, unless we question the ubiquitous and unquestioned assumption of nearly all our modern prophets, unless we judge our prophets by God's prophets instead of vice versa, we will not see ourselves as God sees us, that is, as we are.

And if we do not see ourselves this way, as desperate cases, we are simply not part of the audience Christ came to save. He did not come to give us an aspirin but an operation.

If we do not line up in agreement with Pascal's negative conclusion on the heart of man, we do not line up with the apostles and prophets and saints either—or with Christ. If we do not accept the first half of the *Pensées*, the truth about sin, then the second half, the truth about salvation, will be only a thought-experiment, an "option", not a life-preserver.

Did you notice your first, instinctive reaction to the concluding sentence of this *pensée*?—how patronizing you were to Pascal, how you *excused* his old-fashioned "judgmentalism" or "negativism"—probably with the excuse that Pascal never read modern psychology.

(Psychology, by the way, has a lower proportion of orthodox Christians than any other profession. Ninety percent of cosmologists are theists, nine percent of psychologists are.

There are more Christian prostitutes than Christian psychologists. This is not to disparage psychology as such but to note the need for more Christians to enter that battlefield.)

414

Wretchedness. **The only thing that consoles us for our miseries is diversion. And yet it is the greatest of our miseries. For it is that above all which prevents us thinking about ourselves and leads us imperceptibly to destruction. But for that we should be bored, and boredom would drive us to seek some more solid means of escape, but diversion passes our time and brings us imperceptibly to our death.**

(171)

[414]

Diversion's greatest danger is that it acts like a sedative; it keeps us just content enough so that we don't make waves and seek a real cure. It deadens our spiritual nerves, it muffles our alarm system.

A little respectable religion acts in the same way: as a mild dose of the infection, which builds up antibodies in us to shield us against the real thing. The Devil loves a little religion. He doesn't want us to be too bored and too miserable—yet.

57

It is not good to be too free.
It is not good to have all one needs.

(379)

[57]

The two things people in our society want most are freedom and wealth. Yet for those who have virtually unrestricted freedom and wealth, life is boring. It has no limits to bump up against, like a low-hanging tree branch. Life sets them no busy tasks to keep them diverted by the illusion that they would be happy if only they were rich and free. They *are* rich and free—and miserable. "Blessed are the poor."

622

Boredom. Man finds nothing so intolerable as to be in a state of complete rest, without passions, without occupation, without diversion, without effort.

Then he faces his nullity, loneliness, inadequacy, dependence, helplessness, emptiness.

And at once there wells up from the depths of his soul boredom, gloom, depression, chagrin, resentment, despair.

(131)

[622]

The word "boredom" does not exist in any ancient language. It first appears in the seventeenth century. No one knows its origin.

Since we always invent words for things we experience, it follows that this is a new experience. Until modern times, it seems, people simply were not bored—that is, bored in general, bored with life. Of course they tired of a particular task like cutting wood for ten hours.

The closest thing to it in the Middle Ages is *anomie,* or *acedia,* the deadly sin of *sloth,* spiritual torpitude, lack of care and passion and joy in the face of spiritual good, indifference to our eternal destiny. It is "deadly", or "mortal": it kills souls. This killer is our next topic.

14. Indifference

Indifference is the very nadir of the soul. And it is the very definition of the modern soul.

If diversions do not keep us from Heaven, indifference will.

The first and greatest commandment is to love (seek) God with all our heart (passion). Indifference is the opposite. Indifference is farther from the love of God than hatred of God is. You can love and hate the same person at the same time, but you cannot love and be indifferent to the same person at the same time.

Diversion and indifference are the Devil's two most successful weapons against faith and salvation, the two widest roads to Hell in today's world. It is much harder for him to tempt us with deliberate rebellion against God, for that uses two things that come from God: light and passion. Both can be twisted, but they are not the Devil's natural element. His natural elements are darkness and fog, not light; and sleep and death, not passion. Both diversion and indifference drain off passion and light—not only the light of faith but even the light of simple sanity and natural reason. Indifference is *stupid*.

Indifference is more fashionable today than it ever was before, except perhaps once: as Rome was dying—decadent, sophisticated, skeptical, relativistic, jaded, bored and promiscuous, skidding down its own mudslide of spiritual waste—exactly like us. By contrast, all young and healthy nations, eras, cultures and individuals are simple, strong and passionate—never bland, indifferent and relativistic. If there is any certain symptom of social senility it is indifference, shown in slogans like "anything goes", "do your own thing", "different strokes for different folks", or "live and let live."

We are so afraid that caring about truth and dueling with words will turn into caring about power and dueling with weapons, so afraid that spiritual warfare against evil and falsehood will turn into physical warfare against people, that we have abandoned spiritual warfare altogether, and also real debate, real and serious search for truth (except in science). Pascal is our prophet. No one after this seventeenth-century man has so accurately described our twentieth-century mind.

Both diversion and indifference can be used for good— when the thing we are diverted from, or indifferent to, is bad for us. For instance, the Lamaze method of natural childbirth teaches the mother to divert herself from her labor pains by concentrating on breathing, like yoga. And drugs make us dull and indifferent to pain.

But the only long-range solution to pain, whether physical or spiritual, is to listen to what it is telling us. It is a symptom. We must follow its clue, like a river, or a guide through a jungle, if we want to be healed. Perpetual indifference is like shutting off the alarm clock and going back to sleep when the house you are in, which you have built on the sand, is about to be washed away into the sea.

427

Let them at least learn what this religion is which they are attacking before attacking it. If this religion boasted that it had a clear sight of God and plain and manifest evidence of his existence, it would be an effective objection to say that there is nothing to be seen in the world which proves him so obviously. But since on the contrary it says that men are in darkness and remote from God, that he has hidden himself from their understanding, that this is the very name which he gives himself in Scripture: *Deus absconditus* [the hidden God]; and, in a word, if it strives equally to establish these two facts: that God has appointed visible signs in the Church so that he shall be recognized by those who genuinely seek him, and that he has none the less hidden them in such a way that he will only be perceived by those who seek him with all their heart, then what advantage can they derive when, unconcerned to seek the truth as they profess to be, they protest that nothing shows it to them? For the obscurity in which they find themselves, and which they use as an objection against the Church, simply establishes one of the things the Church maintains without affecting the other, and far from proving her teaching false, confirms it.[A]

In order really to attack the truth they would have to protest that they had made every effort to seek it everywhere, even in what the Church offers by way of instruction, but without any satisfaction. If they talked like that they would indeed be attacking one of Christianity's claims. But I hope to show here that no reasonable person could talk like that. I even venture to say that no one has ever done so. We know well enough how people in this frame of mind behave. They think they have made great efforts to learn when they have spent a few hours reading some book of the Bible, and have questioned some ecclesiastic about the truths of the faith. After that they boast that they have sought without success in books and among men. But, in fact, I should say to them what I have often said: such negligence is intolerable. It is not a question here of the trifling interest of some stranger prompting such behaviour: it is a question of ourselves, and our all.

The immortality of the soul is something of such vital importance to us, affecting us so deeply, that one must have lost all feeling not to care[B] about knowing the facts of the matter. All our actions and thoughts must follow such different paths, according to whether there is hope of eternal blessings or not, that the only possible way of acting with sense and judgement is to decide our course in the light of this point, which ought to be our ultimate objective.[C]

Thus our chief interest and chief duty is to seek enlightenment on this subject, on which all our conduct depends. And that is why, amongst those who are not convinced, I make an absolute distinction between those who strive with all their might to learn and those who live without troubling themselves or thinking about it.[D]

I can feel nothing but compassion for those who sincerely lament their doubt, who regard it as the ultimate misfortune, and who, sparing no effort to escape from it, make their search their principal and most serious business.

But as for those who spend their lives without a thought for this final end of life and who, solely because they do not find within themselves the light of conviction, neglect to look elsewhere, and to examine thoroughly whether this opinion is one of those which people accept out of credulous simplicity or one of those which, though obscure in themselves, none the less have a most solid and unshakeable foundation: as for them, I view them very differently.

This negligence in a matter where they themselves, their eternity, their all are at stake, fills me more with irritation than pity; it astounds and appals me; it seems quite monstrous to me. I do not say this prompted by the pious zeal of spiritual devotion. I mean on the contrary that we ought to have this feeling from principles of human interest and self-esteem.[E] For that we need only see what the least enlightened see.

One needs no great sublimity of soul to realize that in this life there is no true and solid satisfaction, that all our pleasures are mere vanity, that our afflictions are infinite, and finally that death which threatens us at every moment must in a few years infallibly face us with the inescapable and appalling alternative of being annihilated or wretched throughout eternity.[F]

Nothing could be more real, or more dreadful than that. Let us put on as bold a face as we like: that is the end awaiting the world's most illustrious life. Let us ponder these things, and then say whether it is not beyond doubt that the only good thing in this life is the hope of another life, that we become happy only as we come nearer to it, and that, just as no more unhappiness awaits those who have been quite certain of eternity, so there is no happiness for those who have no inkling of it.[G]

It is therefore quite certainly a great evil to have such doubts, but it is at least an indispensable obligation to seek when one does thus doubt; so the doubter who does not seek is at the same time very unhappy and very wrong.[H] If in addition he feels a calm satisfaction, which he openly professes, and even regards as a reason for joy and vanity, I can find no terms to describe so extravagant a creature.[I]

What can give rise to such feelings? What reason for joy can be found in the expectation of nothing but helpless wretchedness? What reason for vanity in being plunged into impenetrable darkness? And how can such an argument as this occur to a reasonable man?

'I do not know who put me into the world, nor what the world is, nor what I am myself. I am terribly ignorant about everything. I do not know what my body is, or my senses, or my soul, or even that part of me which thinks what I am saying, which reflects about everything and about itself, and does not know itself any better than it knows anything else.

'I see the terrifying spaces of the universe hemming me in, and I find myself attached to one corner of this vast expanse without knowing why I have been put in this place rather than that, or why the brief span of life allotted to me should be assigned to one moment rather than another of all the eternity which went before me and all that which will come after me. I see only infinity on every side, hemming me in like an atom or like the shadow of a fleeting instant. All I know is that I must soon die, but what I know least about is this very death which I cannot evade.

'Just as I do not know whence I come, so I do not know whither I am going. All I know is that when I leave this world I shall fall for ever into nothingness or into the hands of a wrathful God, but I do not know which of these two states is to be my eternal lot. Such is my state, full of weakness and uncertainty.[J] And my conclusion from all this is that I must pass my days without a thought of seeking what is to happen to me. Perhaps I might find some enlightenment in my doubts, but I do not want to take the trouble, nor take a step to look for it: and afterwards, as I sneer[K] at those who are striving to this end— (whatever certainty they have should arouse despair rather than vanity)—I will go without fear or foresight to face so momentous an event, and allow myself to be carried off limply[L] to my death, uncertain of my future state for all eternity.'

Who would wish to have as his friend a man who argued like that? Who would choose him from among others as a confidant in his affairs? Who would resort to him in adversity? To what use in life could he possibly be turned?

It is truly glorious for religion to have such unreasonable men as enemies: their opposition represents so small a danger that it serves on the contrary to establish the truths of religion. For the Christian faith consists almost wholly in establishing these two things: The corruption of nature and the redemption of Christ. Now, I maintain that, if they do not serve to prove the truth of the redemption by the sanctity of their conduct, they do at least admirably serve to prove the corruption of nature by such unnatural sentiments. . . .[M]

Thus the fact that there exist men who are indifferent to the loss of their being and the peril of an eternity of wretchedness is against nature. With everything else they are quite different; they fear the most trifling things, foresee and feel them; and the same man who spends so many days and nights in fury and despair at losing some office or at some imaginary affront to his honour is the very one who knows that he is going to lose everything through death but feels neither anxiety nor emotion. It is a monstrous thing to see one and the same heart at once so sensitive to minor things and so strangely insensitive to the greatest. It is an incomprehensible spell, a supernatural torpor that points to an omnipotent[N] power as its cause.[O]

Man's nature must have undergone a strange reversal for him to glory in being in a state in which it seems incredible that any single person should be.[P] Yet experience has shown me so many like this that it would be surprising if we did not know that most of those concerned in this are pretending and are not really what they seem.[Q] They are people who have heard that it is good form to display such extravagance. This is what they call shaking off the yoke, and what they are trying to imitate.[R] But it would not be difficult to show them how mistaken they are to court esteem in this way. That is not how to acquire it, not even, I would say, among worldly people, who judge things sensibly and who know that the only way to succeed is to appear honest, faithful, judicious and capable of rendering useful service to one's friends, because by nature men only like what may be of use to them. Now what advantage is it to us to hear someone say he has shaken off the yoke, that he does not believe that there is a God watching over his actions, that he considers himself sole master of his behaviour, and that he proposes to account for it to no one but himself?[S] Does he think that by so doing he has henceforth won our full confidence, and made us expect from him consolation, counsel and assistance in all life's needs? Do they think that they have given us great pleasure by telling us that they hold our soul to be no more than wind or smoke, and saying it moreover in tones of pride and satisfaction? Is this then something to be said gaily? Is it not on the contrary something to be said sadly, as being the saddest thing in the world?[T]

If they thought seriously, they would see that this is so misguided, so contrary to good sense, so opposed to decency, so remote in every way from the good form they seek, that they would be more likely to reform than corrupt those who might feel inclined to follow them. And, indeed, make them describe the feeling and reasons which inspire their doubts about religion: what they say will be so feeble and cheap as to persuade you of the contrary. As someone said to them very aptly one day: 'If you go on arguing like that,' he said, 'you really will convert me.'[U] And he was right, for who would not shrink from finding himself sharing the feelings of such contemptible people?

Thus those who only pretend to feel like this would be indeed unhappy if they did violence to their nature in order to become the most impertinent of men. If they are vexed in their inmost heart at not seeing more clearly, they should not try to pretend otherwise: it would be no shame to admit it. There is no shame except in having none.[V] There is no surer sign of extreme weakness of mind than the failure to recognize the unhappy state of a man without God; there is no surer sign of an evil heart than failure to desire that the eternal promises be true; nothing is more cowardly than to brazen it out with God.[W] Let them then leave such impiety to those ill-bred enough to be really capable of it; let them at least be decent people if they cannot be Christians; let them, in short, acknowledge that there are only two classes of persons who can be called reasonable: those who serve God with all their heart because they know him and those who seek him with all their heart because they do not know him.[X]

As for those who live without either knowing or seeking him, they consider it so little worth while to take trouble over themselves that they are not worth other people's trouble, and it takes all the charity of that religion they despise not to despise them to the point of abandoning them to their folly. But as this religion obliges us always to regard them, as long as they live, as being capable of receiving grace which may enlighten them, and to believe that in a short time they may be filled with more faith than we are, while we on the contrary may be stricken by the same blindness which is theirs now, we must do for them what we would wish to be done for us in their place, and appeal to them to have pity on themselves, and to take at least a few steps in an attempt to find some light.^Y Let them spend on reading about it a few of the hours they waste on other things: however reluctantly they may approach the task they will perhaps hit upon something, and at least they will not be losing much. . . .^Z

(194)

[427]

A

God's claim is that "you will find me when you seek me with all your heart" (Jer 29:13). This claim is not refuted or fairly tested if we do not fulfill our part of the experiment by seeking. Therefore Christianity can never be refuted by one who is indifferent, no matter how intelligent he is; for the claim to be refuted is that only the key of seeking opens the lock of the knowledge of God.

See Chapters 15 (the opposite of indifference, passion) and 19 (why God hides), especially nos. 160, 444, 446 and 781 (pp. 211, 248, 249, 250).

B

To care is even more important than to know, for it is the only way to know the most important thing: yourself, your soul, your identity, your purpose, your destiny and your immortality. If we are indifferent instead of seeking, we simply will not find, that is, we will not be saved. Hell is not populated mainly by passionate rebels but by nice, bland, indifferent, respectable people who simply never gave a damn.

C

How could anyone act as if it made no difference whether the obscure path through the dark forest of life leads Home or into quicksand; whether the waterslide has a pool at the bottom or rocks? It is insanity to sing "I don't care" while walking along such a path.

D

The absolute distinction, which will become the distinction between the Heavenly and the Hellish, is not between believers and unbelievers but between seekers and nonseekers; for all unbelievers who seek will eventually become believers who find, according to the very highest authority (Mt 7:7–8). The distinction between believers and seeking unbelievers is only temporary; but the distinction between seeking unbelievers and unseeking unbelievers is eternal.

The absolute distinction is between unhappy atheists and happy atheists. Unbelievers who are content and happy now will be unhappy eternally, but those who are unhappy and seeking now will be happy eternally (Lk 6:21–26).

E

Pascal's judgment simply follows God's. God does not judge unbelievers by the supernatural standard of faith but by the natural standard of reason. As St. Paul says in Romans 1, the truth they know by natural reason is what they hold down or suppress because of their unrighteousness (1:18), and this—natural reason, natural law, natural sanity—is enough to condemn them.

The battle for eternal souls is largely decided here in the beginning, in the plain plains of natural reason, rather than later, in the mysterious mountains of faith. If we are honest with truth, reason will lead us to faith.

F

They are annihilated if there is no life after death and wretched if there is, for they have made themselves God's enemies. They will not repent, and God will not or cannot force himself and his happiness on them against their will. For God is a lover, not a rapist.

There are only two possibilities for the indifferent unbeliever, not three:

1. He does not believe, and there is no life after death, only annihilation.

2. He does not believe, and there is life after death, and he has lost it forever because he has refused God's free offer during the only time he had; thus he is without God, and wretched, eternally.

3. The third "possibility" is *im*possible: that he does not believe, and there is life after death, and he has found eternal life in Heaven forever even though he has not sought it or wanted it.

How could it make him happy if it is against his will?

One wonders how much of Christianity's power to win the world has been crippled by the modern fashion of denying or ignoring the reality of Hell. It is certainly a fashion rather than a proof or a discovery. Both reason and faith inform us of Hell: reason, because it is irrational to think that souls created free to refuse God can be compelled to accept him; faith, because if no one goes to Hell, then Jesus is a liar or a fool, for he more than anyone warned against it.

G

Proximately, this is not true, of course. There are many genuinely good finite things in this world, and even unbelievers can derive much pleasure from them: human love, and music, and the stars and the sea. But ultimately, Pascal is right: these are only well-mixed drinks served aboard the *Titanic*.

H

See no. 160 (p. 211). To be "very wrong" is far worse than to be "very unhappy"; we are rightly blamed for being wrong but not for being unhappy.

I

Here is the nadir of the soul. This is why Dante had the lowest circle of Hell as ice, not fire. The argument that now follows, which Pascal puts into the mouth of the self-satisfied, indifferent unbeliever, is in statistical fact *not* "extravagant" or abnormal today at all but is precisely the philosophy of the majority of "educated" people in the secular world, especially the opinion molders, in entertainment, education and journalism, who shape our souls.

J

So far, this unbeliever is only to be pitied, not condemned. He is in terrible deprivation of any certain knowledge about himself and his destiny. What follows, however, is not to be pitied but scorned in horror, like deliberately induced insanity. (It *is* deliberately induced, and it *is* insanity!)

K

A sneer is worse for the soul than a murder. What state of soul can be imagined lower than the sneer? Especially a sneer at reason, faith, humility, hope, righteousness and love of God, which are the ideals pursued by the "religious fanatic" who is being sneered at.

L

Here is the key word. The secularist's soul has turned into a wet noodle.

M

Pascal is using the debater's rhetoric here, but appropriately. It is not even exaggeration; it is literal truth.

N

Pascal does not literally mean "omnipotent" here (though he writes "*toute-puissante*") but "supernatural". The cause of the insanity he is referring to here is not God, who is the only

omnipotent One, but the Devil. And therefore, since the cause
is not omnipotent, it can be opposed. But since it is supernatural, it must be opposed by supernatural means: see Ephesians
6:10–18, especially 12; Matthew 17:21.

O

Again, this is literal truth, not rhetorical exaggeration. Please
pause one minute to reflect on this simple proof of our Original Insanity. Even the believer lives in this inverted consciousness most of the time; but he at least *knows* his insanity, his
intellectual sin, and its supernatural Hellish source and goal,
and he repents and rejects all this.

P

More evidence for a historical Fall. See Kierkegaard, *Philosophical Fragments,* chapter 1, for an extended version of this argument.

Q

This makes the problem worse rather than better in one sense;
for pretense is (a) deliberate, (b) dishonest and (c) scornful of
God for the sake of getting the respect of fools. See Mark 8:38.
If we are ashamed of God, God is ashamed of us.

R

Already in Pascal's time secularists were becoming the new
opinion-molding establishment, the intelligentsia, the envied
sophisticates.

S

A famous atheist said, "I do not believe in God, but I want my
banker, my lawyer and my doctor to do so." Of course there
are very moral atheists and very immoral Christians; there are
also very gentle assassins and very violent philanthropists; hon-
orable thieves and thieving judges. But if there were not para-

doxical exceptions, we would not find them remarkable or bother to remark on them, as we do.

T

One can be honest, intelligent, atheistic and unhappy, but one cannot be honest, intelligent, atheistic and happy. If an atheist is happy, he is either dishonest or unintelligent; either a liar or a fool.

The difference between an unhappy atheist and a happy (contented) atheist is greater than the difference between an unhappy atheist and a theist, for both the unhappy atheist and the theist are at least sane.

U

Nietzsche, for example, has driven more skeptics screaming into the arms of the priests than any preacher of our time. So has Sartre.

V

The prevailing view since Freud is the polar opposite: that there is nothing to feel guilty about except guilt, nothing to fear but fear itself. What wise-sounding foolishness, especially addressed to children playing near a cliff!

W

"The failure to recognize the unhappy state of a man without God" is self-delusion in the face of massive fact; but "failure to *desire* that the eternal promises be true" is scorn or indifference at the very idea of a Heaven of goodness; and "to brazen it out with God" is the last, desperate posturing of a tiny, spoiled child telling his parents he doesn't need their love, thank you.

X

Therefore all reasonable (honest) men go to Heaven, for to be reasonable is to seek, and all seekers eventually find (Mt 7:8).

Y

The Christian attitude toward indifferent, unrepentant sinners laughing on the road to Hell is neither superiority and scorn nor toleration but horror and humility ("There but for the grace of God go I").

Z

Any unbeliever who has taken the trouble to read this book this far has already risen from the ranks of the indifferent to the status of the seeker—if only he does not repent of his repentance.

823
An heir finds the deeds to his house. Will he say, perhaps, that they are false, and not bother to examine them?

(217)

[823]
Proof of the insanity of indifference to Heaven.

The secret of the universe and of your life lies behind this door, according to the wisest and best men who have ever lived; how should we describe someone who won't bother to lift the key to the lock and see whether it opens?

941
We do not grow bored with eating and sleeping every day, for we soon feel hungry or sleepy again, otherwise we should grow bored with it.

Likewise if we do not hunger for spiritual things we find them boring: 'hunger after righteousness,' eighth beatitude.

(264)

[941]
Here is the root of the uniquely modern phenomenon of boredom. We are bored with God because our hearts do not hunger for God, seek God, love God. The ancients were not

bored because they hungered. We are so full of our hunger for earthly riches that we have little hunger for the Heavenly.

Thus our boredom is our *fault*, and we will suffer just punishment for it.

632
Man's sensitivity to little things and insensitivity to the greatest things are marks of a strange disorder.   (198)

[632]

We are more put out at missing a parking place than at missing our place in Heaven; more perturbed at missing the right road to our next appointment than at missing the road to our appointment with God. For "where your treasure is, there will your heart be also" (Mt 6:21).

Of all the obstacles to our sanctification, indifference is the most pervasive and difficult to overcome. It is easier to turn a moving car 180 degrees than to start it up when it has stalled; easier to redirect passion than to create it.

Great saints have often been made out of great sinners (Mary Magdalen, Paul, Augustine, Francis, Ignatius), but not one was ever made out of a wimp. Those who care about foolish little things like fame and sex and money and power, and scorn great things like holiness and wisdom and salvation, can be converted, as a child can be converted from caring about comic books to caring about great literature. Not all indifference is incorrigible. The apologist must find the little flame of passion for some worldly end and explore that, hoping to pass on and convert the flame to greater things. Besides, people listen attentively to you if you talk with any sort of respect or intelligence about what they love.

Kierkegaard started (in *Either/Or*) with writing about seduction, Flannery O'Connor with grotesqueries, C. S. Lewis with fantasy. All effective, because passionate, starting points.

176

Those who do not love truth excuse themselves on the grounds that it is disputed and that very many people deny it. Thus their error is solely due to the fact that they love neither truth nor charity, and so they have no excuse.

(261)

[176]

The fact that people have disputes and contradictory opinions is an immensely popular excuse today for not seeking the truth. Especially moral and religious truth is disputed. Therefore it is thought to be unattainable, or only subjective, "true for me" (whatever *that* could possibly mean). This is exceedingly foolish, for it puts your salvation in the control of *other people*. If these others are foolish enough to deny or dispute what is in fact true, you are lost! Would you risk your body's life on the opinions of others? Why then stake your soul to such a sandy ground?

"They have no excuse."

177

Contradiction is a poor indication of truth.[A]
   Many things that are certain are contradicted.[B]
   Many that are false pass without contradiction.[C]   (384)

[177]

A

That is, the fact that some people contradict X is no proof that X is false.

B

For example, your own mortality.

C

For example, the idea that the earth is the center of the universe (before Copernicus).

150

The ungodly who propose to follow reason. . . .

What do they say then?

'Do we not see,' they say, 'animals live and die like men, Turks like Christians?' . . .[A]

'Is that contrary to Scripture? Does it not say all that?' [B]

If you hardly care about knowing the truth, that is enough to leave you in peace, but if you desire with all your heart to know it, you have not looked closely enough. . . .[C] This would do for a philosophical question, but here where everything is at stake. . . .[D] And yet, after superficial reflection of this kind we amuse ourselves. . . .   (226)

[150]

A

That is, this easy and superficial objection is enough to justify in their minds the abandoning of the search. What visible difference does being a Christian make, anyway? Dogs, Christians and pagans all live and all die, after all.

B

That piece of data which the objector adduces *against* Christianity counts *for* it, for it is data that fit the Christian hypothesis rather than contradicting it. The objection is a stupid one; it shows nothing about Christianity, only something about the objector: his indifference to the truth. He is seizing on any old excuse, however weak, to justify going home without having played the game.

C

The heart that truly desires truth does not give up that easily. Indeed, it *never* gives up.

D

Christianity is not a *philosophy*. It is salvation. It is a matter of life or death, Heaven or Hell.

151

It is absurd of us to rely on the company of our fellows, as wretched and helpless as we are; they will not help us; we shall die alone.[A]

We must act then as if we were alone. If that were so, would we build superb houses, etc? We should unhesitatingly look for the truth. And, if we refuse, it shows that we have a higher regard for men's esteem than for pursuing the truth.[B]　　　　　　　　　　　　　　　　　(211)

[151]

A

This is one reason why modern people are so unprepared for death: death is the one thing society can't do for you, the one thing that forces you to confront your trans-social self. We live as "the lonely crowd", but we die one at a time.

B

Honest confrontation with our mortality would produce a reprioritizing of values. Neither wealth ("superb houses") nor fame and honor ("men's esteem") endures death; but truth does. To have no passion for truth, especially the truth about ourselves and our eternal destiny, even in the face of death, is the "strange disease" Pascal spoke of in no. 427 (see note N, pp. 199–200) and no. 632 (p. 203).

IV

THE WAY TO A REAL SOLUTION:

HOW TO FIND THE TRUTH

This section is not yet the solution, only the way, the method, the epistemology. It is a common confusion in contemporary religious philosophy to confuse the way with the goal; to confuse meditation or contemplation or activism or human love or transformation of consciousness or experience with God. God is not a state of the human soul. "In the heart are the highways to Zion" (Ps 84:5) but not Zion, not Heaven. Else we would be worshiping ourselves.

But we will not get to our end if we do not know the way, the method. So this section is crucial.

Ultimately, the way and the goal are one in Christianity; Christ, who is God, our end, is also our way: "I am the way." But this is letting the cat out of the bag too soon.

15. Passionate Truth-seeking

This is the opposite and alternative to indifference. Indifference and diversion are the first easy steps on the road away from God and Heaven; this is the first step on the road *to* him and Home.

154

Choices. Our life in the world must vary according to these different assumptions:

1. (if it is certain that we shall always be here). . . .

2. (if it is uncertain whether we shall always be here or not).

3. (if it is certain that we shall not always be here, but if we are sure of being here for a long time). . . .

4. if it is certain that we shall not be here for long, and uncertain whether we shall be here even one hour.

This last assumption is ours. (237)

[154]

Each of these four assumptions, or hypotheses, is progressively closer to the truth. And the consequences for "our life in the world" are correspondingly more passionate.

If our geneticists ever discover the artificial immortality they are working on, and our social engineers guarantee it to everyone, assumption number 1 would become true. As a consequence, all passion for truth and for God would cease. Man would turn into a rabbit or a vegetable.

Here is one of the thickest bridges between Pascal's points: death (point 11) creates passion (point 15).

There is one remaining bit of innate sanity in any age, however insane and decadent: the knowledge that we will die. It is wonderful how this one spot of sanity restores a true perspective to everything. Doctor Johnson says, "I know no thought that so wonderfully clarifies the mind as the thought that I shall hang tomorrow morning."

When your doctor tells you that you, or someone you love, has only a short time to live, sanity and sagacity and even sanctity suddenly come flooding in like a wave of wisdom from the sea of Heaven. Suddenly, you stop filling up the boob tube of your consciousness with trivia. Death turns your habitual perspective upside down—that is, really right side up. Tiny things, like economics and technology and politics, no longer loom large, and enormous things, like religion and morality, no longer seem thin and far away. (See *pensées* nos. 43, 164, and 522, pages 75, 144, 76.) In a word, death removes "vanity". One of life's biggest problems, death, solves an even bigger one, vanity.

156
Pity the atheists who seek, for are they not unhappy enough? Inveigh against those who boast about it.   (190)

[156]
Unhappy atheists deserve pity, because they have not yet found God and are therefore unhappy. They do not deserve scorn, because they are seeking God and are therefore wise.

Happy atheists deserve scorn, because they are content and do not seek. But though they do not deserve it, we also give them pity, as God does, and extend the gracious offer to become unhappy, seeking atheists first and Christians later.

158
As far as the choices go, you must take the trouble to seek the truth, for if you die without worshipping the true principle you are lost. 'But', you say, 'if he had wanted me to worship him, he would have left me some signs of his will.' So he did, but you pay no heed. Look for them then; it is well worth it.   (236)

[158]
Unless we seek ("pay heed"), we will not find and will be lost.

The objection in quotation marks is the one addressed by C. S. Lewis' *Till We Have Faces*: "Why must holy places be dark places?" (See point 23 in our Outline for Pascal's more complete answer to that question.)

160

There are only three sorts of people: those who have found God and serve him; those who are busy seeking him and have not found him; those who live without either seeking or finding him. The first are reasonable and happy, the last are foolish and unhappy, those in the middle are unhappy and reasonable. **(257)**

[160]

There is no fourth class, none who find God without ever seeking him.

Group 1 are believers. They are "reasonable" or wise or sane because they seek and happy because they have found.

Group 2 are unhappy atheists and agnostics. They are "reasonable" because they seek and unhappy because they have not yet found.

Group 3 are the happy atheists. They are "unreasonable", foolish, spiritually insane, because they do not even seek the truth; and they are unhappy (forever!) because they do not find.

Thus, paradoxically, unhappy atheists are destined for happiness eternally, and happy atheists are destined for unhappiness eternally (just as Jesus said in Luke 6:21–26).

The great divide, the eternal divide, is not between theists and atheists, or between happiness and unhappiness, but between seekers (lovers) and nonseekers (nonlovers) of the Truth (for God is Truth). Thus it is the heart and not the head that determines our eternal destiny.

We all instinctively know this is right.

193

It is deplorable to see everybody debating about the means, never the end. Everyone thinks about how he will get on in his career. . . .   **(98)**

[193]

The end is more important than the means, for that is what "means" *means*: a means *to the end*. Therefore we should care more about our end.

What we care most about, we debate about and think about and investigate the most. Our mind is moved by our heart, our love, our care. Therefore we should "debate" the most about our end.

But eternity is our end—eternal life or eternal death. Our life in this world is our means, our road. Yet we debate much more about our means than about our end. Why?

Because we care more about it. Our hearts are set on it. We love and care and worry about our job more than our salvation; about our second job (for example, being a good nurse or a good pilot) more than our first job (being a good human being). We worry more about flunking economics than about flunking Life.

386

The enchantment of vanity. **To render passion harmless let us behave as though we had only a week to live.**   **(386)**

[386]

How can we cure our mental illness of indifference and worldliness? Pascal's suggestion here is not game-playing or self-deception but stark realism. For the only thing we can all be infallibly certain of is that some day we *will* have only one week to live. What is more real than that? It is our ordinary worldly consciousness that is unreal, game-playing and self-deceiving.

If you knew you were going to take a one-way trip to

Australia, would it be escapist to inquire about that place and about the way to it? Would it not be escapist to ignore it?

I dare you to try Pascal's experiment, actually to do it, not just read about it. Live this week as if it were your last, so that when you die you have no regrets, no "if onlys"—if only I had done this or said that—no unfinished business. For instance, tell your mother how much you love her. Above all, decide how much you love God, tell him and live that out.

405

I condemn equally those who choose to praise man, those who choose to condemn him, and those who choose to divert themselves, and I can only approve of those who seek with groans. (421)

[405]

Optimism and pessimism are equally condemned because they are equally oversimple, oversatisfied, overcontent, under-amazed, underseeking, *indifferent*. Add the third position of diversion, and we have three follies. The only wisdom for un-believers is to "seek with groans". Whatever is meant by this striking phrase, it does *not* refer to yuppies. Or people who keep using phrases such as "what I'm comfortable with".

429

This is what I see and what troubles me. I look around in every direction and all I see is darkness. Nature has noth-ing to offer me that does not give rise to doubt and anx-iety. If I saw no sign there of a Divinity I should decide on a negative solution: if I saw signs of a Creator everywhere I should peacefully settle down in the faith. But, seeing too much to deny and not enough to affirm, I am in a piti-ful state, where I have wished a hundred times over that, if there is a God supporting nature, she should unequivo-cally proclaim him, and that, if the signs in nature are deceptive, they should be completely erased; that nature should say all or nothing so that I could see what course I ought to follow. Instead of that, in the state in which I am, not knowing what I am nor what I ought to do, I know neither my condition nor my duty. My whole heart strains to know what the true good is in order to pursue it: no price would be too high to pay for eternity.   (229)

[429]

It is unclear whether Pascal here speaks in the person of (that is, impersonating) the groaning, seeking unbeliever or as a believer still perpetually wrestling with rational doubts. The same ambivalence attaches to St. Paul's groans in Romans 7: "The good that I would, I do not; the evil that I would not, that I do."

What state Pascal was in when he wrote this is of interest only to God, to Pascal and to historians. What matters to you is your state of soul, now; how this *pensée* "speaks to your condition", as the Quakers say.

As C. S. Lewis points out in the introduction to *The Problem of Pain*, nature's evidence about God is two-faced. Nature is full of beauty but also of ugliness; of goodness but also of cruelty; of physical law but not moral law: cancer cells and bullets do not ask about the morality or holiness of their victims. No one comes to believe in a loving God simply by contemplating nature. Ecclesiastes, who confined himself to observing nature and life "under the sun" (empirically) concluded that "all is vanity."

God must have deliberately designed nature as a clue, not a manifesto; a puzzle, not a solution. We would have preferred an easier set of signs, one which pointed only in one direction, not two. God must have wanted nature to lead us to puzzlement, not certainty, so that we could "seek with groans". (See point 23).

The two things we need most to know are "our condition and our duty", what we are and what we ought to be. Nature teaches us neither, for both depend on God, not nature. Are we made in the image of King Kong or the image of King

God? Are our duty and our end on earth or in Heaven? Nature tells us neither but sends us elsewhere—first of all, to our own hearts and honest, passionate truth-seeking.

The concluding sentence is a charter, a manifesto, a definition of spiritual sanity. Pascal here bares his deepest heart, with its absolute, uncompromising, unconditional demand "to know what the true good is". How reasonable is this fanaticism! How insane to refuse eternity for fear the earthly price may be too high! (Compare the argument about infinite and finite goods in no. 418, right after the "wager".)

463

It is a remarkable fact that no canonical [Biblical] author has ever used nature to prove God. They all try to make people believe in him. David, Solomon, etc., never said: 'There is no such thing as a vacuum, therefore God exists.' They must have been cleverer than the cleverest of their successors, all of whom have used proofs from nature. This is very noteworthy. (243)

[463]

If Scripture does not use nature to prove God, it can't be the best strategy.

Notice Pascal does not say that there are no good proofs of God or that none of them begin with data from nature. Elsewhere, he specifies merely that such proofs are psychologically weak, but he does not say they are logically weak. (See no. 190, p. 311). More important, they are salvifically weak, they will not save us. Only Christ will save us.

If nature proved God clearly, we would not have to search for him with all our hearts.

631

It is good to be tired and weary from fruitlessly seeking the true good, so that one can stretch out one's arms to the Redeemer. (422)

[631]

Surprise! "Seek and you shall find" is a *koan*, an unsolvable puzzle. If we do not seek, we will not find; but finding God does not come as a direct result of our seeking, either. We don't find God as we find a planet but more as we find a mate. We do not find God, we are found by God. (See the last two paragraphs of chapter 11 of C. S. Lewis' *Miracles*.)

So you can't get God by trying, and you can't get him by not trying. It's an unsolvable puzzle, solvable only by God.

If it is the true God we are dealing with, and not some figment of our comfortable imagination, we will come sooner or later to a turning point in our search where we discover that "you can't get there from here" (in the words of the famous Vermont farmer joke); that our ignorance, our impotence and above all our sin blocks our access to God; and that unless God has stretched out his hand to us to save us, we cannot stretch out our hand to him and be saved.

At this point we discover what we can do: just say Yes, accept, believe, receive, open our tight-clenched hands and hearts and let him enter.

If you have never done that, it's not too late—yet.

739

Truth is so obscured nowadays and lies [are] so well established that unless we love the truth we shall never recognize it. **(864)**

[739]

This is why the discovery of truth depends on the heart and will, not just the head and mind. This is why the prime requisite for finding any great truth (like God, or the meaning of life or death, or who we are and what we ought to do, or even finding the right mate and the right career) is love, passion, questing and questioning. Once we pursue a question with our whole being, as Socrates pursued "know thyself", we will find answers. Answers are not as hard to come by as we think; and questions, real questioning, is a lot more rare and precious than we think. Finding is not the problem, seeking is. For truth is hidden, ever since the Fall but especially "nowadays", now that our secular society no longer helps us to God, as traditional societies did. Lies are well established on the level of appearance (for example, movies); truth and reality are hidden, behind the lies. No one will find the truth today just by listening to the media, which are largely in the power of the Father of Lies. We have to ignore the pervasive chatter and seek the countercultural, unfashionable, media-scorned truth behind these obstacles.

Clearly, this situation has become vastly exacerbated since Pascal's day. Here again he plays the prophet; he is more relevant to our time than to his own.

If we do not love the truth, we will not seek it. If we do not seek it, we will not find it. If we do not find it, we will not know it. If we do not know it, we have failed our fundamental task in time, and quite likely also in eternity.

16. Three Levels of Reality: Body, Mind and Heart

We must not be indifferent but must seek the true and the good, our own true good, with passion.

But where shall we seek? Pascal gives us a crude map of three possible lands in which we may seek our true home and happiness; three levels of reality, three dimensions—thus classifying all mankind into three types: those who seek their end in the goods of the body; those who seek their end in the goods of the mind; and those who seek their end in the goods of the heart or spirit.

All people, all goods and all realities fit into one of these three dimensions. They are similar, though not exactly identical, to Kierkegaard's three "stages on life's way", the "aesthetic" (pleasure-seeking), the "ethical" (abstract duty) and the "religious" (God-seeking). (Kierkegaard would classify Pascal's second type, those who seek the goods of the mind, as a sophisticated subdivision of his first, "aesthetic", category; and Pascal would classify Kierkegaard's second stage, the "ethical", as the beginning of his third, "heart", category.)

Essentially, Pascal is taking the famous mind-body dualism of his contemporary Descartes (and, more generally, of his seventeenth-century outlook) and expanding it one dimension "up". What matters for apologetics is not the theoretical inadequacy of this Cartesian dualism but the practical advice given along the way.

308

The infinite distance between body and mind symbolizes the infinitely more infinite distance between mind and charity, for charity is supernatural.[A]

All the splendour of [worldly] greatness lacks lustre for those engaged in pursuits of the mind.[B]

The greatness of intellectual people is not visible to kings, rich men, captains, who are all great in a carnal sense.

The greatness of wisdom,[C] which is nothing if it does not come from God, is not visible to carnal or intellectual people. They are three orders differing in kind.

Great geniuses have their power, their splendour, their greatness, their victory and their lustre, and do not need carnal greatness, which has no relevance for them. They are recognized not with the eyes but with the mind, and that is enough.

Saints have their power, their splendour, their victory, their lustre, and do not need either carnal or intellectual greatness, which has no relevance for them, for it neither adds nor takes away anything. They are recognized by God and the angels, and not by bodies or by curious minds. God is enough for them.[D]

Archimedes[E] in obscurity would still be revered. He fought no battles visible to the eyes, but enriched every mind with his discoveries. How splendidly he shone in the minds of men!

Jesus without wealth or any outward show of knowledge has his own order of holiness. He made no discoveries; he did not reign, but he was humble, patient, thrice holy to God, terrible to devils, and without sin. With what great pomp and marvellously magnificent array he came in the eyes of the heart, which perceive wisdom!

It would have been pointless for Archimedes to play the prince in his mathematical books, prince though he was.

It would have been pointless for Our Lord Jesus Christ to come as a king with splendour in his reign of holiness, but he truly came in splendour in his own order.

It is quite absurd to be shocked at the lowliness of Jesus, as if his lowliness was of the same order as the greatness he came to reveal.

If we consider his greatness in his life, his passion, his obscurity, his death, in the way he chose his disciples, in their desertion, in his secret resurrection and all the rest, we shall see that it is so great that we have no reason to be shocked at a lowliness which has nothing to do with it.[F]

But there are some who are only capable of admiring carnal greatness, as if there were no such thing as greatness of the mind. And others who only admire greatness of the mind, as if there were not infinitely higher greatness in wisdom.

All bodies, the firmament, the stars, the earth and its kingdoms are not worth the least of minds, for it knows them all and itself too, while bodies know nothing.

All bodies together and all minds together and all their products are not worth the least impulse of charity. This is of an infinitely superior order.

Out of all bodies together we could not succeed in creating one little thought. It is impossible, and of a different order. Out of all bodies and minds we could not extract one impulse of true charity. It is impossible, and of a different, supernatural, order.[G]   (793)

[308]

A

Pascal is making two points here, a metaphysical point and a psychological point. There are three levels or dimensions of reality, and three corresponding levels or dimensions of human awareness. We can seek our fulfillment and end and good in any one of these three dimensions: body (matter), mind (truth), or heart (goodness, charity). We can seek health, happiness or holiness; physical health, mental health or spiritual health as our *summum bonum*, our greatest good.

"Charity" is the proper and essential action of the "heart". For more on the meaning of "heart", see the next section (point 17). "Charity" = *agapē*, the kind of love that is God's essential nature (1 Jn 4:8, 16) and God's essential work in the world (Jn 3:16) and in the human heart (1 Jn 4:12). See C. S. Lewis' *The Four Loves* for how charity is related to other loves.

Briefly, "charity is supernatural" to the mind or ego, as the mind is supernatural (transcendent) to the body.

B

St. Thomas Aquinas was traveling across the mountains. As the sun suddenly came out, it revealed the shining splendors of hundreds of miles of rooftops, fields and palaces below. Thomas' traveling companion remarked, "Wouldn't it be grand to own all the kingdoms your eye can see?" Thomas retorted, "I'd find it far grander to own that missing page of that Aristotle manuscript!"

But St. Thomas also understood how all his magnificent works of the mind—the greatest that any man has ever produced—were mere "straw" compared to the living God he had met in contemplative prayer; that's why he could not even finish his *Summa*. Like Pascal, he would say *at that stage* that all of philosophy is not worth half an hour's trouble compared to *that*. (See *pensée* no. 84, p. 115.)

C

By "wisdom" Pascal here means the moral and religious wisdom of charity, not the intellectual achievements of intelligence; sanctity, not scholarship. This "wisdom" is in a different *dimension* than knowledge or intelligence.

D

When God said to St. Thomas, "You have written well of me, Thomas; what will you have as a reward?" Thomas answered, with perfect, saintly boldness and perfect, saintly humility: "Only yourself, Lord." He never said a wiser word.

Augustine says: "Lord God of truth, is any man pleasing to you for knowing such things? Surely a man is unhappy even if he knows all these things but does not know you; and that man is happy who knows you even though he knows nothing of them. And that man who knows both you and them is not the happier for them but only on account of you" (*Confessions* V, 4).

God is enough. God plus x is no more than God alone. Infinity plus one is not one greater than infinity, for infinity already includes all ones.

E

The great scientist Archimedes was visited by Alexander the Great, who asked him what he could do for him. Archimedes replied, "You could get out of my sun." (Alexander was blocking the sunlight on the geometrical diagrams Archimedes was drawing in the sand.) The scientist sought none of the things Alexander had—power, riches, fame, honor—only truth. All true scientists and scholars, as distinct from the vast crowd of intellectual prostitutes, do the same.

F

Those who rejected Christ (and still do) because he did not fulfill their political and worldly expectations reveal much about themselves and their god but nothing about Christ or the nature of the true God. Christ's first question in John's Gospel is the crucial one: "What do you seek?" (1:38). This question determines what we will find, determines our eternal destiny, determines everything.

There are still many who are disappointed with Christ for not solving the world's political and social problems and who try to remedy his "failure" by the use of the worldly powers he disdained. These range from right-wing Moonies to left-wing "liberation theologians". There are also many who are disappointed that he taught mysteries in parables rather than systems in syllogisms and who try to remedy this "failure". All these people reveal themselves but not him. They do not stoop to his lowliness but try to recast his image into their own greatness. St. Paul knew better: see 1 Corinthians 2.

G

These last three paragraphs are the metaphysical, cosmic, objective background for Pascal's personal, pastoral, practical, psychological point about three seekings. The three levels are discontinuous, like the three dimensions of space. You cannot get one bit closer to breadth by any extension of length, however great. You do not come any closer to depth by any extension of breadth. You do not come any closer to time by any enlargement of space. Out of all the inorganic rocks in the world you cannot squeeze one atom of organic life: "You can't get blood out of a stone." Similarly, out of all merely material bodies you cannot make one iota of thought (computers do not think *at all*), and out of all merely intellectual minds you cannot produce one iota of will or love.

Quantity cannot substitute for quality. Complexity in one dimension does not produce another dimension. No matter how much you rearrange and complexify matter in a computer, you do not create consciousness. Computers know absolutely nothing at all, just as library buildings and books know nothing. Computers are only mobile books.

And even if computers did think, they could not love. (See no. 741, p. 225).

Pascal accepts, perhaps too simply and uncritically, Descartes' absolute qualitative dualism between mind and body, thought and spatial extension; but he adds a third level, which Descartes neglected, namely, charity. Descartes never delivered on his promise in *Discourse on Method* to give us an *ethic* constructed by his new scientific method. (The promise comes in part I and II; the nonfulfillment comes in part III, where the only ethic he ever gives us is purely provisional and pragmatic.) For he never climbed above level two to level three, where alone can be found true ethics, in charity and in the heart.

377

What a long way it is between knowing God and loving him!   (280)

[377]

The length of this gap is infinite. The most brilliant theological mind in the universe is also the one with the least love: his name is Lucifer.

407

The Stoics say: 'Withdraw into yourself, that is where you will find peace.' And that is not true.[A]

Others say: 'Go outside: look for happiness in some diversion.' And that is not true: we may fall sick.[B]

Happiness is neither outside nor inside us: it is in God, both outside and inside us.[C]   (465)

[407]
A

This corresponds to Pascal's second level, greatness of intellect and its works, including Stoic self-control and pop psychology's "self-esteem".

B

This corresponds to Pascal's first level, pleasure and power, "worldly greatness"—what traditional moralists call "the gifts of fortune". (See Aquinas, *Summa Theologica* I–II, 2, the most perfect summary I know of life's greatest debate, on the *summum bonum*.)

C

God escapes the "inside/outside" dilemma. "The God within" and "the God without" are both idols. The true God is everywhere, both within and without, for he is not in us (as *contained* by us) or outside us (as *absent* from us), but we (and the whole universe) are in *him*. He is the absolute, not us. Our innate tendency to begin all our thinking and writing with the human "I" exhibits our inherent illusion of perspective, our egocentric predicament from which we cannot escape (for it would always be *we* who escaped), and from which we can be delivered only by God's initiative.

613b
Philosophers: they surprise the ordinary run of men.
Christians: they surprise the philosophers.   **(443)**

[613b]
Surprise (*thauma*, "wonder") is an index of a dimensional interface, a leap, a confrontation with a new dimension. Therefore we fear ghosts with wonder, but we fear poverty without wonder.

741
The adding-machine produces effects closer to thought than anything done by the animals, but it does nothing to justify the assertion that it has a will like the animals. (340)

[741]
From the inventor of the world's first working computer comes the simplest, most obviously true and most unanswerable answer to the question that, quite incredibly, many otherwise quite sane and intelligent thinkers are all wrapped up in knots about: What is the difference, if any, between "AI", "artificial intelligence", and natural intelligence; between computer consciousness and human consciousness?

The philosophical answer is that there is no such thing as computer consciousness. But that involves us in great philosophical questions. Those who say there is no difference between computer consciousness and human consciousness usually mean, not that computers have what ordinary people call consciousness, but that people do not have it. In other words, they are materialists and behaviorists. A good philosophical answer to them is Joseph Wood Krutch's chapter "The Stubborn Fact of Consciousness" in *The Measure of Man*. But a simpler answer is Pascal's.

Pascal's answer is more empirical than philosophical. It has the advantage of not getting involved in controversial definitions of "consciousness". It is the simple observation that computers are never disobedient, never give any evidence of having a will of their own. They always obey their programming—which comes from the *will* as well as the mind of the human programmer.

This is manifested most clearly in the fact that men question and computers do not. Questioning is the *will* to know; this is not merely intellectual but also volitional. No computer will ever ask a question unless programmed to do so. You can program a computer to question its previous programming, but a computer will never question its most recent, or its priority, program. We will. Even God's program for us, we question and disobey.

Even animals have a rudimentary will (though it is not free, rational and moral), so they are superior to computers. Computers exist wholly on Pascal's first level. His point in this *pensée* is that even if computers function on the second level (which I do not think he thinks they do), they do not function on the third level.

(By the way, animals also mess up and falsify the absolute Cartesian dualism between the first two levels, mind and matter. Animal life and sensation and instinct are not mere matter, nor are they yet conscious intelligence. Descartes thought animals were only complex machines. It would follow then that breaking a lever off a machine, a limb off a tree or a leg off a dog would be essentially the same kind of act!)

23

Vanity of science. **Knowledge of physical science will not console me for ignorance of morality in time of affliction, but knowledge of morality will always console me for ignorance of physical science.** (67)

[23]

As you lie dying, you can no more take consolation in your knowledge of science than in your money. As Charles Péguy says, in the end, life offers only one tragedy: not to have been a saint.

Therefore parents should not only worry less about their children's ability to get a well-paying job than about their education, less about their bodies and monies than their minds, but also less about their minds than about their morals, their hearts and wills. Pascal's map of three dimensions has radical social consequences. Society (merely an abstract word for "parents and teachers") should prepare its members for death; if it cannot do that, it cannot prepare them for life. This is the fundamental task of education, and it is totally and fatally refused by modernity's educational establishment. We know more and more about less and less. We dare not teach anything worth teaching—wisdom, morality and religion. If the reasons for this are political—*if* pluralistic democracy is incompatible with learning true wisdom—then by all means and for the sake of saving our children's souls, let us quickly sweep away pluralistic democracy. For what does it profit a man to gain the whole world's approval and lose his own soul?

17. The Heart

Pascal means by the "heart":

1. The "intuitive" mind as vs. the "geometrical" (that is, calculating, reasoning) mind; right-brain as vs. left-brain. By this work of the heart, we know unprovable, self-evident "first principles" like the law of noncontradiction in logic and "do good and avoid evil" in ethics. (See no. 110, p. 229, for an extended treatment of this aspect of the "heart".)

2. The perception of God by faith, the awareness that God is real. (See no. 110, last paragraph, p. 229, and no. 424, p. 232.)

3. That which hopes in God, invests its goodness, end, purpose and fulfillment in God as its *summum bonum*; that which "wagers" on God and his promises. (See no. 418, the "wager" [pp. 293–95], vs. no. 427, "indifference" [pp. 189–96].)

4. The will, that which chooses to love, to commit, to say Yes or No to another person, human or divine. (See no. 423, p. 231.)

Thus the three "theological virtues"—faith, hope and charity—the three greatest things in the world (1 Cor 13:13), all are found in the heart.

The ultimate premises and standards of all the intellect's knowledge also come from the heart (meaning number 1 above); for all reasoning depends on axioms. The work of calculation depends on the work of intuition.

Solomon, the wisest man in the ancient world, says: "Keep your heart with all diligence, for from it spring the issues of life" (Prov 4:23 NKJV).

We have seen (1) life's pressing problems—death, wretchedness, uncertainty, and so on; (2) the folly of diversion and indifference as ways of coping with them; (3) the need for passionate truth-seeking; and (4) the three levels on which we may seek and the superiority of the level of "heart". We now need to know (5) what this "heart" is and what it can do, and then (6) to do it (= the rest of the *Pensées*).

110

We know the truth not only through our reason[A] but also through our heart. It is through the latter that we know first principles, and reason, which has nothing to do with it, tries in vain to refute them.[B] The sceptics have no other object than that, and they work at it to no purpose. We know that we are not dreaming,[C] but, however unable we may be to prove it rationally, our inability proves nothing but the weakness of our reason, and not the uncertainty of all our knowledge, as they maintain.[D] For knowledge of first principles, like space, time, motion, number, is as solid as any derived through reason, and it is on such knowledge, coming from the heart and instinct, that reason has to depend and base all its argument. The heart feels [intuits] that there are three spatial dimensions and that there is an infinite series of numbers, and reason goes on to demonstrate that there are no two square numbers of which one is double the other. Principles are felt [intuited], propositions proved, and both with certainty though by different means. It is just as pointless and absurd for reason to demand proof of first principles from the heart before agreeing to accept them as it would be absurd for the heart to demand an intuition of all the propositions demonstrated by reason before agreeing to accept them. . . .

[T]hose to whom God has given religious faith by moving their hearts are very fortunate, and feel quite legitimately convinced, but to those who do not have it we can only give such faith through reasoning, until God gives it by moving their heart, without which faith is only human and useless for salvation.[E]   (282)

[110]

A

That is, reason*ing.* "Reason" meant something broader to premoderns than it has since Descartes narrowed it to scientific analysis and calculation (*Discourse on Method* I, 1, 1). Plato, Aristotle, Augustine and Aquinas, for example, all meant by "reason" intellectual intuition as well as calculation, and moral intuition as well—that is, intuitive knowledge of moral first principles. Pascal uses "reason" in the new, modern, narrower way, to refer to what medieval Scholastic-Aristotelian logic calls "the third act of the mind" only: discursive reason*ing*, not the understanding of the meaning of an essence (= "the first act of the mind") or the affirmation of the truth of a proposition (= "the second act of the mind"), but the process by which we discover or prove one truth (the conclusion) from another (the premise). When Pascal demeans the power of reason in relation to our knowledge of God, he means this narrow, modern "reason", not the broad, ancient "reason". The difference between Pascal and Aquinas is mainly a verbal rather than a real contradiction.

B

Reasoning can neither prove nor disprove first principles like the law of noncontradiction, for these principles are presupposed in all reasoning. Trying to prove them would be "begging the question" and arguing in a circle. Since they cannot be rationally proved, they cannot be rationally disproved either, for such attempts at disproof, like all reasoning, necessarily presuppose these first principles.

C

Descartes' famous "universal doubt"—how do we know anything at all? how do we know anything is real and not a mere dream?—is answered first of all by *data*: We *do* know, by whatever means. The means happens to be the heart. We intuitively and indubitably recognize some truths (first principles) when we meet them. We recognize reality, as distinct from dreams, when we meet it. We may mistake the dream for the reality, but we do not in fact mistake the reality for the dream. This is because it is impossible for the authentic and the real to dress up in deceptive appearances of unreality, although it is possible for the inauthentic and the unreal to dress up in deceptive appearances of reality. Idols appear like the real God, but the real God never appears like an idol. All deception works one way.

It is the "heart", or right-brain, that "just knows". The head, or left-brain, proceeds *from* that foundation.

D

But even though we *know* we are not dreaming, we may not be able to *prove* it. See no. 131.

E

Pascal distinguishes here between *intellectual* faith, mere *belief*, based on our own reasoning, and *saving* faith, which is a gift of God. Jesus (Mt 7:21) and James (2:14–19) make the same distinction. See no. 424, p. 232.

The strategy of Pascal's apologetics is to strew palm branches and coats on the road to prepare for the coming of the Messiah humbly, on a donkey, into the Holy City of the unbeliever's heart.

423

The heart has its reasons of which reason knows nothing:[A] **we know this in countless ways.**[B]

I say that it is natural for the heart to love the universal being or itself, according to its allegiance, and it hardens itself against either as it chooses. You have rejected one and kept the other. Is it reason that makes you love yourself? [C]   (277)

[423]
A

This, the most famous of Pascal's sayings, is also the one most frequently misunderstood. It is *not* sentimentalism or irrationalism. Pascal does not oppose the heart to reason and demean reason by exalting the heart. On the contrary, he says the heart has its *reasons*. The heart does not only *feel*, it *sees*. The heart has an eye in it.

See the next section (point 18), on faith and reason, for a refutation of the notion that Pascal is a fideist or anti-intellectualist.

B

Here is one of the "countless ways" we know this. We all know that a friend who loves you deeply *knows* you more adequately than a scientist who only studies you as a specimen. A psychologist is someone who knows *about* you; a friend is someone who *knows* you. Other languages than English make this clear: the distinction is between *wissen* and *kennen* in German, *savoir* and *connaître* in French.

C

It is with our heart that we make the fateful choices of our God, our mate and our career. It is with our heart that we choose our eternal destiny, our "fundamental option" (Rahner), our "city" (Augustine). All the members of "the City of the World" (*civitas mundi*) have chosen in their heart of hearts to love and worship and hope in and believe in and obey themselves above God. Those in "the City of God" (*civitas Dei*) have chosen the opposite. Is it reason that determines this most fateful of all choices, the choice between Hell and Heaven? Only as the navigator; the captain is the heart. Therefore our eternal destiny depends, not on our intelligence, which we largely inherited, but on our heart and will and love, which are freely chosen and for which we are justly responsible forever.

424

It is the heart which perceives God and not the reason. That is what faith is: God perceived by the heart, not by the reason.   **(278)**

[424]

This is "the gift of faith" as distinct from intellectual *belief* or *opinion*. Saving faith is not an *opinion*. It does not opine; it sees, it understands. "If you do not believe, surely you will not understand" (Is 7:9 KJV), implying that if you do believe, you will understand.

751

Those who are accustomed to judge by feeling [intuition] have no understanding of matters involving reasoning. For they want to go right to the bottom of things at a glance, and are not accustomed to look for principles. The others, on the contrary, who are accustomed to reason from principles, have no understanding of matters involving feeling, because they look for principles and are unable to see things at a glance. (3)

[751]

Until the rise of radical feminism, everyone in the world knew that women tended to be more intuitive and men more rational; that women tended to judge by feeling and context, in a kind of global motherly embrace, while men tended to analyze and focus from without, objectively. Even the "feminists" are rediscovering this: see Carol Gilligan, *In a Different Voice*.

Pascal oversimplifies the difference here for clarity's sake. The ideal, of course, is to do *both*; and the ideal is not totally unattainable.

975

Men often take their imagination for their heart, and often believe they are converted as soon as they start thinking of becoming converted. (275)

[975]

The heart intuits immediately and directly, rather than reasoning mediately and indirectly; but not all direct and immediate intuition is from the heart. Imagination also intuits rather than reasons. It "sees pictures". But it is not the heart. And we can easily mistake it for the heart. This is why we can imagine ourselves to be saints. We can easily imagine, think of, contemplate and be attracted to the idea of giving our whole selves and lives over to God without actually *doing* it, and think we have done it because we have imagined it. Our imagination can even become an idol, a substitute. Dostoyevsky says: "Love in action is a harsh and dreadful thing compared with love in dreams [that is, imagination]." We can think we love God when we are only dreaming about it.

Here is a test whether you really love God. Have you done or avoided or given up a single thing today solely because you believed that God wanted you to?

18. Faith and Reason

Pascal is neither a fideist nor a rationalist.

There are many Christian fideists today. In the current climate of skepticism and relativism, weakness and despair in philosophy, many Christians are seizing on the conclusions of relativists like Richard Rorty and the Deconstructionists to justify their own inability to obey the Apostle Peter's command to be ready to give a reason for the hope and faith that is in us.

They attack "Foundationalism", which is their term for the commonsensical teaching that reason has foundations in objective reality that can be known; and that our faith can and should therefore have foundations in reason (and via reason, in reality). More technically, they oppose the Aristotelian answer to skepticism, which is that we can know some absolutely certain, rationally self-evident, undeniable first principles like the law of noncontradiction, thereby answering the skeptic's challenge that every argument is uncertain and "iffy" because it assumes without proof that its premises are true.

Kant is the major villain here. He divorced reason from reality and reduced it to a subjective (though universal) grid our mind imposes upon an unknown and unknowable reality ("things-in-themselves"). In this post-Kantian climate, reason, no longer anchored in reality, floats on a subjective sea, blown by every wind: sociological, psychological, "politically correct", or even hormonal.

Some Christian fideists want to kidnap Pascal and pin their label on him.

It cannot be done, as the following *pensées* will make clear. Like Augustine, Pascal knows that the heart is deeper than the head, but like Augustine he does not cut off his own head, or so soften it up with relativism and subjectivism and "open-mindedness" that his brains fall out.

170

Submission. One must know when it is right to doubt, to affirm, to submit. Anyone who does otherwise does not understand the force of reason. Some men run counter to these three principles, either affirming that everything can be proved, because they know nothing about proof, or doubting everything, because they do not know when to submit, or always submitting, because they do not know when judgement is called for.   **(268)**

[170]

How balanced Pascal is! And how commodious, how large! He ignores or cavils at no one of the three possible attitudes toward truth, but sees a proper place and time for each: doubting, affirming (claiming certainty) and submitting (faith).

Those who "run counter to these three principles" are fanatics, either (1) of reason and proof (like Descartes) or (2) of doubt and skepticism (like Montaigne) or (3) of submission and faith (the naive, who will believe anything).

The rationalist (the type-1 fanatic) lacks doubt. Descartes should have had a Socrates looking over his shoulder.

The skeptic (the type-2 fanatic) lacks faith. Montaigne should have met Abraham.

The naive sucker (the type-3 fanatic) lacks reason. He needs an Aquinas. Why believe in Christianity rather than Hinduism or Mormonism or atheism or Satanism?

This latter point is expanded in no. 174 (next), a surprisingly "rationalistic" *pensée* to those who misjudge Pascal to be a fideist; and by no. 187:

> There is nothing unusual in having to reproach people for being too docile. It is a vice as natural as incredulity and just as pernicious.

173

If we submit everything to reason our religion will be left with nothing mysterious or supernatural.

If we offend the principles of reason our religion will be absurd and ridiculous. (273)

183
Two excesses: to exclude reason, to admit nothing but reason. (253)

[173, 183]
Balance. The Golden Mean. Avoidance of opposite bad extremes. Very Thomistic as well as Aristotelian. What Pascal says here about faith and reason is exactly what Aquinas says in *Summa contra Gentiles* I, 7: that some of the tenets of the Christian faith (for example, the Trinity) cannot be discovered, adequately understood, or proved by human reason, but are "mysterious and supernatural"; and that others (like monotheism) can; and that *all* of them at least do not "offend the principles of reason", that is, none can be *refuted* or disproved by reason. (If one could, it would be proved *to be untrue*, and Christianity would be a lie.) Not all of Christianity can be proved, but some of it can, and none of it can be disproved. If it could, faith would indeed be "absurd and ridiculous".

This is neither fideistic religion, rationalistic religion, fideistic irreligion, nor rationalistic irreligion—the four miserable alternatives, all irrational, that we see sprawled around on every side while the truth stands erect and serene in the middle.

185
Faith certainly tells us what the senses do not, but not the contrary of what they see; it is above, not against them.
(265)

[185]
Faith has the same relation to reason as it has to the senses: it exceeds and surpasses but does not contradict.

174

St. Augustine. Reason would never submit unless it judged that there are occasions when it ought to submit.[1]

It is right, then, that reason should submit when it judges that it ought to submit.   (270)

[174]

Reason takes you to the beach via land transportation; faith jumps into the ocean. Reason takes you to the diving board and even tells you when to jump, but it does not jump. Reason is like dating, faith is like marrying. How blind and foolish to marry someone you never dated and don't know! Scripture itself commands us to give, and therefore to have, reasons for our faith (1 Pet 3:16).

175

One of the ways in which the damned will be confounded is that they will see themselves condemned by their own reason, by which they claimed to condemn the Christian religion.   (563)

[175]

Reason is so valid, so powerful, that it can determine our damnation by itself (Rom 1), though not our salvation by itself.

188

Reason's last step is the recognition that there are an infinite number of things which are beyond it. It is merely feeble if it does not go as far as to realize that.

If natural things are beyond it, what are we to say about supernatural things?   (267)

[188]

The most rational of theologians, St. Thomas Aquinas, says that "it is impossible for any created intellect to see the

[1] *Letters,* CXXII. 5.

essence of God by its own natural power" (*S.T.* I, 12, 4);
that "the divine essence cannot be known through the nature
of material things" (*S.T.* I, 12, 11); and that "no name is uni-
vocally predicated of God and of creatures" (*S.T.* I, 13, 5).
Reason itself tells us that God transcends reason. How irrational to think that a being that did not transcend our reason's ability to know it deserved the name of God! How
irrational to claim to know that there is no more than your
reason knows!

The greatest philosophers, apostles of reason, have always
been the most humble, beginning with Granddaddy Socrates.
The most arrogant and rationalist philosophers have always
been feeble, brittle and thin.

Pascal's last paragraph is straight from Jesus (Jn 3:12).

<h2 style="text-align:center">420</h2>

'Do you believe that it is impossible for God to be infinite
and indivisible?—'Yes.'—'Very well, I will show you
something infinite and indivisible: it is a point moving
everywhere at an infinite speed.

'For it is one and the same everywhere and wholly
present in every place. From this natural phenomenon
which previously seemed impossible to you you should
realize that there may be others which you do not yet
know. Do not conclude from your apprenticeship that
there is nothing left for you to learn, but that you still
have an infinite amount to learn.'   (231)

<h3 style="text-align:center">[420]</h3>

This is a lesson in intellectual humility, Socrates' Lesson One.

Like Pascal, Socrates was balanced between Dogmatism and
Skepticism, Rationalism and Irrationalism, arrogance and
naiveté. He revered and used reason, as Pascal did and advised
(see nos. 184, 187), yet he knew how little he knew (see no.
188, p. 238). Both points are balanced in nos. 184, 170 (p. 236)
and 173 (pp. 236–37).

7

**Faith is different from proof. One is human and the other
a gift of God. . . . This is the faith that God himself puts
into our hearts, often using proof as the instrument. (248)**

[7]

To think that faith is a proof is like thinking a man is a microphone, or that Christ on Palm Sunday is a donkey. It confuses
the instrument with the user.

Yet man does use a microphone, and Christ does use a donkey to ride to his death and our salvation. And God sometimes
rides into a human heart on the back of the plodding donkey
of proofs. He uses them.

Therefore apologetic proofs are noble and great. But they
are mere means, often used and often dispensed with. Like
road maps.

172

**The way of God, who disposes all things with gentleness,
is to instil religion into our minds with reasoned arguments and into our hearts with grace, but attempting to
instil it into hearts and minds with force and threats is to
instil not religion but terror. (185)**

[172]

There are three ways to faith: (1) reasoned arguments, (2) divine grace, and (3) human coercion and pressure. The history
of religion is a sad record of reliance on (3), based on lack of
confidence in ourselves to do (1) and God to do (2).

Coercion and indifference, like pride and despair, their
respective roots, are equally deadly errors.

769

*'Stand ye in the ways, and see, and ask for the old paths, and
walk therein.' But they said: 'We will not walk therein.'* [1] *'But*

<hr>

[1] Jer. VI. 16.

we will walk after our own devices.' [2] They said to the nations of the world: 'Come unto us, follow the opinions of these new authors. Natural reason will be our guide. We also shall be like other nations, who all follow their natural light.'

Philosophers and all the religions and sects in the world have taken natural reason for their guide. Christians alone have been obliged to take their rules from outside themselves and to acquaint themselves with those which Christ left for us with those of old, to be handed down again to the faithful. Such constraint irks these good Fathers ["dissenting" theologians]. They want to be as free as other people to follow the imagination of their hearts. In vain we cry out to them as the prophets of old said to the Jews: 'Go into the midst of the Church, ask for the old paths and walk therein.' They have answered like the Jews: 'We will not walk therein, but will walk after the devices of our own hearts.' And they said: 'We also shall be like all the nations.' [3]   (903)

[769]

Faith is distinctive, reason is not.

The special gift God gave to Jews and Christians was supernatural revelation, and the gift of faith to believe it. Yet modernity is embarrassed at this special gift—at its specialness even more than at its supernaturalness—and longs to be "just like everybody else"—which thus means dependent on common human reason alone. The desire "to be like all the other nations", with which the Chosen People grieved God in the Old Testament, the love of equality and the fear of "elitism", is one of the Devil's most effective deterrents to faith today. Many theologians lean over backward to "nuance" Christianity's distinctive dogmas, such as miracles, and emphasize its nondistinctive ones, like peace and justice. They fear being right where "the nations" are wrong more

[2] Jer. XVIII. 12.   [3] I Sam. VII. 20.

than they fear being wrong where "the nations" are wrong; they fear nonconformity to the world more than nonconformity to God.

Not Pascal.

V

SIX CLUES ALONG THE WAY

19. Why God Hides

Why are there so few clues to God? And why are they so obscure? "Why must holy places be dark places?" Why does God hide?

Bertrand Russell, on his deathbed, was visited by a friend who asked him, "You've been the world's most famous atheist most of your life, and now you're about to die. What if you were wrong? What would you say to God if you met him? Don't you think it's prudent at least to raise that question now, before it's too late?" Russell replied: "I think I should say to him: Sir, it appears that my atheistic hypothesis was erroneous. Would you mind answering me one wee little question? Why didn't you give us more *evidence*?"

Very good question. If you were God and you wanted all your children to know you and believe in you, wouldn't you give them more evidence? A miracle every day at six o'clock sharp, for instance?

Pascal has a very good answer, which turns the objection *against* the faith into a clue *for* it. Essentially, it comes down to this: If God did not conceal himself, he would not reveal himself truly; only by partial concealing can there be revealing of God to man in his present state.

How can this paradox be? Read on and see.

228

What do the prophets say about Jesus Christ? That he will plainly be God? No, but that he is a truly hidden God, that he will not be recognized, that people will not believe that it is he, that he will be a stumbling-block on which many will fall, etc.

Let us not then be criticized for lack of clarity, since we openly profess it.[A] 'But,' they say, 'there are obscurities, and but for that Jesus would not have caused anyone to stumble.' And this is one of the formal intentions of the prophets.[B] (751)

[228]

A

Thus the fact that Christ's divinity is not plain and obvious is not something that counts against the Christian claim, but for it. For the claim, and the prophecy of it, is not that he will be "the plain God" but "the hidden God". The prophecy is fulfilled perfectly.

B

We tend to assume that Christ acted as we would have acted; that he would do *anything* to attain the end of universal acknowledgment, allegiance and discipleship, like a modernist theologian, desperate to be fashionable and accepted. Instead, like the prophets, he says he comes to do two things: open some eyes and shut others, reveal himself to some and conceal himself from others, simultaneously and by the same words and works.

He came to *give* light, as a gift, not to force light on us. A gift must appeal to freedom. It must be freely accepted as well as freely given. Thus there must be the freedom to refuse it.

235

Jesus came to blind those who have clear sight and to give sight to the blind; to heal the sick and let the healthy die; to call sinners to repentance and justify them, and to leave the righteous to their sins; to fill the hungry with good things and to send the rich empty away.   (771)

[235]

This is exactly what Scripture says.

But what does it mean?

It means that the same light that fulfills some threatens others; that the same divine nature, the same justice and righteousness and holiness, the same unselfish love and self-surrender and willingness to suffer that is Heaven to the saints, is Hell to sinners.

Christ does not deliberately and delightedly hide from the wicked or blind them. He can't help it, just as the sun can't help shining. Too bad the bat's eyes can't take it. He blinds sinners simply by being what he is.

234
God wishes to move the will rather than the mind. Perfect clarity would help the mind and harm the will.

Humble their pride. (581)

[234]
Here is one reason God hides, that is, does not reveal himself more clearly. If he did, we would have more knowledge but less humility and thus less wisdom. Humility is the beginning of wisdom. He sees that we need the beginning the most.

236
There is enough light to enlighten and enough obscurity to humiliate them. There is enough obscurity to blind the reprobate and enough light to condemn them and deprive them of excuse.[A]

The genealogy of Jesus in the Old Testament is mixed up with so many others that are irrelevant that it is indistinguishable. If Moses had recorded only the ancestors of Jesus it would have been too obvious; if he had not indicated Jesus's genealogy it would not have been obvious enough. But, after all, anyone who looks closely can see Jesus's genealogy easily distinguished through Thamar, Ruth, etc. . . .[B]

If God had permitted only one religion, it would have been too easily recognizable. But, if we look closely, it is easy to distinguish the true religion amidst all this confusion.[C] (578)

[236]

A

He gives exactly the right amount of light. If he gave less, even the righteous would be unable to find him, and their will would be thwarted. If he gave more, even the wicked would find him, against their will. Thus he respects and fulfills the will of all.

If he gave more light, the righteous would not learn humility, for they would know too much. If he gave less light, the wicked would not be responsible for their wickedness, for they would know too little.

B

See the following subpoint on the deliberate obscurity of Scripture. Jesus' genealogy is one specific example of this principle, typical of many. The reader is invited to find and interpret many others.

C

The same principle applied to the thorny question of "comparative religions". See also point 23.

444

It is true then that everything teaches man his condition, but there must be no misunderstanding, for it is not true that everything reveals God, and it is not true that everything conceals God. But it is true at once that he hides from those who tempt him and that he reveals himself to those who seek him, because men are at once unworthy and capable of God: unworthy through their corruption, capable through their original nature.

(557)

[444]

We can learn something from everything. Everyone knows that already. But we can learn everything from something—or rather, from Somebody. Only Christians know that. (See no. 417, p. 313.)

Everything both conceals and reveals God. To everything in the world we can say, with Charles Williams, "This also is Thou" *and* "Neither is this Thou." God is both immanent (present) and transcendent.

But this is true for everyone. The point Pascal makes here is that the same things reveal God to some (the seekers: see no. 236 [p. 247] and no. 446 [below]) and conceal him from others (the nonseekers).

And that this revealing is itself double: because it is obscure, it reveals not only God in his greatness but also ourselves in our wretchedness and ignorance—exactly as it did to Job (42:1–6). (See also no. 192, pp. 279–80.)

446

If there were no obscurity man would not feel his corruption:[A] if there were no light man could not hope for a cure.[B] Thus it is not only right but useful for us that God should be partly concealed and partly revealed, since it is equally dangerous for man to know God without knowing his own wretchedness as to know his wretchedness without knowing God.[C] **(586)**

[446]

A

Therefore to reveal fully and adequately the truth about ourselves to ourselves in our present state, it was necessary for God to use obscurity. To reveal fully, he had to conceal partly.

B

See no. 192, pp. 279–80, and no. 121, p. 52.

C

Note how economical God's teaching is! The very same thing—the obscure revelation he gives us in nature, in Scripture, in the Church and in conscience—at once works multiple purposes; just as the same miracle of Jesus often gave to different people exactly what each needed: hope to the despairing, humility to the proud, condemnation to the hypocritical, adequate clues to the honest seeker, and confirmation in faith to his disciples. For instance, in John 8:1–8, the adulteress got both forgiveness and a stern warning; the Pharisees got a lesson in their own hypocrisy; the bystanders who were tempted to be like the Pharisees got a lesson in humility; and the disciples got a lesson on Christ's authority to forgive sins. The very same word or deed of Christ in the Gospels frequently both comforts the afflicted and afflicts the comfortable.

781

I marvel at the boldness with which these people presume to speak of God.[A]

In addressing their arguments to unbelievers, their first chapter is the proof of the existence of God from the works of nature. Their enterprise would cause me no surprise if they were addressing their arguments to the faithful, for those with living faith in their hearts can certainly see at once that everything which exists is entirely the work of the God they worship.[B] But for those in whom this light has gone out and in whom we are trying to rekindle it,[C] people deprived of faith and grace, examining with such light as they have everything they see in nature that might lead them to this knowledge, but finding only obscurity and darkness; to tell them, I say, that they have only to look at the least thing around them and they will see in it God plainly revealed; to give them no other proof of this great and weighty matter than the course of the moon and the planets;[D] to claim to have completed the proof with such an argument; this is giving them cause to think that the proofs of our religion are indeed feeble, and reason and experience tell me that nothing is more likely to bring it into contempt in their eyes. This is not how Scripture speaks, with its better knowledge of the things of God.[E] On the contrary it says that God is a hidden God, and that since nature was corrupted he has left men to their blindness, from which they can escape only through Jesus Christ, without whom all communication with God is broken off. *Neither knoweth any man the Father save the Son, and he to whomsoever the Son will reveal him.* [1]

This is what Scripture shows us when it says in so many places that those who seek God shall find him. This is not the light of which we speak as of the noonday sun. We do not say that those who seek the sun at noon or water in the sea will find it, and so it necessarily follows that the evidence of God in nature is not of this kind.[F] It tells us elsewhere: *Verily thou art a God that hidest thyself.* [2]   (242)

[781]

A

"These people" presumably are theologians who know theology but not the human heart; absent-minded professors.

B

St. Thomas wrote his *Summa* to believers, not to unbelievers. Good arguments seldom convince atheists. This is a fact. Pascal is not saying that the arguments from nature to prove God's existence are *logically* weak, but *psychologically* weak. There is nothing wrong with some of the arguments (indeed, St. Paul uses them himself in Romans 1:19–20). But there's something wrong with *us*. If we don't *want* to believe, we don't, and therefore we don't *see* God in nature. If we don't *want* to believe that we are murdering our son or daughter when we have an abortion, we *don't* believe that, and we then don't *see* the evident fact that it's a baby, a human being.

---

[1] Matt. XI. 27.   [2] Is. XLV. 15.

The Nazis *wanted* to kill the Jews, so they *saw* them as subhuman. The white slavers *wanted* to treat Blacks as subhuman, so they *saw* them as subhuman.

Then, the atheist, the aborter, the Nazi and the slaver give arguments to rationalize what they see. This is the way our psychological mechanisms usually work. Living apologetics with live people dare not ignore this.

C

This light—wisdom, understanding, *seeing*—is no more kindled by logical arguments than physical blindness is healed by eyeglasses, or prisoners are freed by being given a road map of the outside world.

D

Pascal perhaps has in mind here the argument from motion: if there are moving bodies, there must be a first, unmoved Mover. His point seems to be, not that the conclusion does not follow from the premise, but that the conclusion is a million miles from the God of Christianity.

E

On every point God's word has always proved wiser than man's words, especially the points where it contradicts the highest human wisdom the most surprisingly and the most scandalously. See 1 Corinthians 1:18–2:16.

F

The rationalist expects God to be like the light of the noonday sun. (He is, but not to us.) The skeptic expects God to be like the darkness of the night. (He is to the wicked, but not in himself.) According to Scripture, God is like the shadows or fogs of early morning before sunrise (to us, but not in himself).

Therefore the rationalist thinks we can find God by reason alone, without the heart, without passionate and loving seeking. The skeptic does not think we can find God by any kind of seeking, so he gives up. So neither the rationalist nor the skeptic seeks God, for opposite reasons; and therefore neither finds him.

But the Christian believes (because he has been told, by God's word) two things: that *only* those who seek God find him, and that *all* those who seek God find him. The first eliminates rationalism, the second eliminates skepticism.

God, who alone knows hearts, knows who seeks him and who does not.

13

'Why does God not show himself?'—'Are you worthy?'—'Yes.'—'You are very presumptuous, and thus unworthy.'—'No.'—'Then you are just unworthy.'

[ADDITION NO. 13]

(Thirteen additional *pensées* were discovered by M. Jean Mesnard, first published in 1962, and included in Krailsheimer's edition—p. 357, Penguin edition.)

Which are you: wise or foolish?
  Wise.
  Then you are a fool, for you are proud.
  No, foolish.
  Then you are a fool. You have said so yourself. In either case, you are a fool.

Are you a saint or a sinner?
  A saint.
  Then you are the most desperate sinner, for you are proud.
  No, a sinner.
  Then you are a sinner. In either case, you are a sinner.

What matters is what kind of a fool and what kind of a sinner you are. There are two kinds of fools: foolish and wise. There are two kinds of sinners: unrepentant and repentant.

There once lived a people who believed that no man could see God and live. These were the wisest people on earth, not from themselves, but because God chose them. What does this mean, that no one can see God's face and live? God does not show his face clearly, not only because we are *unworthy* to see him, but also because we are *unable* to endure the light of his countenance, his holiness, his justice, his perfection. If we saw God face to face, we would wither and disappear like a flea in a fire. It is God's mercy and kindness and love, as well as our sin, that hide his face from us. He "tempers the wind to the shorn lamb." "A bruised reed he will not break" (Is 42:3).

That is why we need Purgatory: to become the kind of creature that would *not* wither and die when we meet God face to face in Heaven. Purgatory can begin on earth, and for some it may be completed here; but most of us seem hardly finished, not completely baked, when we are removed from the oven. Do you really think you are ready to stand in that light? If so, you are proud and not ready. If not, you are not ready. In either case, you are not ready, and you need purging.

I do not see how one can deny Purgatory thoughtfully without pride or at least tremendous naiveté about who we are and who God is.

149

. . . 'If he had wished to overcome the obstinacy of the most hardened, he could have done so by revealing himself to them so plainly that they could not doubt the truth of his essence, as he will appear on the last day with such thunder and lightning and such convulsions of nature that the dead will rise up and the blindest will see him. This is not the way he wished to appear when he came in mildness, because so many men had shown themselves unworthy of his clemency, that he wished to deprive them of the good they did not desire. It was therefore not right that he should appear in a manner manifestly divine and absolutely capable of convincing all men, but neither was it right that his coming should be so hidden that he could not be recognized by those who sincerely sought him. He wished to make himself perfectly recognizable to them. Thus wishing to appear openly to those who seek him with all their heart and hidden from those who shun him with all their heart, he has qualified our knowledge of him by giving signs which can be seen by those who seek him and not by those who do not.

'There is enough light for those who desire only to see, and enough darkness for those of a contrary disposition.'

(430)

[149, LAST 2 PARAGRAPHS]

If God wanted to get our attention, he could have become a mile-high green giraffe instead of a man; then even the indifferent sophisticate would have taken notice.

Why didn't he perform more miracles? How many blind men did he leave unhealed? Why did he raise only Lazarus and the widow's son from death? Why doesn't he create great gold letters in the sky every evening at 8, spelling out "I AM WHO AM", and invite scientists to send up rockets and investigate them, and annihilate them every night at 8:30? Why didn't Jesus stay on earth and invite us to experiment on him in any laboratory?

There are three answers.

First, he wants to give us time to repent. This is Pascal's point here. It is also Scripture's point: Genesis 15:16; Isaiah 48:9; Luke 13:7–9; Romans 2:4. He *will* show himself clearly one day. But then it will be too late.

Second, he wants to effect a true relationship with us, not one merely of intellectual belief but of personal faith, hope, love and trust. The propositions of lovers are different from the propositions of syllogisms. (This is Kierkegaard's point in *Philosophical Fragments,* chapter 2: the beautiful parable of the king wooing the humble maiden.)

Third, he is both love and justice; if he manifests himself

truly, it cannot be without love or without justice. His love led him to save all who will have him, and his justice led him to punish those who will not have him. Thus he respects our free choice. He deprives the damned only of the good that they themselves do not desire.

(See C. S. Lewis, *The Problem of Pain*, chapter on "Hell".)

(See also *pensées* no. 236, p. 247, no. 444, p. 248 and no. 446, p. 249.)

Why Scripture Is Obscure;
How to Interpret Scripture

Scripture is obscure for the same reason God is obscure.

Christ and Scripture are both called "the Word of God". Both have a double nature and a double origin, human and divine. One is the Word of God in the flesh of man, the other is the Word of God in the words of man.

255

In order to make the Messiah recognizable to the good and unrecognizable to the wicked God caused him to be foretold in this way. If the manner of the Messiah had been clearly foretold, there would have been no obscurity even for the wicked.

If the time had been foretold obscurely, there would have been obscurity even for the good. . . . But the time was foretold clearly, while the manner was figurative.

As a result, the wicked, taking the promised good to be a material one, have gone astray. . . .

For an understanding of the promised good depends on the heart, which calls good that which it loves, but an understanding of the promised time does not depend on the heart. Thus foretelling the time clearly and the good obscurely deceived none but the wicked. **(758)**

[255]

Here again we see, applied to the Messianic prophecies, the same two principles we saw before concerning God's obscurity:

1. There is enough light for seekers and not so much that it compels even nonseekers. Scripture is full of clues. Clues must be followed, like sheet music, rather than just heard, like finished performances on records or tapes. Scripture is more like a laboratory manual than like a science textbook, and the

laboratory is our own souls. It is more like a cookbook than like a dinner, and the kitchen is our own lives.

2. Correct interpretation of Scripture depends on the heart as well as the head; that is why saints are more accurate than theologians. Scripture is a love letter, not a business report.

The two points are connected. God foretold the time of the Messiah clearly and the manner obscurely, because the correct time does not depend on the heart, but the true manner—in humility and suffering, not in glory and prosperity—does.

What style! What grace! What economy! He is perfect in all his works, revelation as well as creation. He is truly "full of grace and truth" (Jn 1:14).

269

There are some who see clearly that man has no other enemy but concupiscence, which turns him away from God, and not [human] enemies, no other good but God, and not a rich land.[A] Let those who believe that man's good lies in the flesh and his evil in whatever turns him away from sensual pleasures take their fill and die of it. But those who seek God with all their hearts, whose only pain is to be deprived of the sight of him, whose only desire is to possess him, whose only enemies are those who turn them away from him, who grieve at finding themselves surrounded and dominated by such enemies, let them take heart, for I bring them glad tidings. There is one who will set them free. . . .[B]

When David foretold that the Messiah would deliver his people from their enemies, we may believe that, according to the flesh, he meant the Egyptians. And in that case I could not prove the fulfillment of the prophecy,[C] but we may also very well believe that he meant iniquities, because in fact the Egyptians are not enemies, while iniquities are.

The word 'enemy' is therefore ambiguous, but if he says elsewhere, as he does, that he will deliver his people from their sins, [1] as do Isaiah [2] and others, the ambiguity is removed, and the double meaning of enemies reduced to the single meaning of iniquities. For, if he had sins in mind, he might quite well describe them as enemies, but if he was thinking of enemies he could not refer to them as iniquities.[D]   (692)

[269]

A

These alone understand and correctly interpret Scripture when it promises a Messiah who will deliver us from our "enemies".

B

Thus, "seek and you shall find" means—according to the electronic evangelists with their "name it and claim it" gospel of health, wealth and prosperity—that faith will make you rich and protect you from tragedy. But it means to the Christian that God will give you what he gave to Christ: himself, spiritual prosperity and worldly crosses. Even the peace he promised us, he warned, is "not as the world gives" (Jn 14:27)—that is, it is not the end of war but a new *kind* of war: a war "not against flesh and blood but against principalities and powers" (Eph 6:12).

The Gospel is Good News indeed to the good, but bad news indeed to the bad.

C

If we interpret Scripture's promises in a worldly way, with a worldly heart, we will find them false. The Jews, promised victory, *succumbed* to their worldly enemies. Christians, promised all good, are *not* protected from suffering. Thus Scripture is obscure and false to the worldly and selfish heart but clear and verified to the heart that loves God and fears only evil.

[1] Ps. cxxx. 8.   [2] Is. xliii. 25.

D

Thus there is even adequate textual evidence for the correct interpretation. The only readers who are victimized are those who deserve to be. A heart set on goodness will understand what God means by "enemies" and will also understand the text, without contradiction, as Pascal does.

286

Two kinds of men in every religion.

Among the heathen those who worship animals and others who worship the one God of natural religion.

Among the Jews those who were carnal and those who were spiritual. . . .

The carnal Jews awaited a carnal Messiah, and the gross Christians believe that the Messiah has dispensed them from loving God. True Jews and true Christians worship a Messiah who makes them love God.   (609)

[286]

It is not true that only Christians understand their Scriptures, and it is not true that only Jews understand their Scriptures. God is too just and too much an equal-opportunity employer for that. Spiritual Christians, that is, God-seeking Christians, and spiritual Jews and spiritual pagans all fundamentally understand their data; and carnal Christians, Jews and pagans all fundamentally misinterpret it. This applies to data in nature and life as well as data in Scripture.

Thus, spiritual Jews, Christians and pagans all find the God they seek: the God whose nature is Truth and self-giving love; while carnal Jews, Christians and pagans do not find the God they seek—the God who gives worldly contentment and pleasure—for the simple reason that such a God does not exist.

The "gross Christians" Pascal has in mind in the last paragraph are probably the moral minimalists. His *Provincial Letters* are a biting and brilliant satire (but much more technical and theological than the *Pensées*) on Jesuit casuistry, which in his day amounted to minimalism. His lengthy analysis finally lets the cat out of the bag: the Jesuits have invented a new religion, one in which we are dispensed from the onerous obligation to love God more than ourselves. (Ironically, this "new religion" sounds uncannily like modern theopsychobabble, and it is not only Jesuits who teach it as Christianity. Pascal the prophet again!)

252

Two errors: 1. to take everything literally, 2. to take everything spiritually. **(648)**

[252]

Christians have data. God has spoken; his Word is our data.

How are we to interpret this data? With a loving heart, as we have seen. But how are we to use our heads?

Pascal mentions two obviously wrong answers here. But two popular answers come close to these extremes: fundamentalists interpret almost everything literally (except John 6:31–68), and modernists interpret everything supernatural nonliterally. Both are bad literary criticism, for both are determined by prior ideology, not by the text. Both interpret the text by the interpreter's beliefs rather than by the author's; that is, they are eisagesis (reading-into), not exegesis (reading-out-of).

Sometimes it is easy to discriminate between passages the author meant literally and passages meant figuratively just by asking this question: Does the passage claim to be an eyewitness description or not? If yes, it is meant literally, whether it is a miracle or not. (Miracles are *visible* events, after all!) If not, not.

Therefore, the creation story in Genesis 1 and 2 is figurative, since no human eye observed it. (It is *historical*, it is true, it happened; but it is described in symbols.) The same is true of the explicitly visionary images in the Book of Revelation: the author says he saw them in a dream or vision, not in the outside world.

But sometimes the discrimination is not so easy and depends on the heart, not the head; on what the reader loves, not on what kind of literary critic he is. This is the situation with the Messianic prophecies, as Pascal explains (no. 255).

Above all, we must not make the elementary but common mistake of confusing *interpretation* with *belief* and interpreting Scripture—or any book—in light of our beliefs. The fact that such a procedure sounds right to many of us should show us how foolish we are and how far from basic competence to interpret Scripture.

For the author is trying to break into the house of our mind with *his* ideas. How dare we close the door and substitute *our* ideas, our beliefs, for his? How dare we substitute our fantasies of what he ought to mean for his intentions, his meanings? How dare we look at him through the colored glasses of our categories and presuppositions, our prejudices, rather than looking at ourselves through his? That would turn dialogue into monologue. And that is exactly what Deconstructionism advocates and exalts. It is the death of objective truth. That is the philosophy of Hell.

20. Reliability of Scripture

Though *obscure*, Scripture is *reliable*.

Though it gives us clues and data rather than proofs, the clues are reliable and the data are true.

This is especially so for the crucial center of Scripture, the thing God wants to reveal the most: Christ. Pascal, Christocentric like Scripture itself, focuses on the Gospel accounts, especially the key claim of the Resurrection.

Modernist Scripture scholarship doubts and impugns the reliability of the scriptural records, especially the Gospels, and has made many Catholic and main-line Protestant colleges and seminaries into the most effective places in the world to lose your faith. Pascal comes to grips with the heart of the current scriptural issue in defending the reliability of Scripture by simple and commonsensical rather than technical and scholarly arguments.

332

Prophecies. **If a single man had written a book foretelling the time and manner of Jesus's coming and Jesus had come in conformity with these prophecies, this would carry infinite weight.**

But there is much more here. There is a succession of men over a period of 4,000 years, coming consistently and invariably one after the other, to foretell the same coming; there is an entire people proclaiming it, existing for 4,000 years to testify in a body to the certainty they feel about it, from which they cannot be deflected by whatever threats and persecutions they may suffer. This is of a quite different order of importance. (710)

[332]

Like most premodern Christian apologists, Pascal laid heavy emphasis on Christ's fulfillment of Old Testament prophecies and also on his miracles—two emphases currently unfashion-able with scholars but perennially powerful arguments to common sense. We here include only one *pensée* and omit dozens of others because of their great detail, number and specialized nature. (For Pascal's treatment of miracles, see point 22.)

If you were to calculate the probability of any one person fulfilling, sheerly by chance, all the Old Testament Messianic prophecies that Jesus fulfilled, it would be as astronomical as winning the lottery every day for a century. Even if Jesus deliberately tried to fulfill the prophecies, no mere man could have the power to arrange the time, place, events and circum-stances of his birth or events after his death.

However, prophecies are usually somewhat obscure, and even after they are fulfilled there is a little room for doubt, for God gave them as strong clues, not compelling proofs.

303
An artisan speaking of riches, a lawyer speaking of war, or kingship, etc., but the rich man can well speak of riches, . . . and God can well speak of God.   **(799)**

[303]
Authority is based on experience. When you want the authori-tative word about a novel, listen to the author.

Thus, the rich man, not the artisan, is the authority on riches; the soldier, not the lawyer, is the authority on war; and God, not man, is the authority on God.

This is an argument for the necessity of revelation. A three-year-old's guesses about a thirty-year-old's life are found to be ridiculously off the mark, unless the thirty-year-old *tells* the three-year-old. Even less hope is there for our understanding of God unless he takes the initiative and tells us, that is, reveals himself.

When we want to know something much less than our-selves—for example, a rock—it is easy. All the activity is ours;

the rock cannot hide. When we want to know an animal, it's harder. It's active. It can run away. It can hide. We have to win its confidence. Yet most of the activity is on our side. When it comes to knowing another human being, the activity is shared fifty–fifty. Unless both parties open up, there is no communication. When it comes to knowing God, all the activity is his. There must be revelation.

310

Proofs of Jesus Christ. **The hypothesis that the Apostles were knaves is quite absurd. Follow it out to the end and imagine these twelve men meeting after Jesus's death and conspiring to say that he had risen from the dead. This means attacking all the powers that be. The human heart is singularly susceptible to fickleness, to change, to promises, to bribery. One of them had only to deny his story under these inducements, or still more because of possible imprisonment, tortures and death, and they would all have been lost. Follow that out.** (801)

[310]

The fundamental point of all Scripture is Christ, according to Christianity.

The fundamental Christian claim about Christ is that he is divine.

If he is not divine, he cannot save us from sin and death and Hell.

The clearest and simplest and most powerful proof that he is divine is his Resurrection. This is also the consummation of his work of saving us from sin and death and Hell.

Every sermon preached by every Christian in the New Testament centers on the Resurrection. The Resurrection was so central to Paul's preaching that the Athenians thought he was preaching *two* new gods, "Jesus and Resurrection [*Anastasis*]" (Acts 17:18).

If Christ really rose, Christianity is true; if not, it is false.

There are only two alternatives to a real resurrection. If Christ did not really rise, as the writers of the New Testament, his apostles, say that he did, then the apostles were either deceived or deceivers. Either they did not know their story was false, or they did.

Pascal refutes both possibilities. The "conspiracy theory"—that they conspired to deceive the world—is absurd; for people conspire to lie only to gain some advantage. What advantage did Christ's apostles gain? Excommunication, persecution, hatred, torture, imprisonment, crucifixion—hardly a list of perks! The amazing historical fact that not one of them ever confessed to the conspiracy, even under torture—neither did any of their successors—is very powerful evidence.

The alternative, that they were deceived (the "hallucination theory"), Pascal refutes in no. 322.

322

The Apostles were either deceived or deceivers [if Jesus didn't really rise]. Either supposition is difficult, for it is not possible to imagine that a man has risen from the dead.

While Jesus was with them he could sustain them, but afterwards, if he did not appear to them, who did make them act?   **(802)**

[322]

If the apostles imagined the Resurrection, they were either the stupidest men in history, unable to distinguish a corpse from a triumphant, resurrected Lord of life and death; or else their hallucination behaved very differently from any hallucination in history, appearing many times, to many people (Paul mentions five hundred in 1 Corinthians 15:6 and challenges his readers to interview them by noting that "many of them are still alive"), eating real fish (Lk 24:26–43), remaining forty days (Acts 1:3), and—as Pascal points out in the last sentence—transforming them from a rabble as scared as rabbits, running away at the crucifixion, denying their Lord (Lk 22:54–62), cowering behind locked doors (Jn 20:19)—transforming them into a force that conquered the world, softening hard Roman hearts and hardening martyrs' resolve, going to lions and crosses with hymns of joy on their lips. If Jesus did not really rise from the dead, then an even greater miracle happened to them, without a cause: they and thousands of others gave up worldly pleasures, acceptance, security, prestige, power, wealth and very often life itself for nothing and from nothing. No one has ever answered Pascal's simple question at the end: "Who did make them act?"

21. The Jews

Unlike many Christian theologians in his era, Pascal looks on the Jews with love, respect and wonder, not loathing, contempt and resentment. For they are our fathers in the faith. They taught us the true God. And our Savior chose to be one of them. Christian anti-Semitism is an oxymoron and the blackest page in Christian history.

451

Advantages of the Jewish people. In this inquiry the Jewish people first attract my attention through a number of striking and singular features apparent in them.

[1] I see first of all that they are a people wholly composed of brothers, . . . entirely descended from one individual, and . . . of a single family. . . .

[2] This family, or people, is the oldest known to man. . . .

[3] This people is not only of remarkable antiquity but has also lasted for a singularly long time, extending continuously from its origin to the present day. For whereas the peoples of Greece and Italy, of Sparta, Athens, Rome, and others who came so much later have perished so long ago, these still exist, despite the efforts of so many powerful kings who have tried a hundred times to wipe them out. . . . They have always been preserved, however, and their preservation was foretold. . . .

[4] The law by which this people is governed is at once the oldest law in the world, the most perfect, and the only one which has been continuously observed in any state. . . .

[5] But this law is at the same time the most severe and rigorous of all as regards the practice of their religion. . . . Thus it is a really amazing thing that the law has been constantly preserved for so many centuries, by a people as

rebellious and impatient as this one, while all other states have from time to time changed their laws, although they were very much more lenient.

[6] The book containing this first of all laws is itself the oldest book in the world; those of Homer, Hesiod, and others coming only six or seven hundred years later.

(620)

452

[7] *Sincerity of the Jews.* Lovingly and faithfully they hand on this book in which Moses declares that they have been ungrateful towards God throughout their lives, that he knows they will be still more so after his death, but that he calls heaven and earth to witness against them that he told them so often enough. . . .

(631)

[451, 452]

These two *pensées* mention, and we have numbered, seven historically observable features of this people that are remarkable. The one that is the most striking to us who have seen "the century of genocide" is probably number 3, their survival. No people has ever been hated by so many others, for so many reasons, for so long. No one else has been more targeted for extinction. Yet no other people has survived and thrived so spectacularly: so long, so continuously, so resiliently and so brilliantly. Their influence on the world, even in secular areas, is vastly out of proportion to their numbers. They are the exception to nearly every known historical law. They are history's abiding miracle.

And they point to the Messiah, the Christ, for those who have the eyes to see, to follow the signs.

453

To show that true Jews and true Christians have only one religion.

The religion of the Jews seemed to consist essentially in the fatherhood of Abraham, circumcision, sacrifices, ceremonies, the Ark, the Temple, Jerusalem and finally the law and covenant of Moses.

I say that it consisted in none of these things, but only in the love of God, and that God rejected all the other things. (610)

[453]

A charter for Jewish-Christian dialogue and cooperation.

Judaism and Christianity are not two different religions! Christ never said he came to found a new religion. He never asked Jews to convert from Judaism to Christianity, but from sin to God. He said he came not to destroy the Jewish law and the prophets but to fulfill them.

The essence, point, purpose, end, goal, heart and reason for existence of Judaism is the same as that of Christianity: to make us into lovers of God and man.

The essential Jewish prayer, lovingly ensconced in mezuzahs and phylacteries throughout time and space, is the "Shema" (Dt 6:4–9: "Hear, O Israel: The Lord our God is one Lord; and you shall love the Lord your God with all your heart, and with all your soul, and with all your might. And these words which I command you this day shall be upon your heart; and you shall teach them diligently to your children, and shall talk of them when you sit in your house, and when you walk by the way, and when you lie down, and when you rise. And you shall bind them as a sign upon your hand, and they shall be as frontlets between your eyes. And you shall write them on the doorposts of your house and on your gates"). Jesus was the perfect Jew; he taught this prayer as the heart of the law, as the whole of the law. He did not give us a new law but a new power to fulfill it; not a new goal, a new God, but a new means, a new bridge to God: himself.

454

I see then makers of religions in several parts of the world and throughout the ages, but their morality fails to satisfy me and their proofs fail to give me pause. . . .

But as I consider this shifting and odd variety of customs and beliefs in different ages, I find in one corner of the world a peculiar people, [1] separated from all the other peoples of the earth, [2] who are the most ancient of all and whose history is earlier by several centuries than the oldest histories we have.

I find then this great and numerous people, [3] descended from one man, [4] worshipping one God, and [5] living according to a law which they claim to have received from his hand. They maintain that [6] they are the only people in the world to whom God has revealed his mysteries; [7] that all men are corrupt and in disgrace with God, that they have all been abandoned to their senses and their own minds; and that this is the reason for the strange aberrations and continual changes of religions and customs among them, whereas these people remain unshakeable in their conduct; but that God will not leave the other peoples for ever in darkness, [8] that a Redeemer will come, for all; that they are in the world to proclaim him to men; that they have been expressly created to be the forerunners and heralds of this great coming, and to call all peoples to unite with them in looking forward to this Redeemer.

My encounter with this people amazes me and seems worthy of attention.

I consider this law which they boast of receiving from God, and I find it admirable. It is the first of all laws, so much so that even before the word 'law' was in use among the Greeks they had received it and had been observing it for nearly a thousand years without interruption. Therefore I find it strange that the first law in the world should also happen to be the most perfect.

(619)

[454]

Here Pascal mentions eight great Jewish clues to the truth: (1) their separation, (2) their antiquity, (3) their genetic unity, (4) their monotheism, (5) their law's perfection and antiquity, (6) their claim to a unique divine revelation, (7) their consciousness of sin and (8) their hope of salvation through a Messiah.

Significantly, Pascal uses the same word ("amazement") that everyone who met Jesus used for him. His enemies, his disciples and his puzzled audiences all found him "wonderful".

22. Miracles

Pascal says in no. 859,

> Miracles are more important than you think. They were used to found the Church and will be used to continue it until Antichrist, until the end.

On the other hand, he is also aware of the *limitation* of arguing from miracles: see no. 378 (pp. 274–75).

The clinching argument for the importance of miracles is that *God* thought they were important enough to use them to found and perpetuate his Church.

In fact, all the essential and distinctive elements of Christianity are miracles: creation, revelation (first to the Jews), the giving of the law, prophecies, the Incarnation, the Resurrection, the Ascension and the Second Coming and Last Judgment.

Subtract miracles from Islam, Buddhism, Confucianism or Taoism, and you have essentially the same religion left. Subtract miracles from Christianity, and you have nothing but the clichés and platitudes most American Christians get weekly (and weakly) from their pulpits. Nothing *distinctive*, no reason to be a Christian rather than something else.

568

It is not possible to have reasonable grounds for not believing in miracles. (815)

[568]

This is a challenge; if there *are* such "reasonable grounds", as distinct from fear or fashion, it is incumbent on the unbeliever to produce them. Science cannot disprove miracles, any more than the science of accounting and the calculation of a bank balance can prove that it is impossible for someone to add extra money to that bank account from the outside.

The most famous argument against miracles is Hume's. For an account of the argument, see Hume's *Dialogues concerning Natural Religion*; for a refutation of it, see C. S. Lewis' *Miracles*; also Richard Purtill, *Thinking about Religion*, and Kreeft and Tacelli, *Handbook of Christian Apologetics*.

168

How I hate such foolishness as not believing in the Eucharist, etc. If the Gospel is true, if Jesus Christ is God, where is the difficulty? (224)

[168]

How irrational to swallow a camel and strain at a gnat!—to believe the greater miracle, the oneness of the man Christ with God, and not the lesser one, the oneness of bread with his body. If God can leap the infinite gap into man, he can surely leap into the appearances of bread and wine.

I think Pascal would like the following little poem, which connects the miracle at Cana, the Eucharist and our own resurrected body:

> The Resurrection of the Body
>
> He's a terror, that one—
> Turns water into wine,
> Wine into blood—
> I wonder what He turns blood into?
>
> (Christopher Derrick)

378

'If I had seen a miracle,' they say, 'I should be converted.' How can they be positive that they would do what they know nothing about? They imagine that such a conversion consists in a worship of God conducted, as they picture it, like some exchange or conversation. True conversion consists in self-annihilation before the universal being whom we have so often vexed and who is perfectly entitled to

destroy us at any moment, in recognizing that we can do
nothing without him and that we have deserved nothing
but his disfavour. It consists in knowing that there is an
irreconcilable opposition between God and us, and that
without a mediator there can be no exchange.   (470)

[378]

This *pensée*, on the limitations of miracles, balances no. 859, on
the importance of miracles.

Miracles convert only the mind, by force of evidence. Even
then, the hardened heart, determined not to believe, can over-
rule the mind, as it did with the Pharisees.

God wants to convert hearts. Humility, repentance, self-
surrender and love are what God wants and what conversion
consists in. These are not caused by seeing miracles. Miracles
do not address our major problem, *sin*.

Yet miracles are useful. They are powerful clues for seekers.
They are attention grabbers. They are like the famous argument of the "wager": if you don't expect too much of them,
they are very effective. (The "wager" does not convert the
heart to *saving* faith But it is a powerful *beginning*.)

734

After considering what makes us trust impostors claiming
to have cures, to the extent that we often put our lives
into their hands, it seemed to me that the real reason is
that some of them are genuine, for there could not possibly be so many false ones, enjoying so much credit, unless
some of them were genuine. If there had never been a
cure for any ill, and all ills had been incurable, men could
not possibly have imagined that they could provide any,
still less could so many others have given credence to
those who boasted of having such cures. Similarly, if a
man boasted that he could prevent death, no one would
believe him, because there is no example of that happen-
ing. But as numerous cures have been found genuine, to

the knowledge of even the greatest men, this has inclined men to be more trusting; from the fact that this was known to be possible, it was concluded that it actually is. For the people normally argue like this: 'Something is possible, therefore it is.' Because a thing cannot be denied in general, certain particular effects being genuine, the people, unable to distinguish which of the particular effects are genuine, believe in them all. Similarly, the reason we believe in so many false effects of the moon is that there are some genuine ones, like the tides of the sea. It is the same with prophecies, miracles, divination by dreams, spells, etc., for, if none of this had ever been genuine, none of it would ever have been believed. Thus instead of concluding that there are no true miracles because there are so many false ones, we must on the contrary say that there certainly are true miracles since there are so many false ones, and that false ones are only there because true ones exist. The same argument must be applied to religion, for men could not possibly have imagined so many false religions unless there were a true one. (817)

[734]

Fake miracles, exposed, seem to constitute an argument *against* believing in miracles, but they are really a probable argument *for* them, just as the existence of counterfeit money is evidence for, not against, the existence of real money.

Notice the last sentence especially—a very important clue for the seeker.

23. Uniqueness of Christianity

Under this heading, Pascal includes especially these five strong points. They are quite clear, so rather than comment at length on each one, I simply summarize them here, then print them.

1. Christianity understands both halves of human nature (no. 215).

2. Christianity teaches, not "self-fulfillment", but self-abnegation and the Cross (no. 220).

3. All other religious "enlightenments" (for example, monotheism, morality) are Christianity's kindergarten (no. 229).

4. Christianity puts into martyrs' lips hymns of triumph and into believers' lives "joy unspeakable and full of glory" (1 Pet 1:8 KJV) (no. 357).

5. Christianity does not teach human clichés and platitudes but divine mysteries, wonders and paradoxes (no. 817).

There are, of course, many more unique and distinctive features of Christianity. (See, for example, no. 733, pp. 322–23.) Many of them are more important than these—most notably Christ himself, the only man who ever rose from the dead, the only man who was God and the only man who can save us from sin. The five unique features Pascal mentions are only clues, pointing fingers. Christ is the one they all point to. (See point 26.)

215

[1] **(After hearing the whole nature of man.) For a religion to be true it must have known our nature; it must have known its greatness and smallness, and the reason for both. What other religion but Christianity has known this?**

(433)

220

[2] **No other religion has proposed that we should hate ourselves. No other religion therefore can please those**

who hate themselves and seek a being who is really worthy of love. And if they had never [before] heard of the religion of a humiliated God, they would at once embrace it.   (468)

229

[3] This religion taught its children what men had managed to know only at their most enlightened.   (444)

357

[4] No one is so happy as a true Christian, or so reasonable, virtuous, and lovable.   (541)

817

[5] There is no denying it; one must admit that there is something astonishing about Christianity. 'It is because you were born in it,' they will say. Far from it; I stiffen myself against it for that very reason, for fear of being corrupted by prejudice. But, though I was born in it, I cannot help finding it astonishing.   (615)

24. How the Christian Key Fits the Human Lock: The Two Essential Truths

We have seen the essential human paradox, "the greatness and wretchedness of man". Pascal now brings the Christian key and this lock together. The Christian key, like the human lock, is strange, wonderful, paradoxical and double: very good news and very bad news. There are two ways to put it: (1) The good news is that we are ontologically very good, created in God's image, and the bad news is that we are morally very bad, rebellious sinners; that is why we are wretched. (2) The bad news is that we are sinners, but the good news is that God has become a man to die to save us from sin and its consequence, eternal death.

The story of finding a strange and beautiful key first, and searching for a lifetime to find the lock it opens, is told in George Macdonald's beautiful little Christian allegory, *The Golden Key*. (The key, of course, is Christ.)

351

Christianity is strange; It bids man to recognize that he is vile, and even abominable, and bids him want to be like God. Without such a counterweight his exaltation would make him horribly vain or his abasement horribly abject.

(537)

[351]

Christianity blames man more than any other religion does. Man killed God.

Christianity also exalts man more than any other religion does. Man is to be married to God, united to God, to share in God's own life, "perfect even as the Father in Heaven is perfect".

192

Knowing God without knowing our own wretchedness makes for pride.

Knowing our own wretchedness without knowing God makes for despair.

Knowing Jesus Christ strikes the balance because he shows us both God and our own wretchedness. (527)

[192]
To avoid both pride and despair, we need to know both our wretchedness and our greatness. Christ alone shows us both at once. How godlike he is, how far above all other men, how perfect! And how wretchedly he in his humanity suffers everything we suffer, to the very dregs!

352
Wretchedness induces despair.

Pride induces presumption.

The Incarnation shows man the greatness of his wretchedness through the greatness of the remedy required. (526)

[352]
Christ shows us both our greatness (thus destroying our despair) and our wretchedness (thus destroying our pride) *together*.

358
How little pride the Christian feels in believing himself united to God! How little he grovels when he likens himself to the earthworm! A fine way to meet life and death, good and evil! (538)

[358]
No pride because we are united to God wholly by grace, not by nature or our worthiness.

No despair because we are miserable only by our fall into sin, not by our origin and our destiny, both of which are divine.

To be children of Adam is both greatness enough to raise any head and shame enough to lower it.

712

Someone told me one day that he felt full of joy and confidence when he had been to confession. Someone else told me that he was still afraid. My reaction was that one good man could be made by putting these two together, for each of them lacked something in not sharing the feelings of the other. The same thing often happens in other connexions.   (530)

[712]

The fear of God and the love of God are related in the same way in Scripture. Christian truth is always paradoxical, double-sided, "good news and bad news", greatness and wretchedness. Yet not by compromise. As Chesterton says, Christianity is like a checkerboard, very red and very white; it has always had a healthy hatred of pink.

398

The philosophers did not prescribe feelings proportionate to the two states.

They inspired impulses of pure greatness, and this is not the state of man.

They inspired impulses of pure abasement, and this is not the state of man.

There must be impulses of abasement prompted not by nature but by penitence, not as a lasting state but as a stage towards greatness. There must be impulses of greatness, prompted not by merit but by grace, and after the stage of abasement has been passed.   (525)

[398]

Where else but in Christianity are we so strongly headed off from both pride and despair (*and* dull compromise)?

282 *Christianity for Modern Pagans*

Non-Christian philosophies of abasement, or wretchedness, are "prompted by nature"—they teach that man is only a machine, or only an animal, or only selfishness, or a diseased wart on the planet, or a mere cog in the social wheel, totally determined by forces of heredity and environment.

The Christian philosophy of abasement is "prompted by penitence", which insults not God's work but man's, not God's creation but man's fall. "God don't make no junk."

Non-Christian philosophies of greatness are prompted by merit—they teach that man is innocent and blameless (Rousseau), a spark of God himself (pantheism), inherently omniscient (Platonism), his own standard of goodness (subjectivism), the highest being and his own end (humanism).

The Christian philosophy of greatness is prompted by grace, by God's work.

The last part of Pascal's last sentence means that Christians go *through* abasement to greatness, through despair to hope, through Purgatory to Heaven, through the Cross to the Resurrection. Like good roads. Like life.

430

No other has realized that man is the most excellent of creatures. Some, fully realizing how real his excellence is, have taken for cowardice and ingratitude men's natural feelings of abasement; while others, fully realizing how real this abasement is, have treated with haughty ridicule the feelings of greatness which are just as natural to man.

'Lift up your eyes to God,' say some of them, 'look at him whom you resemble. . . . 'Hold your heads high, free men,' said Epictetus. And others say, 'Cast down your eyes towards the ground, puny worm that you are, and look at the beasts whose companion you are.'

What then is to become of man? Will he be the equal of God or the beasts? What a terrifying distance! What then shall he be? Who cannot see from all this that man is lost, that he has fallen from his place, that he anxiously seeks it, and cannot find it again? And who then is to direct him there? The greatest men have failed.   (431)

[430]

Other philosophies of greatness criticize Christianity for too much wretchedness; and other philosophies of wretchedness criticize Christianity for too much greatness.

Chesterton says (in *Orthodoxy*): Suppose you heard of a man whom some criticized for being too tall, while others said he was too short; some said he was too fat, while others said he was too thin. One possible explanation would be that he was an extremely strange shape. But most likely he was just the right shape, perfect. Fat people say he is too thin, thin people say he is too fat. The criticisms bounce off the man and back to the critic.

399
If man was not made for God, why is he only happy in God?
If man was made for God, why is he so opposed to God?
(438)

[399]

The first question shows that God is man's end. The second shows that man is in sin, separation from his end. Only Christianity explains why we are so opposed to the very thing that is our end, our happiness, our supreme joy.

449
The Christian religion consists of two points, which it is equally important for man to know and equally dangerous not to know; and it is equally merciful of God to have given signs of both.

And yet they [unbelievers] take occasion to conclude that one of these points is not true from facts which should lead them to conclude the other. . . .

And on this basis they take occasion to blaspheme against the Christian religion, because they know so little about it. They imagine that it simply consists in worshipping a God considered to be great and mighty and eternal, which is properly speaking deism, almost as remote from the Christian religion as atheism, its complete opposite. . . .[A]

But let them conclude what they like against deism, their conclusions will not apply to Christianity, which properly consists in the mystery of the Redeemer, who, uniting in himself the two natures, human and divine, saved men from the corruption of sin in order to reconcile them with God in his divine person.[B]

It teaches men then these two truths alike: that there is a God, of whom men are capable, and that there is a corruption in nature which makes them unworthy. It is of equal importance to men to know each of these points: and it is equally dangerous for man to know God without knowing his own wretchedness as to know his own wretchedness without knowing the Redeemer who can cure him. Knowing only one of these points leads either to the arrogance of the philosophers, who have known God but not their own wretchedness, or to the despair of the atheists, who know their own wretchedness without knowing their Redeemer. . . .[C]

Let us go on to examine the order of the world, and see whether all things do not tend to establish the two main tenets of this religion: Jesus Christ is the object of all things, the centre towards which all things tend. Whoever knows him knows the reason for everything.[D]

Those who go astray only do so for want of seeing one of these two things. It is then perfectly possible to know God but not our own wretchedness, or our own wretchedness but not God; but it is not possible to know Christ without knowing both God and our wretchedness alike.

And that is why I shall not undertake here to prove by reasons from nature either the existence of God, or the Trinity or the immortality of the soul, or anything of that kind: not just because I should not feel competent to find in nature arguments which would convince hardened atheists, but also because such knowledge, without Christ, is useless and sterile.[E] Even if someone were convinced that the proportions between numbers are immaterial, eternal truths, depending on a first truth in which they subsist, called God, I should not consider that he had made much progress towards his salvation.

The Christian's God does not consist merely of a God who is the author of mathematical truths and the order of the elements. That is the portion of the heathen and Epicureans. He does not consist merely of a God who extends his providence over the life and property of men so as to grant a happy span of years to those who worship him. That is the portion of the [worldly] Jews. But the God of Abraham, the God of Isaac, the God of Jacob, the God of the Christians is a God of love and consolation: he is a God who fills the soul and heart of those whom he possesses: he is a God who makes them inwardly aware of their wretchedness and his infinite mercy: who unites himself with them in the depths of their soul: who fills it with humility, joy, confidence and love: who makes them incapable of having any other end but him.

All those who seek God apart from Christ, and who go no further than nature, either find no light to satisfy them or come to devise a means of knowing and serving God without a mediator, thus falling into either atheism or deism, two things almost equally abhorrent to Christianity.

But for Christ the world would not go on existing, for it would either have to be destroyed or be a kind of hell.

If the world existed in order to teach man about God, his divinity would shine out on every hand in a way that could not be gainsaid: but as it only exists through Christ, for Christ, and to teach men about their corruption and redemption, everything in it blazes with proofs of these two truths.

What can be seen on earth indicates neither the total absence, nor the manifest presence of divinity, but the presence of a hidden God. Everything bears this stamp. . . .

He must not see nothing at all, nor must he see enough to think that he possesses God, but he must see enough to know that he has lost him. For, to know that one has lost something one must see and not see: such precisely is the state of nature.[F]   (556)

[449]

A
Why does Pascal say this? The answer is in point c.

B
How could a reasonable man confuse Christianity with deism? Deism has a Creator without a Redeemer, transcendence without immanence or Incarnation, God without Christ. Imagine confusing Christianity with Christianity-minus-Christ!

Deism is still more *respectable* than Christianity today, just as it was in the seventeenth century, when it was invented. It avoids "the scandal of particularity", the crime of concreteness, the odium of distinctiveness. It is generic religion. And its god is not a crucified criminal.

And after creating the world, the deist god no longer gets his divine hands dirty doing miracles in it. Its god is aloof, "the snob god", while the god of pantheism is "the blob god".

You see, we make gods in our own image. As one wag said, "God created man in his image and man has been returning the compliment ever since."

But the Christian God is hardly made in our image. Who wants to be a God who suffers Hell on a Cross for man's sin?

Deism avoids the two fundamental truths of Christianity, sin and salvation. It avoids *blood*. It is not—as one of its twen-

tieth-century proponents describes orthodox Christianity—
"butcher-shop theology".

C

This is why Pascal says deism and atheism are opposites, rather
than deism and pantheism. *Theologically* and theoretically, the
opposites are deism (divine transcendence without immanence)
and pantheism (immanence without transcendence); but existentially and practically and humanly, the opposites are deism
(human greatness without wretchedness) and atheism (wretchedness without greatness).

D

Christianity is like no other religion. Instead of the founder
pointing to the religion, the religion points to the founder.
Buddha said: "Look not to me, look to my *dharma* (doctrine)";
Christ said: "Come unto me. . . . I am the way, the truth and
the life."

   If he is *not* God, as he claims, then he is an idiot, not a sage.
If he *is* God, then all other religions, however many great
truths they may contain, can be nothing more than torn pieces
from Christ's seamless garment—for example, insights into
man's greatness *or* man's wretchedness, but never both at once,
with the reason for both.

   The traditional Christian "triumphalistic" claim of superiority over all other religions is not a claim about *Christianity* (and
certainly not about *Christians*), but about *Christ*. That's why it's
nonnegotiable. Christianity reduces to Christ, and if Christianity is reduced to equality with Buddhism, Christ is thus
reduced to equality with Buddha.

E

The deepest reason why we find so few traditional philosophical arguments in Pascal is *not* that he is a skeptic. He isn't. (See
no. 131, p. 54.) Rather, the reason is existential and practical:
rational knowledge without Christ is not useful. Nothing is.

The whole point of every word in the *Pensées* is to lead us to The Word; nothing more, nothing less.

F

Here is another reason why God hides (point 19): to teach us that we have lost him, to teach us our sin and fallenness.

How subtle God is! He reveals himself most fully to us by partly concealing himself, thus revealing not only who he is but also who we are. He reveals his own unrevealedness-to-sinful-human-hearts, and he reveals this to those very hearts.

VI

THE TURNING POINT,
THE DECISION

25. The Wager

This is the most famous of all Pascal's ideas, the one history associates with his name. Yet it is not his central concern, the thing closest to his heart. It is only one step on the way, one possible means to the end. The end, the point, the goal, is Christ. This comes in the three next (and last) points of our Outline.

A further limitation of the Wager is that it is only for some people: for those who are (1) interested, not indifferent, and (2) doubtful, not certain, either by faith or by reason, concerning the existence of the God of the Bible. We all start in a pit; but some are not even interested in investigating whether or not there is a way out of the darkness into the light of the sun, and others already have climbed out by the ladder of reason or the ladder of faith. For those still in the pit, eager to escape, and doubtful of these two ladders, Pascal provides a third ladder in the Wager.

The Wager is not an attempt to prove that God exists. It is not a new argument for the existence of God. Rather, it tries to prove that it is eminently reasonable for anyone to "bet" on God, to *hope* that God is, to invest his life in God. It moves on the practical, existential, human level rather than the theoretical, metaphysical, theological level.

It is not an alternative to the traditional arguments for the existence of God, all of which move on the latter level. It is also addressed to a different audience than are Aquinas' arguments, for instance. Aquinas' famous "five ways" of demonstrating that God exists are part of the *Summa Theologica*, a work of theology, addressed to believers, to show them that purely logical reasoning confirms the faith they already have in divine revelation. Pascal's Wager, on the other hand, is addressed to unbelievers, to those who are skeptical of both theoretical reason and revelation.

These two great Christian philosophers do not contradict

each other but address very different audiences with very different needs. Their common goal, the goal of all Christians, is to bring men to Christ and to "do all for the glory of God" (1 Cor 10:31).

387

Order. **I should be much more afraid of being mistaken and then finding out that Christianity is true than of being mistaken in believing it to be true.**   **(241)**

[387]

The Wager in a nutshell.

We can be wrong in two ways: by "wagering" on God when there is no God or by "wagering" on there being no God when there is a God. The second mistake loses everything, the first loses nothing. The second is therefore the stupidest wager in the world, and the first is the wisest.

We can also be right in two ways: by wagering on God when there is a God or by wagering on no God when there is no God. If we are right in the first way, we gain everything; if we are right in the second way, we gain nothing, for there is nothing to gain. Therefore the first is the world's wisest wager and the second is the stupidest.

Remember, the Wager is not just about there being some sort of God, but the God of Christianity, the God who promises salvation and threatens damnation. In other words, the Wager is not just about God but about Christ, the man who claimed to be God and said that if and only if we believe in him will we be saved.

Pascal assumes, by the way, that we have our data straight; he assumes biblical literacy—common in his day even among unbelievers but uncommon in our day even among believers. So perhaps we should take a moment to review the relevant data first, so that we know exactly what we are wagering on. See John 3:16–18; 1:12; 4:24; 6:40, 47; 8:46–59; 9:35–39; 10:24–31; 11:25–27; 20:28–31; Acts 4:12; 13:39; 16:31; Mat-

thew 28:17–19; Mark 16:15–16; Luke 22:66–71; Romans 10:9;
1 John 5:9–13.

418

The finite is annihilated in the presence of the infinite and
becomes pure nothingness. So it is with our mind before
God. . . .[A]

We know that the infinite exists without knowing its
nature, just as we know that it is untrue that numbers are
finite. Thus it is true that there is an infinite number, but
we do not know what it is. It is untrue that it is even,
untrue that it is odd, for by adding a unit it does not
change its nature. Yet it is a number, and every number is
even or odd. . . .

Therefore we may well know that God exists without
knowing what he is. . . .

Let us now speak according to our natural lights.[B]

If there is a God, he is infinitely beyond our compre-
hension. . . .

Who then will condemn Christians for being unable to
give rational grounds for their belief. . . . They declare
that it is a folly, *stultitiam*, in expounding it to the world,
and then you complain that they do not prove it. . . .

Let us then examine this point, and let us say: 'Either
God is or he is not.' But to which view shall we be
inclined?[C] Reason cannot decide this question.[D] Infinite
chaos separates us.[E] At the far end of this infinite distance
a coin is being spun which will come down heads or tails.[F]
How will you wager?[G] Reason cannot make you choose
either, reason cannot prove either wrong.[H]

Do not then condemn as wrong those who have made a
choice, for you know nothing about it. 'No, but I will
condemn them not for having made this particular choice,
but any choice, for, although the one who calls heads and
the other one are equally at fault, the fact is that they are
both at fault: the right thing is not to wager at all.'[I]

Yes, but you must wager. There is no choice, you are already committed.[J] Which will you choose then? Let us see: since a choice must be made, let us see which offers you the least interest. You have two things to lose: the true and the good; and two things to stake: your reason and your will, your knowledge and your happiness; and your nature has two things to avoid: error and wretchedness.[K] Since you must necessarily choose, your reason is no more affronted by choosing one rather than the other. That is one point cleared up. But your happiness? Let us weigh up the gain and the loss involved in calling heads that God exists. Let us assess the two cases: if you win you win everything, if you lose you lose nothing.[L] Do not hesitate then; wager that he does exist.[M] 'That is wonderful. Yes, I must wager, but perhaps I am wagering too much.' Let us see: since there is an equal chance of gain and loss, if you stood to win only two lives for one you could still wager, but supposing you stood to win three? . . .

But here there is an infinity of infinitely happy life to be won, one chance of winning against a finite number of chances of losing, and what you are staking is finite. That leaves no choice; wherever there is infinity, and where there are not infinite chances of losing against that of winning, there is no room for hesitation, you must give everything. And thus, since you are obliged to play, you must be renouncing reason if you hoard your life rather than risk it for an infinite gain. . . .

Thus our argument carries infinite weight, when the stakes are finite in a game where there are even chances of winning and losing and an infinite prize to be won.[N]

This is conclusive and if men are capable of any truth this is it.[O]

'I confess, I admit it, but is there really no way of seeing what the cards are?'—'Yes. Scripture and the rest, etc.'[P]—'Yes, but my hands are tied and my lips are sealed; I am being forced to wager and I am not free; I am being held fast and I am so made that I cannot believe. What do you want me to do then?' Q—'That is true, but at least get it into your head that, if you are unable to believe, it is because of your passions, since reason impels you to believe and yet you cannot do so. Concentrate then not on convincing yourself by multiplying proofs of God's existence but by diminishing your passions.R You want to find faith and you do not know the road. You want to be cured of unbelief and you ask for the remedy: learn from those who were once bound like you and who now wager all they have. These are people who know the road you wish to follow, who have been cured of the affliction of which you wish to be cured: follow the way by which they began.S They behaved just as if they did believe, taking holy water, having masses said, and so on. That will make you believe quite naturally,T and will make you more docile.' U—'But that is what I am afraid of.'—'But why? What have you to lose? . . .' V

'Now what harm will come to you from choosing this course? You will be faithful, honest, humble, grateful, full of good works, a sincere, true friend. . . . It is true you will not enjoy noxious pleasures, glory and good living, but will you not have others? W

'I tell you that you will gain even in this life, and that at every step you take along this road you will see that your gain is so certain and your risk so negligible that in the end you will realize that you have wagered on something certain and infinite for which you have paid nothing.' X

'How these words fill me with rapture and delight!—'

'If my words please you and seem cogent, you must know that they come from a man who went down upon his knees before and after to pray this infinite and indivisible being, to whom he submits his own,Y that he might bring your being also to submit to him for your own good and for his glory.' Z

(233)

[418]

A

Pascal begins with reasons for theological skepticism. There is no *proportion* between our minds and God, the object we are trying to ascertain. Therefore there is no possibility of our understanding or comprehending God, any more than there is of an ant comprehending an angel.

Yet we can know God *exists* without knowing *what* he is. Pascal shows this by the analogy with an infinite number.

St. Thomas would not disagree with any of this, by the way. Pascal is not denying that there may be logical proofs of God's existence. He is denying (as Aquinas does also) that reason can understand his nature or his will.

Furthermore, the Wager "bets" on not just theism (which may be rationally provable) but Christianity and salvation (which is *not* provable by reason alone). It is a bet not just on God but on Christ, on the God of our salvation, on God-and-salvation. It is like a leap out of a burning building into a cloud of smoke on the street below, out of which has come a voice saying: "Jump! I'm holding a safety net. I see you even though you can't see me. Trust me. Jump!" Faith is a leap, not a demonstration.

B

Pascal appeals only to natural reason, not supernatural faith, in the Wager.

The most common criticism of the Wager is that it is selfish and does not lead you to true faith and love. This is perfectly true; it leads only to natural faith, selfishly motivated faith. It appeals not to the love of God but to the fear of Hell. But

1. Even this is a *beginning*, and one Jesus himself often appealed to. Should we be more "proper" than he was? God will of course not be *content* with this first step, but he will surely honor it and use it. Like a parent watching baby toddle, God our Father is "easy to please but hard to satisfy" (George Macdonald).

2. The Wager can easily be recast to appeal to a higher motive than the fear of Hell. One could wager as follows: If God exists, he deserves all my allegiance and faith. And I don't know whether he exists or not. Therefore, to avoid the terrible injustice of refusing God his rights, I will believe. Thus, we can simply substitute the "high" motive of love of justice (giving God his due) and fear of injustice for the love of Heaven and the fear of Hell, and everything in the Wager remains unchanged.

C

See diagram below.

Objectively, there are only two possibilities: either God exists, or not.

Subjectively, there are only two possibilities: either I believe, or not.

Thus, combining the two sets of variables, we get four possibilities:

1. God exists and I believe in him.
2. God exists and I do not believe in him.
3. God does not exist and I believe in him.
4. God does not exist and I do not believe in him.

		OBJECTIVELY	
		God exists	*God does not exist*
SUBJECTIVELY	*I believe*	**GAIN:** everything (eternal happiness) **LOSE:** nothing	**GAIN:** nothing **LOSE:** nothing
	I do not believe	**GAIN:** nothing **LOSE:** everything (eternal happiness)	**GAIN:** nothing **LOSE:** nothing

D

If theoretical, objective, logical, scientific reason could decide this question, we would not need to "wager". If we had proof, we would not need to take a chance. The Wager is addressed only to those who are not convinced that reason can prove theism (God exists) or atheism (God does not exist).

E

The reason Pascal gives for reason's impotence is that "infinite chaos separates us." This "infinite chaos" is the infinite difference between our minds and God's, finitude and infinity; and also the infinite distance (and worse, divorce) between God's holiness and our sinfulness. According to Christianity, God has bridged both gaps. He has bridged the first "infinite chaos" by revealing himself, especially in the Incarnation; and the second (sin) by Christ's death. But both these truths are known by faith, not by reason. Thus to the unbeliever, "infinite chaos separates us" still.

F

That is, at death we will find the coin of life coming down in one of two ways: either "heads"—you see God face to face—or "tails"—God's retreat, God's death, God's nonexistence. At death you will find out which of the two possibilities is true, atheism or theism.

G

But now, before death, you must choose to believe one way or the other. Both theism and atheism are leaps of faith, bets, wagers, chances.

H

Thus neither atheists nor theists can be refuted and proved wrong. Thus both options remain open, and a "bet" is possible as well as necessary.

I

In this paragraph, Pascal's imaginary objector defends a third possibility, neither atheism (which is betting against God) or theism (which is betting on God) but agnosticism (which is not betting at all).

Although theoretically and objectively this is agnosticism, yet practically and existentially it is withdrawal, noncommitment, noninvolvement—something close to "indifference". Pascal's refutation of this "existential agnosticism" is simple and stunning and is repeated by nearly all later "existentialists", atheistic as well as theistic: "Yes, but you *must* wager." "Not to wager at all" is simply not an option any human being can live, though he can think it. The option of agnosticism is closed to us, not by thought but by life—or, rather, by death (as we shall see in the next note).

J

We are "condemned to freedom" (to use Sartre's formula). "There is no choice", says Pascal; that is, we cannot choose whether or not we must choose. We *must* choose, though we are free to choose unbelief or belief.

Why can't we choose not to choose? Why can't we choose agnosticism?

Because we are "already committed", that is, "embarked" (*embarqué*), as on a ship. The ship is our life. The sea is time. We are moving, past a port that claims to be our true home. We can choose to turn and put in at this port (that is, to believe) or to refuse it (that is, to disbelieve), but we cannot choose to stay motionless out at sea. For we are not motionless; we are dying.

Our journey—and our fuel—is finite. Some day soon the fuel will run out, and we will no longer be *able* to choose to put in at the port of God, to believe, for we will have no more time. There is a point of no return.

In other words, to every possible question life presents three possible answers: Yes, No and Evasion. Death removes the third answer.

This "home port", you see, is not just an *idea* (that God exists). It is a marriage proposal from this God. Not to say Yes is eventually to say No. Suppose Romeo proposes to Juliet, and she says neither Yes nor No, but Wait. Suppose the "wait" lasts and lasts—until she dies. Then her "wait" becomes No. Death turns agnosticism into atheism. For death turns "Tomorrow" into "Never".

Once this is clear, that a choice *must* be made, that there are only two alternatives, not three, the next step is easy. Once Pascal has you out of indifference and onto the battlefield, it becomes very clear which side is the wise one to choose. Not choosing sides is much more popular than choosing the wrong side; agnosticism is more respectable than atheism. Even though his refutation of atheism takes fifty sentences and his refutation of agnosticism takes only one, the crucial battle is here, in this one.

K

We are all playing the same game (life) for the same two prizes. We all have two things we absolutely demand to win and not to lose: truth and happiness. No one wants to be deceived and no one wants to be miserable.

Imagine the two prizes we are playing for as blue chips (truth) and red chips (happiness). Now we cannot calculate our chances of winning the blue chips. Reason cannot prove the truth of either theism or atheism. Therefore we must calculate our chances of winning the red chips, happiness.

These are the two things everyone wants absolutely. No one wants to be a fool, stupid, ignorant, in error. "All men by nature desire to know"—this is Aristotle's premise and first line in the *Metaphysics*. And no one wants to be wretched and miserable. St. Thomas observes, in the *Summa*, that since no one can live without joy, one deprived of true joys necessarily seeks false joys in the form of worldly and carnal pleasures. We seek truth with our reason and joy with our will, and these are the two things that raise us above the animal. That is why they are absolute and nonnegotiable to us: they are the fulfillment of our essence. If we attain them, we are a success, no matter how else we fail. If we fail at them, no other success can compensate for this loss. For "what does it profit a man if he gain the whole world and lose his own soul?" (Mk 8:36 KJV).

L

The red-chip calculation is as certain as the blue-chip calculation is uncertain. The only chance of winning the happiness we crave—adequate, total, eternal, unending, unlimited, infinite happiness—is the first of the four possibilities delineated in note c, namely, the combination "God exists and I believe." And the only possibility of losing this happiness *and finding eternal unhappiness* is possibility number 2, "God exists and I do not believe." In possibilities number 3 and number 4, there is no God, and therefore no eternity, no Heaven and no Hell, no reward and no punishment, nothing to win and nothing to lose, no payoff for the wager.

Suppose you were offered a lottery ticket for free. Suppose you knew there was a 50 percent chance it was worth a million dollars, and a 50 percent chance it was worth nothing. Would it be reasonable to take the trouble to accept the gift, to *hope* at least in it, to trust the giver enough to accept the gift?

It would be obvious insanity not to.

M

To the objection that such "belief" is not yet true faith, the reply is: Of course not, but it is a step on the road to it. Even if it is sheer fear of God's justice in Hell, "the fear of the Lord is the beginning of wisdom" (Prov 1:7). It is certainly not the end. Love is that. But "love stoops to conquer" and can use even fear as a beginning—like a loving parent shouting to a toddler to get out of the street.

True faith is not a wager but a relationship. But it can begin with a wager, just as a marriage can begin with a blind date.

Suppose you had to pay $2 for the lottery ticket that had a 50 percent chance of being worth $1,000,000. It would still be a great bet. Suppose I had to give up something if I became a Christian—adultery, for instance. It would still be a great exchange. Even if I had to pay $100 for a 50 percent chance of winning a million, it would be a good bet. In fact, anything less than half a million is a good risk for a 50 percent chance of winning a million.

But here we are betting not on a million dollars but on infinite and eternal joy. Even if Romeo had to give up Juliet to get God, that would be like giving up one cigarette to get Juliet.

The objector may retort that Pascal leaves something out of this simple calculation. If we take the leap of faith and wager on God, we *may* gain something infinite, but we *will* have to give up something finite (which he calls "noxious pleasures"). The reply is that we also *will* gain something finite, namely, a moral meaning to life and the deep happiness of virtue. ("You will be faithful, honest, humble, grateful, full of good works, sincere, a true friend.") So even on the level of finite gain and loss, faith is a good bet. Converts are always happier as well as better after conversion.

By the way, Pascal is not implying that we have to attain moral perfection to be saved, only that if we are saved we will make a sincere effort to practice the Savior's moral principles. Sanctification is the effect of salvation, not the cause. But it is part of the package deal. Christ saves us *from sin*, not just from *punishment*. We must go into it with open eyes, counting the cost.

This statement is so unusual for Pascal that it is as startling as a coarse curse from a Victorian matron. Pascal is dogmatic about very little. In fact, so far in the *Pensées* he has been dogmatic about almost nothing but this, the simplest and crudest argument of all for faith.

Remember, it is not an argument for the existence of God but an argument for *faith*. Its conclusion is not "Therefore God exists" but "Therefore you should believe."

P

Back to the blue chips. Can't we calculate with them at all? Pascal's answer is: Yes, we can. There are clues, there is evidence. But there is not proof, only probabilities. So even the blue-chip calculation leads to the same conclusion. If it is *probable* that the lottery ticket is a winner, it is reasonable to buy it.

Q

Now the objector gets to the psychological root of the matter, and of his unbelief. The rational considerations all tell him to believe, yet he does not. So what holds him back then must not be rationality but irrationality; not reason but passion. Cardinal Newman noted that atheism's roots are almost always moral rather than intellectual. St. Paul said the same thing in Romans 1:18f., and Jesus in John 3:16–21.

R

If the skeptic is honest and wants to know the truth, conform his mind to the truth, believe only the truth, then he must overcome whatever force prevents him from doing that. We have just discovered that that force is not reason and argument but passion (greed, lust, fear, pride). Therefore he must overcome his slavery to his passions.

S

A very common road to faith is morality. The road to the true is the good. If you live morally, you will find the truth. Good behavior gives you clear eyes. Goodness and truth are allies, not enemies; each one helps you to the other. Many have trod this road; Pascal asks only that we imitate their success, learn from their experience.

T

The principle Pascal appeals to here is a kind of "feedback effect". Brain damage is sometimes treated by exercising the limbs that the damaged parts of the brain are unable to control, thus educating the brain through the limbs, like educating the teacher through the students. Normally, faith produces good works, as a root produces flowers or the brain controls limbs. But sometimes we can also work backward and get a new root by planting a flower. So also we can grow faith by planting good works.

What makes this work is something we have already seen regarding the heart: the heart has eyes, the heart can see. If you love God, you will see God (Mt 5:7); if you will God's will, you will understand his teaching, his mind (Jn 7:17); if you begin to obey, you will begin to believe.

Father Zossima teaches this "feedback" principle to "a lady of little faith" in *The Brothers Karamazov*. Madame Hohlokov comes to him distraught at losing her childish faith by exposure to science and philosophy, which have destroyed her faith in God and immortality. "What if when I come to die there are only the flowers on my grave? How can I get back my faith? How can I prove it to myself? It's agonizing!"

Wise old Zossima tells her that it is not possible simply to go back to her childhood, forget her doubts and believe naively. Neither is it possible for him to prove God and immortality to her. But there is a third way, a way to become certain. It is the way of active love, acting as if she believed, loving her neighbors indefatigably. Then she will come to see the image of God in the soul of her neighbors. Love will grow eyes in her heart. But only if she exercises it, only if she loves in action, not just in thought; actively, not passively and sentimentally. "I can tell you nothing more comforting than this. For love in action is a harsh and dreadful thing compared with love in dreams."

This is scriptural love. Scripture *never* tells us to love

"humanity" or to love "ideals", only to love our *neighbors*, all of them, one by one. "Humanity" is a dream, neighbor is a fact.

The actions Pascal recommends are religious rather than ethical, directed to God rather than neighbor. But they exemplify the same principle. Love of God in action or love of neighbor in action will release the irrational chains that bind us, will open our eyes and enable us to believe. For they will diminish selfish passions, which are the chains that bind us and blind us like an addiction.

U

"Docile" means "teachable". It is not *passivity* but *receptivity*, like a woman's body in intercourse. Teachability (docility) is a highly active virtue. You can't teach a rock.

V

What, exactly, is the unbeliever afraid of at this point? To find out, read Augustine's *Confessions* VIII, 5–11, and *pensée* no. 816 (next).

W

See the end of note N (last two paragraphs).

X

What a deal! What good news this Gospel is! How could any bet be better? The next words, from the now-converted skeptic, may seem exaggerated or artificial to the uninvolved spectator, but they emerge inevitably and naturally from the lived movement of the argument.

Y

Now Pascal lets the cat out of the bag and blows his cover. He is not a gambler but a matchmaker! The Wager is not a worldly calculation after all, but a divinely inspired fishnet to catch souls. Pascal got his Wager from the same source Anselm got his "ontological argument", according to his own testimony (*Proslogion* 1–2): from prayer.

An example of one of the very principles of the Wager itself, the principle that love gives you eyes (note T).

z

The ultimate point, end, purpose and goal of the Wager is God's glory—the same end as the end of all things. Pascal paid his debt to the Jesuits, whom he so severely maligned in his *Provincial Letters*, by dedicating his most famous argument, his whole book and indeed his whole life to *their* essential maxim and end: "*ad majorem Dei gloriam.*"

816

'I should soon have given up a life of pleasure,' they say, 'if I had faith.' But I tell you: 'You would soon have faith if you gave up a life of pleasure.[A] Now it is up to you to begin.[B] If I could give you faith, I would. But I cannot,[C] nor can I test the truth of what you say, but you can easily give up your pleasure and test whether I am telling the truth.'[D]

(240)

[816]

A

Pascal, like any psychologist whose ideas are based on experience rather than theory, is more of a voluntarist than an intellectualist; that is, he sees that our moral choices have more causal power over our mental beliefs than our mental beliefs have over our moral choices.

This practical voluntarism, by the way, does not contradict Aquinas' theoretical intellectualism. Augustine, for instance, clearly manifests both.

B

Voluntarism entails the conclusion that we begin the process of education by willing it.

C

No man can convert another. Only God can convert. Faith is a gift of God, not a gift of man. But we can get the obstacles out of the way, especially the addictions that blind us.

D

If you are honest and scientific and really want to know the truth, then you will perform the relevant and requisite experiment. Faith need not be based on authority, it can be based on experiment—*if* you will let the experiment happen by removing the irrational obstacle, let go your drug, your toy, your closed fist. Faith (and its consequence, salvation) is thus up to you. Though it is a gift of God, it is freely accepted as well as freely given. It takes two to tango, or to marry, both on Earth and in Heaven.

917

The Christian's hope of possessing an infinite good is mingled with actual enjoyment. . . . Christians hope for holiness, and to be freed from unrighteousness, and some part of this is already theirs. (540)

[917]

The Wager thus is not wholly a leap in the dark but is partially testable and confirmable experientially in this life.

VII

THE END OF THE ROAD:

THE POINT OF IT ALL

26. Christ

Pascal is Christocentric because Christianity is Christocentric. Christianity is Christocentric because Christ was Christocentric. He did not say "I come to teach the way, the truth and the life", but "*I AM* the way, the truth and the life" (Jn 14:6). The Apostle does not say that God had Christ *give* us wisdom, righteousness, sanctification and redemption, but he speaks of "Jesus, whom God made [to *be*] our wisdom, our righteousness and sanctification and redemption" (1 Cor 1:30). The essential Christian affirmation is that of "Doubting Thomas" to Christ: "My Lord and my God!" (Jn 20:28).

190

The metaphysical proofs for the existence of God are so remote from human reasoning and so involved that they make little impact, and, even if they did help some people, it would only be for the moment during which they watched the demonstration, because an hour later they would be afraid they had made a mistake.

What they gained by curiosity they lost through pride.

That is the result of knowing God without Christ. (543)

[190]

Pascal does not say that the traditional philosophical proofs of the existence of God are logically weak, just (a) psychologically weak, that is, not *permanently* convincing, and (b) spiritually weak, that is, not converting the heart from pride to humility.

Suppose you knew you were to be roasted on a giant barbecue spit naked for fourteen hours every day for fifty years if you had made a mistake in thinking that the philosophical proofs for the existence of God were valid. Would you stake your life on that? We cannot pin our salvation on our reason's infallibility.

Christ overcomes both weaknesses above. (a) He does not *prove* God, he *is* God. And (b) he converts hearts as well as minds.

212

Jesus is a God whom we can approach without pride and before whom we can humble ourselves without despair.

(528)

[212]

Without Christ we are sinners without a Savior standing before the face of absolute holiness and infinite, uncompromisable justice. If we do not despair at this, we are proud fools. If we are not proud fools, we despair.

We can approach Christ without pride because it is his command for us to approach him; we approach him out of obedience, which is humility. And we can approach Christ without despair for the same reason: because he invites us.

Thus just as both pride and despair stem from the same source—the lack of a Savior—so our overcoming of pride and of despair also stems from the same source—the presence of a Savior.

309

Proofs of Jesus Christ. **Jesus said great things so simply that he seems not to have thought about them, and yet so clearly that it is obvious what he thought about them. Such clarity together with such simplicity is wonderful.**

(797)

[309]

A purely objective comparison of Christ to all other sages shows no equality, even on a human level, no other such combination of (a) greatness, profundity of mystery, (b) simplicity and naturalness of person, and (c) clarity and penetration of teaching. Buddha was great and simple but not as clear. Socrates was simple and clear but not as great and mysterious. The greatest philosophers, like Aquinas, are sometimes both profound and clear but not simple.

321

Any man can do what Mahomet did. For he performed no miracles and was not foretold. No man can do what Christ did. (600)

[321]

Christ's miracles most simply and absolutely distinguish him from all other sages and prove his divinity, as speech proves rationality. The only animal that can speak is man, the rational animal; the only man who can perform miracles is Christ, the divine man.

417

Not only do we only know God through Jesus Christ,[A] but we only know ourselves through Jesus Christ;[B] we only know life[C] and death[D] through Jesus Christ. Apart from Jesus Christ we cannot know the meaning of our life or our death, of God or of ourselves.[E]

Thus without Scripture, whose only object is Christ, we know nothing, and can see nothing but obscurity and confusion in the nature of God and in nature itself.[F] (548)

[417]
A

For Christ is our only clear window to God. "No one has ever seen God; the only Son, who is in the bosom of the Father, he has made him known" (Jn 1:18). "No one comes to the Father but by me" (Jn 14:6).

B

For Christ shows us what we were designed to be—perfect—and the depth of our sin—the Cross. We are half-men, he is perfect man. We are inhuman humans, he is perfect humanity. We are alienated from ourselves, he is perfectly himself, perfect man, perfect *ourselves*. He is more us than we are.

C

For Christ shows us the meaning of life, the ultimate end of human life and history, which is union with him, the marriage of the Lamb (Christ) and his Bride, his Church (Rev 21:9).

D

For Christ alone can save us from eternal death. Christ alone can lead us through this life, which is "the valley of the shadow of death" (Ps 23:4) to resurrection.

E

Thus the four most important things we must know—the *only* four things we absolutely must know—are all knowable only through Christ.

F

Christ is "the Word of God" (Jn 1:1). Scripture is also "the Word of God" (Heb 4:12). But Scripture is a sign of Christ (Jn 5:39–40). Scripture is the Word of the Word of God, the window onto the window.

Catholics, who make greater claims for the Church than Protestants do, do not make lesser claims for Scripture than Protestants do.

291

This religion so great in miracles, in men holy, pure and irreproachable, in scholars, great witnesses and martyrs, established kings—David—Isaiah, a prince of the blood; so great in knowledge, after displaying all its miracles and all its wisdom, rejects it all and says that it offers neither wisdom nor signs, but only the Cross and folly.

For those who by this wisdom and these signs have

deserved your trust, and who have proved their character, declare to you that none of this can change us and make us capable of knowing and loving God, except the virtue contained in the folly of the Cross, without wisdom or signs, and not the signs without this virtue.

Thus our religion is foolish judged by its effective cause, and wise judged by the wisdom which prepares for it.

(587)

[291]

See 1 Corinthians 1:18–2:9.

The Cross of Christ is the greatest power in the universe— greater than wisdom, greater than miracles, greater than virtue, greater than the Big Bang of creation itself, greater even than sin (Rom 5:20).

842

Our religion is wise and foolish: wise, because it is the most learned and most strongly based on miracles, prophecies, etc., foolish, because it is not all this which makes people belong to it. This is a good enough reason for condemning those who do not belong, but not for making those who do belong believe. What makes them believe is the Cross. . . .

And so St Paul, who came with wisdom and signs, said that he came with neither wisdom nor signs, for he came to convert, but those who come only to convince may say they come with wisdom and signs. (588)

[842]

Pascal himself exemplifies this principle, as did Christ, Paul, Socrates and St. Thomas.

Christ would not exercise his power and come down from the Cross so that the skeptics could believe in him. Only because of that can we believe in him.

Paul, the great Apostle with knowledge and wisdom and

authority, comes to the sophisticated, philosophical Corinthians and says: "I decided to know nothing among you except Jesus Christ and him crucified" (1 Cor 2:2).

When the god of the Delphic oracle, who Socrates believed "cannot lie" (*Apology* 21b), declared that no one was wiser than Socrates, Socrates declared his only wisdom must be the knowledge of his unwisdom (*Apology* 20e–23b).

St. Thomas, greatest of theologians, declared all his writings to be but "straw" once he saw God.

One has a right to disdain what he surpasses.

Miracles are like arguments: they do not create faith, though they can refute errors and unfaith. The Cross is more powerful than any miracle or any argument. Ultimately, what makes us believe is not miracles or arguments but the power of the Cross.

27. The Body of Christ (the Church)

Pascal would have thought it to be just as absurd and impossible to be united to Christ without being united to his Body, the Church, as for Juliet to marry Romeo without ever touching his body. To love Christ without loving his Church is abstract, "spiritual", Gnostic. It is "Platonic love", not marriage. "Love me, love my body", says Romeo to Juliet—and says Christ to the Christian.

Superstitious, materialistic, merely institutional Catholicism is like carnal love. "Spiritual", noninstitutional Protestantism is like "Platonic love". Orthodox Catholicism is like marriage to Christ.

Pascal not only believed all Catholic dogmas because he believed the authority of the Magisterium, the teaching authority of the Church; but he also had a Catholic sensibility and vision of the Church. This vision emerges in the following *pensées*. It *emphasized* the mystical and moral more than the institutional and theological, but without denying the latter. Pascal cared less about structures and controversies than about life in Christ.

But he did not separate the Church from Christ. In fact, he identified the two, just as Christ himself did. When Christ appeared to Paul, who was persecuting the Church, he said, "Paul, Paul, why are you persecuting *me*?" (Acts 9:4). And he also said, "Verily I say unto you [that is, I'm not exaggerating; take this literally!], inasmuch as ye have done it unto one of the least of these my brethren, ye have done it unto me" (Mt 25:40 KJV). (An appropriate sign for abortion clinics!)

For Pascal, the Church is not man's God-society but God's man-body, not "man at worship" but God at work.

359

Example of noble deaths of Spartans and others hardly affects us, for what good does it do us?

But the example of the deaths of martyrs affects us for they are our members. . . .

There is none of this in heathen examples. We have no connexion with them, just as we do not become rich through seeing a rich stranger, but through seeing a father or husband rich.   (481)

[359]

The Church is a family. Christ is not our *hero* but our *head*; not our example or model or ideal merely (like the ancient Spartans) but the very vine of which we are branches (Jn 15:5).

If you discovered Adolf Hitler was your grandfather, *you* would be ashamed. If you discovered that your husband was a millionaire, *you* would be rich.

We are the King's kids!

360

Beginning of thinking members. Morality. When God had made heaven and earth, which are not conscious of the happiness of their existence, he wanted to create beings who would realize it and compose a body of thinking members. For our own members are not conscious of the happiness of their union, their wonderful understanding, the care taken by nature to infuse them with spirits and make them grow and endure. How happy they would be if they could feel and see all this! But for that they would have to have the intelligence to know it and the good will to fall in with that of the universal soul. If, when they had been given intelligence, they used it to retain nourishment for themselves without letting it pass on to the other members, they would be not only wrong but wretched, and would hate rather than love themselves; for their delight as much as their duty consists in consenting to the guidance of the whole soul to which they belong, which loves them better than they love themselves.   (482)

[360]

When St. Paul says we are "members" of Christ, he does not mean "members" of a *group*, a *society*; he means "members" of a *body*: limbs, lungs, toes, ears, kidneys.

If each member (organ) in our body had conscious thought and free will, that would be the kind of thing the Church is.

It's all in St. Paul: Romans 12:4–5; 1 Corinthians 6:15; 12:27; Ephesians 1:22–23; 5:28–32; Colossians 1:24; 2:19. Paul even dares to speak concretely of "ligaments", not abstractly of "society".

372

To be a member is to have no life, no being and no movement except through the spirit of the body and for the body. The separated member, no longer seeing the body to which it belongs, has only a wasting and moribund being left. . . .[A]

It could not by its very nature love anything else except for selfish reasons and in order to enslave it, because each thing loves itself more than anything else.

But in loving the body it loves itself, because it has no being except in the body, through the body, and for the body. . . .[B]

We love ourselves because we are members of Christ. We love Christ because he is the body of which we are members. All are one. One is in the other like the three persons [of the Trinity].[C] (483)

[372]

A

When a machine gains or loses a part, the part still maintains its own life and identity. Its union with the machine is accidental.

The same is true of individuals in a social group. I am I, whether or not I am a part of a party, a club or a nation.

But this is not true of members (organs) in a body. Remove heart, lungs or kidneys from the body and they die.

A member of a group has a life outside the group; an organ in a body has no life outside the body. An eye removed from the body and put on a plate no longer lives. It is even no longer an eye. It cannot see outside the body, it loses its identity.

This is how we are related to the Church. The Church is not essentially an organization but an organism. The Church is not Christ's *society* but Christ's *Body*.

The Christian has no life or identity apart from Christ (and therefore apart from his Body). If I were to die and discover that there was no Christ, that Christ was dead, that Christ was not God, that I was not alive with his life in his Body, then I would not be I, I would be another person.

B

God's integration of individuals into Christ's Body solves the problem of love. He does not destroy the principle of self-love, which is inherent in our being as in the being of every thing in the universe (even bubbles strive to survive!); but he enables us to love others *as ourselves*. By putting myself and my neighbor into Christ's Body, God enabled me to extend the love I have toward myself to my neighbor too. We are "members of one another" (Rom 12:5). I am his arm, he is my leg; I am his eye, he is my ear.

This is true most intimately of marriage. The two become "one flesh", that is, one body, one new person. So that when a man loves his wife, he loves himself (Eph 5:28). This is literal, not symbolic; real, not "as if ".

C

The ultimate model for the organic principle is the Creator of everything, who is a Trinity. Reality can't help being one-in-many, many-in-one. For the origin and designer and archetype of all reality is one-in-many, many-in-one. This is what love is. And love is not in us, we are "in Love". Love is not a sentiment, love is a metaphysic.

373

If the foot had never known it belonged to the body, and that there was a body on which it depended, if it had only known and loved itself, and if it then came to know that it belonged to a body on which it depended, what regret, what shame it would feel for its past life, for having been useless to the body which poured life into it, and would have annihilated it if it had rejected and cut it off as the foot cut itself off from the body! How it would pray to be kept on! How submissively it would let itself be governed by the will in charge of the body, to the point of being amputated if necessary! Otherwise it would cease to be a member, for every member must be willing to perish for the sake of the body, for whose sake alone everything exists.   (476)

[373]

Therefore conversion means conversion to the Church, to the Body of Christ, to the new relationship with Christ, the relationship of dependence on and incorporation into him. Repentance means, among other things, repenting our separate existence outside his Body, "being useless to the body".

The Church is not an addition *after* conversion; the Church is an aspect *of* conversion. Romeo doesn't marry Juliet's body *after* he marries Juliet!

927

The slightest movement affects the whole of nature; one stone can alter the whole sea. Likewise, in the realm of grace, the slightest action affects everything because of its consequences; therefore everything matters.   (505)

[927]

Here is the great principle of solidarity, spiritual and mystical and universal. Every sin harms everyone in the Body, and every act of love and obedience to the Head helps every organ in the Body.

Even the physical universe works this way. Gravity is universal. Every particle of matter in the universe "loves" and gravitationally affects every other particle of matter in the universe, and we can calculate exactly how much if we only know their mass and distance. How much more must there be a universal spiritual gravity.

When you put down this book and say a loving and helpful word to your family, some martyr three thousand miles and three hundred years away may receive enough grace to endure his trials because of you. And if instead you sin one more time this afternoon, that martyr may weaken, compromise and be broken. If there is a universal spiritual gravity, if we all help or harm each other, there must be some one straw that breaks the camel's back, one vote that decides the election.

Everything matters. There are no "victimless crimes". Every sin against Christ harms his Body and every member in it.

733

The Church has always been attacked by contrary errors. . . .

Faith embraces many apparently contradictory truths, 'a time to weep and a time to laugh,' [1] etc., 'answer, answer not.' [2]

The origin of this is the union of two natures in Christ.

And also the two worlds. The creation of a new heaven and a new earth. New life, new death. . . .

And finally the two men who are in the righteous [Rom. VI, 7]. For they are the two worlds, and a member and image of Christ. Thus all the names fit them: righteous sinners; living dead; dead living; reprobate elect, etc. . . .

The source of all heresies is the exclusion of certain of these truths.

And the source of all the objections levelled at us by heretics is their ignorance of certain of our truths.

[1] Eccl. III. 4.   [2] Prov. XXVI. 4, 5.

It usually happens that, being unable to imagine the connexion between two opposing truths, and thinking that the acceptance of the one entails the exclusion of the other, they hold on to one and exclude the other, and think that we are doing just the opposite. Now this exclusion is the cause of their heresy, and ignorance of the fact that we hold the other causes their objections.

First example. Jesus Christ is God and man. The Arians, unable to combine two things which they believe to be incompatible, say that he is man, and in this are Catholic, but they deny that he is God, and in that they are heretical. They claim that we deny his humanity, and in that they are ignorant.

Second example. On the subject of the Blessed Sacrament. We believe that, the substance of bread being changed and transsubstantiated into that of Our Lord's body, Jesus Christ is really present in it: that is one of the truths. Another is that this sacrament also prefigures that of the Cross, and glory, and is a commemoration of both. Here we have the Catholic faith embracing two apparently opposing truths.

Modern heresy, unable to conceive that this sacrament contains at once the presence and the figuration of Jesus Christ, and is both a sacrifice and a commemoration of a sacrifice, believes that one of these truths cannot be admitted without thereby excluding the other.

They fix on the single point that the sacrament is figurative, and in this they are not heretical. They think that we exclude this truth, and hence raise so many objections about passages in the Fathers which attest it. Finally they deny the real presence and in this they are heretical. . . .

That is why the shortest way to prevent heresy is to teach all truths, and the surest way of refuting it is to proclaim them all.   (862)

[733]

Here Pascal treats the Church on a second level, as visible teacher, as Magisterium, as the *mind of* the Body.

Chesterton, in *Orthodoxy*, has explored this principle of the paradoxes of the faith with unsurpassed vigor.

From this principle all heresies can be identified and classified. All heresies are half-truths.

An entire theology course can (and should) be structured around this single principle. The entire history of theology has in fact been structured around this principle for two thousand years.

28. The Experience of Christ

Christ is our God. Experience is not our God. Contemporary theopsychobabble substitutes experience for Christ, pop psychology for revealed religion.

Yet we need to experience Christ, meet Christ, touch Christ, not just believe correct theology about Christ. What we need is not experience without Christ, nor Christ without experience, but the experience of Christ; not psychology or theology but religion, lived relationship.

We do not all need, or get, the same experience of Christ. But we all need, and get, the same Christ. Pascal's experience of Christ was a special, divine gift. Yet in many ways it is a universal, and not just a singular and quirky, Christian experience. The Godly "fire", the joy, the tears, the concreteness and specificity and definiteness of Pascal's experience as recorded in the "Memorial" (no. 913) are for all.

913[A]

The year of grace 1654.

Monday, 23 November, feast of Saint Clement, Pope and Martyr, and of others in the Martyrology.

Eve of Saint Chrysogonus, Martyr and others.

From about half past ten in the evening until half past midnight.[B]

Fire[C]

'**God of Abraham, God of Isaac, God of Jacob,**'[1] **not of philosophers and scholars.**[D]

Certainty, certainty,[E] **heartfelt, joy, peace.**[F]

God of Jesus Christ.[G]

God of Jesus Christ. . . .

Joy, joy, joy, tears of joy. . . .[H]

'**And this is life eternal, that they might know thee, the only true God, and Jesus Christ whom thou has sent.**'[2]

---

[1] Ex. III. 6.   [2] John XVII. 3.

Jesus Christ.
Jesus Christ. . . .

[913]

A

Of all the *pensées*, this one is certainly the closest to Pascal's
heart, figuratively and even literally, since he kept it sewn into
his coat pocket; he kept it close to his heart physically at all
times because he kept it close to his heart spiritually at all
times. It is of all the *pensées* the most intimately revealing and
the most mystically exalted.

B

Note how concrete and specific and factual it is—like the
Incarnation! "The God of the philosophers" is a timeless principle; "the God of Abraham, Isaac and Jacob" is a historical
fact. We *think* the God of the philosophers, we *meet* the God
of Abraham.

C

The key word. It is like a sacrament, it effects what it signifies.
It penetrates and burns into our heart, this word—like fire
itself. What a shocking word for God, yet what a true one.
God is not a pale light but a life-creating and consuming fire, a
volcano. Those who frown or sniff at this crude God prefer the
beautiful perfume to the beautiful woman, the portrait to the
person, as the Pharisees did (Jn 5:39–40).

D

Not that there are two Gods, but that "the God of the philosophers" is only an abstract concept, a picture, while the God of
Abraham is a concrete person. ("Concrete" means "individual", not "corporeal".) The God of the philosophers is only a
thin slice of the God of Abraham.

E

Certainty eluded Pascal until now. Or, rather, in light of this experience and this certainty, Pascal could never again claim certainty for any pale philosophical concepts.

F

Joy and peace are fruits and marks of the Holy Spirit.

G

The summit of revelation, the summit of mystical experience for the Christian, is not a God beyond Christ, an abyss of abstract "being", but Christ's Father, fully revealed only by Christ, even in the heights of mystical experience. Christocentrism more clearly distinguishes orthodox Christian mysticism from all other forms than anything else does. (See Thomas Dubay, *The Fire Within*.)

H

Pascal can only stammer and weep like a child.

There are no "adult Christians". It is an oxymoron. The higher we climb, the more childlike we are.

Perhaps the profoundest possible prayer, perfectly appropriate for the deepest depths of sorrow and despair *and* the highest heights of mystical graces of joy, is simply "Jesus, I love you; Jesus, I love you", again and again forever.

919
The Mystery of Jesus [A]

Jesus suffers in his passion the torments inflicted upon him by men, but in his agony he suffers the torments which he inflicts on himself. *He was troubled.* [1] This punishment is inflicted by no human, but an almighty hand, and only he that is almighty can bear it.

Jesus seeks some comfort at least from his three dearest friends, and they sleep: he asks them to bear with him a

[1] John. XI. 33.

while, and they abandon him with complete indifference, and with so little pity that it did not keep them awake even for a single moment. And so Jesus was abandoned to face the wrath of God alone.

Jesus is alone on earth, not merely with no one to feel and share his agony, but with no one even to know of it. Heaven and he are the only ones to know.

Jesus is in a garden, not of delight, like the first Adam, who there fell and took with him all mankind, but of agony, where he has saved himself and all mankind.

He suffers this anguish and abandonment in the horror of the night.

I believe that this is the only occasion on which Jesus ever complained. But then he complained as though he could no longer contain his overflowing grief: 'My soul is exceeding sorrowful, even unto death.' [2]

Jesus seeks companionship and solace from men.

It seems to me that this is unique in his whole life, but he finds none, for his disciples are asleep.

Jesus will be in agony until the end of the world. There must be no sleeping during that time.[B]

Jesus, totally abandoned, even by the friends he had chosen to watch with him, is vexed when he finds them asleep because of the dangers to which they are exposing not him but themselves, and he warns them for their own safety and their own good, with warm affection in the face of their ingratitude. And warns them: 'The spirit is willing but the flesh is weak.' [3]

Jesus finding them asleep again, undeterred by consideration either for him or for themselves, is kind enough not to wake them up and lets them take their rest.

Jesus prays, uncertain of the will of the Father, and is afraid of death. But once he knows what it is, he goes to meet it and offer himself up. *Let us be going.*[4] *He went forth.* (John) [XVIII.4.]

---

[2] Matt. XXVI. 38.	[3] Matt. XXVI. 41.	[4] Matt. XXVI. 46.

Jesus asked of men and was not heard.

Jesus brought about the salvation of his disciples while they slept. He has done this for each of the righteous while they slept, in nothingness before their birth and in their sins after their birth.

He prays only once that the cup might pass from him, even then submitting himself to God's will, and twice that it should come if it must be so.

Jesus weary at heart.

Jesus, seeing all his friends asleep and all his enemies watchful, commends himself utterly to his Father.

Jesus disregards the enmity of Judas, and sees only in him God's will, which he loves; so much so that he calls him friend.

Jesus tears himself away from his disciples to enter upon his agony: we must tear ourselves away from those who are nearest and dearest to us in order to imitate him.

While Jesus remains in agony and cruellest distress, let us pray longer.

We implore God's mercy, not so that he shall leave us in peace with our vices, but so that he may deliver us from them.

If God gave us masters with his own hand, how gladly we ought to obey them! Necessity and events are infallibly such.[C]

'Take comfort; you would not seek me if you had not found me.'[D]

'I thought of you in my agony: I shed these drops of blood for you.'[E]

'It is tempting me rather than testing yourself to wonder if you would do right in the absence of this or that. I will do it in you if it happens.'

'Let yourself be guided by my rules. See how well I guided the Virgin and the saints who let me work in them.'

'The Father loves all I do.'

'Do you want it always to cost me the blood of my humanity while you do not even shed a tear?'

'My concern is for your conversion; do not be afraid, and pray with confidence as though for me.'

'I am present with you through my word in Scripture, my spirit in the Church, through inspiration, my power in my priests, my prayer among the faithful.'

'Physicians will not heal you, for you will die in the end, but it is I who will heal you and make your body immortal.'

'Endure the chains and bondage of the body. For the present I am delivering you only from spiritual bondage.'

'I am a better friend to you than this man or that, for I have done more for you than they, and they would never endure what I have endured from you, and they would never die for you, while you were being faithless and cruel, as I did, and as I am ready to do, and still do in my elect, and in the Blessed Sacrament.'

'If you knew your sins, you would lose heart.'—'In that case I shall lose heart, Lord, for I believe in their wickedness on the strength of your assurance.'—'No, for I who tell you this can heal you, and the fact that I tell you is a sign that I want to heal you. . . .

'I love you more ardently than you have loved your foulness. . . .'

Do small things as if they were great, because of the majesty of Christ, who does them in us and lives our life, and great things as if they were small and easy, because of his almighty power.   (553)

[919]

A

Another famous and intimate *pensée*. Its vision of Jesus continuing to suffer in his Body follows from the previous point of the union of the Head with the Body (point 27). There are more than nineteen hundred nails in the Cross.

B

How can we not be haunted by this line?

C

Therefore, Romans 8:28.

D

Christ says this to us who seek him. The very act of seeking him can come only from his presence in the soul. "I sought the Lord, and afterward I knew/ He moved my soul to seek him, seeking me./ It was not I that found, O Savior true;/ No, I was found by thee."

E

You individually, by name! If you were the only one he had created, or the only one who had sinned (like the one stray sheep in his parable [Lk 15]), he would have done all that he did for you alone. Indeed, he did do all he did for you alone, for each one individually, not for "mankind" (which does not exist except in thought and which he *never* mentions).

God's love letter is never addressed "Dear occupant". If every cell in our body is genetically coded individually, so is every drop of his blood individually coded for *your* salvation.

And he still bleeds, whenever his Body bleeds.

924

It is true that there is something painful in beginning to practise piety, but this pain does not arise from the beginnings of piety within us, but from the impiety that is still there. . . . We only suffer in so far as our natural vice resists supernatural grace: our heart feels torn between these contrary forces, but it would be very wrong to impute this violence to God, who draws us to him, instead of attributing it to the world which holds us back. It is like a child snatched by its mother from the arms of robbers. . . . The cruellest war that God can wage on men in this life is to leave them without the war he came to bring. 'I came not to send peace but a sword,' he said. . . . Before his coming the world lived in a false peace.

(498)

[924]

The pains of piety are like the withdrawal symptoms when an addict goes clean and sober. God does not cause pain; sin causes pain. But the juxtaposition of God and sin also causes pain.

The surgeon who does not cut out the cancer is not kind but cruel. The God of mere kindness whom we long for, the Grandfather God who leaves us alone to enjoy ourselves rather than the Father God who constantly interrupts us and interferes with our lives is really not kind but cruel. (He is also nonexistent!) The "cruel" God of the Bible is a God of battles. He fights a spiritual war for us against the demons of sin in us. This God is not cruel but kind, as kind as he can possibly be. The sword he comes to us with (Mt 10:34) is a surgeon's scalpel, and this Surgeon's hands are covered with his own blood.

946

Consider Jesus Christ in every person, and in ourselves. Jesus Christ as father in his father, Jesus Christ as brother in his brothers, Jesus Christ as poor in the poor, Jesus Christ as rich in the rich, Jesus Christ as priest and doctor in priests, Jesus Christ as sovereign in princes, etc. For by his glory he is everything that is great, being God, and by his mortal life he is everything that is wretched and abject. That is why he took on this unhappy condition, so that he could be in every person and a model for every condition of men. (785)

[946]

We can consider him there only because he really is there. He is in his whole Body as your soul is in your whole body. We really do meet and touch and help or harm Christ in our neighbors. If we lived this one thought, we would convert and transform the world.

INDEX
by Krailsheimer Numbers

INDEX
by Brunschvicg Numbers